My Gorbals Life

My Gorbals Life

Allan Gilfillan McLachlan

First published 2024 by Allan Gilfillan McLachlan

Paperback: 978-0-473-72419-1

eBook: 978-0-473-72421-4

Kindle: 978-0-473-72422-1

Cover Images:

Glasgow City Archives, used with permission

© CSG CIC Glasgow Museums and Libraries Collection: The Mitchell Library, Special Collections, used with permission.

Cover design and typesetting by Holly Dunn Design.

Chapter 1

I was born into a troubled world in the very early morning of the 7th of October 1938, in a ward of Rotten Row Maternity Hospital, Glasgow, Scotland. During the years of 1938, 1939, and 1940, when my younger brother Bobby was born, my mother (Mammy) and I shared the ground level, two-roomed apartment of my paternal grandmother situated at 25 McDuff Street, in Parkhead. I have only the vaguest memories of this.

Due to the efforts of my mother's elder sister, Annie, we moved to a tiny 'single-end', one-roomed 'hoose', at 29 Kidston Street, Gorbals. It was located on the first floor, directly above the common 'close'. We moved in on the afternoon of 28 November 1940.

Moving house, for us, consisted of Mammy pushing an old well- used hand-me-down pram containing Bobby, plus our meagre worldly possessions tied on top, with me either holding on like grim death to the pram rail, or at intervals trotting alongside. It was a three-hour trudge but, to Mammy's great relief, we were at long last going to a home of our own. I can remember how excited she was.

Arriving at Kidston Street, after heaving the laden pram up the stairs, we found that the hoose, when the door was opened with the massive iron key which we had just collected from the 'Factor', was chock full of rags, from floor to ceiling. The previous tenant must have been a rag dealer who had used the place as a cheap storehouse.

Mammy burst into tears, slumped to her knees, and sobbed bitterly, until our Auntie Annie, who lived 'up the sterrs', and who had got us the single end, arrived. "Dinnae worry, wee yin", she said, "thae rags are worth plenty, jist ye wait fur a few hoors, an' see".

We spent some hours sorting out the rags into manageable bundles, which we wrapped up in some of the old sheets and tablecloths found amongst the rag pile. Carting these in relays, to one of the numerous rag stores which dotted the neighbourhood, using the empty pram as a cart, we ended up very tired, but fifteen shillings richer, which was, in our terms, an awful lot of money. To put this sum into perspective, our rent for the single end was one shilling and sixpence per week. We were fed and scrubbed by Auntie Annie, before being tucked up, totally exhausted, in someone's bed for the night.

Our 'new hoose', consisted of one single room, with a built-in recess bedspace, a cast iron sink (cold water tap only), a fireplace, a solitary single broken gas mantle for lighting, and a single gas ring for cooking, which was located on the floor next to the sink. A single window let sufficient gloomy light in from the street, to show up the peeling plaster walls and scuffed bare damp floorboards. It stank!!

The toilet was outside, to be shared with the other two families on the first-floor common entry area, known as a landing.

Clothes washing facilities were located in the wash house situated in the 'back coort', known as 'the back'. This was an ancient, dilapidated brick shed with a sheet iron roof, containing a bricked-in circular copper boiler, with a wood fired grate underneath. The other fixtures were two large, galvanised sinks, and a real honest-to-goodness mangle. When we were old enough to turn the crank handle, operating this bulky contraption would be our responsibility.

Tenants had to supply their own firewood, washboard, soap etc. and chase the hordes of incumbent rats outside until the washing was finished. The only alternative to using the wash house was to cart the weekly wash, bundled up in a sheet, to the nearest corporation 'Steamie', where for a small sum the washing could be done on a self-service basis. Transportation would have been the ubiquitous old pram chassis and wheels on which a galvanised tub would somehow be mounted, instead of the original pram body. Mammy thought that this was far too common, and never ever did this.

The only means of drying the washing was to use the 'Back', which was surfaced with muck. A rope was tied between rusty iron rings set into the tenement walls, supported in the middle by a wooden pole. When you consider that rain is endemic to Glasgow, not to mention that we were surrounded by all sorts of industrial enterprises belching thick black smoke without any restriction whatsoever. The most prominent of these factories was the Govan Ironworks, known universally as Dixons Blazes, which was literally only a single tenement block away.

Drying of clothes and sheets was a constant problem and a perennial topic of conversation between neighbours. The washing got filthy whilst drying, due to the filthy environment and mobs of grubby kids rushing through the hanging sheets and clothes. Each tenant was allocated the same half day each week to use the wash house and clothesline. If it rained, as it usually did, then the only available option was to take the dripping washing inside and attempt to dry it by hanging it in stages on the clothes pulley, which was suspended from the kitchen ceiling. In our case, we only had one room so almost always had to share our meagre living space with dripping washing which took forever to dry.

Soot, cinders, and God-only-knows what else, rained down twenty-four hours a day. Every available surface of local buildings was thickly coated with a black crust. This state of affairs was universally accepted as normal by the tenement dwellers. Buildings which had been originally solidly constructed using beautiful cream or pink sandstone had always been black within the collective memory of the local inhabitants. As far as the slum dwellers were concerned, buildings were grimy black, had always been grimy black, and always would be grimy black.

Children are amazingly adaptive, especially in situations where everyone is in the same boat. Luckily for us, my mother was the youngest member of an extended nuclear family. All the medically fit adult male family members were serving overseas, in all three services. This resulted in a totally female dominated environment being the status quo, which I thought of as a child, and still do, as being just fine.

We had 'Big Granny', Granny Cunningham, my mother's mother, who I worshipped; Auntie Annie; Auntie Phamie; Auntie Marion [pronounced Murn]; Auntie Bella; and our totally outrageous hard case Auntie Jean. Auntie Nellie Kerr was the wife of Mammy's only brother, my favourite uncle Rab (Robert).

Auntie Nellie much preferred to be called Helen, her given name, but despite this she was always referred to as Nellie Kerr, by everyone from our side of the family. She and Mammy had been best friends and had both worked together at Coats cotton mills since they were thirteen years old.

On my absent father's side, we had 'Wee Granny', Granny McLachlan, who had to be kept away from any type of alcoholic beverage at all costs; Auntie Mary, who at that time lived and worked in Dumfries, and Auntie Annie McEwan, my father's sister-in-law. Even as tiny tots, we were always warned, if out walking with Wee Granny for any reason, to hold on to her hand tightly at all times, not for our safety, but to prevent her from swiftly slipping sideways through the ladies saloon door of any pub which we might pass.

This was quite a task, as at that time in the Gorbals there was a pub on every corner, plus numerous ones in between. We did our very best but sometimes failed. This meant that we had to run home quickly to tell Mammy that Granny was missing in action. Mammy would invariably go berserk, pulling on her coat furiously, which always frightened me, as she was of a mild disposition normally, while we raced down Crown Street to the pub where Granny had last been seen.

Now came the difficult part, for my mother did not hold with drink, and would never under any circumstances enter a pub. We would wait outside until a woman was entering the pub. Mammy would diffidently ask her to see if a wee wumman was inside, and if so, could she tell her to come outside immediately. If we were on the spot quickly enough, and the lady's saloon had only one door, we might be lucky, otherwise we would wait outside until Granny had spent our money, and came tottering out of the pub.

Mammy would say not a word, but would take Granny firmly by the arm, looking around constantly in dread, in case a neighbour might see us, and steer the staggering Granny to the nearest tram stop. When the next tram arrived, Mammy would, blushing to the roots of her auburn hair, ask the conductor to put Granny off at Glasgow Cross, where she could then get a number 9 Auchenshuggle tram home. How she got home we never knew, but she invariably did. When we next saw her the previous incident was never mentioned.

Wee Granny was stone deaf. To communicate with her, you had to cup your hands, and shout into her best ear, which was okay in private, but highly embarrassing in public.

My mother's family were considerably older than she was, and each had a reasonably large number of offspring. The number of older cousins was overwhelming to small children at family gatherings, which were held at the drop of a hat, and for the slightest excuse. We all got on extremely well despite the great disparity in ages and would play outside (there was insufficient room inside for both offspring and adults), for hours without complaint, the younger kids being happily spoiled by the older ones.

Having two small children, my mother could not work. We had to survive on the pittance of my father's army pay. This is where the family support system kicked in. We had a whole tribe of older cousins, ranging in age from slightly older than us to teenagers and up to some in their twenties, who were serving in the forces. Within the extended family system, nothing of any use, particularly clothing, was ever discarded but was passed on to the most needy.

Since I was the offspring of my mother, the youngest, and the favourite 'Wee Yin' of the Cunningham family, all of our clothing consisted of 'hand me downs', which had already had at least one prior owner, if not more, and not necessarily of the same sex. The one exception to this was footwear, which never survived long in the harsh environment, being made of cheap substandard materials in the first place. Ploughing through the omnipresent puddles, and constantly kicking ball substitutes such as tin cans, and pieces of brick or stones, meant that broken, scuffed, leaky, boots, shoes or clogs, were the norm. There were always the cold wet socks and feet, which we regarded as situation normal.

During the war years everything was rationed. Because we never bought clothing, except for footwear, Mammy traded our clothing coupons for food coupons or cash. Wartime shopping consisted of women carrying at all times, at least one, but normally two, 'message bags'. Queues formed as if by magic, outside a butcher's or grocery shop, if it was even rumoured that they had something to sell. As kids, or 'weans' (in the vernacular, pronounced 'wains'), we were conditioned to spending hours at a time waiting in queues with Mammy.

Butcher's queues were the best fun, as the floors were thickly covered with sawdust which we would play in, building castles, moats, and roads, which had to be abandoned and rebuilt, as the queue shuffled slowly on. Another feature of the butcher shop was the fact that the animal carcasses were hung on hooks and rails on the customer side of the shop where we queued. We could climb into the rib cages and swing until Mammy, or anyone else who thought fit, would smack us out of it.

In regard to shopping (which was not referred to as shopping, but as 'going for the messages') nothing was pre-packed, except such items as jams or sauces. Everything else was weighed and wrapped as you were being served. Fresh fruit and eggs, amongst many other items, were totally unobtainable. For many years we presumed that apples and pears, etc, were a shade of grey in colour, as we had only ever seen these on the black and white screen at the pictures.

Another fact of wartime life was the almost universal use of horse-drawn vehicles for just about every task imaginable. Large stables were dotted around our neighbourhood, which accommodated not only the majestic Clydesdales which pulled the majority of drays, or 'larries' as these were known locally, but a wide range of smaller horses suitable for lighter work. These horses, which knew nothing but congested city streets, must have had a grim life.

For the drivers of these vehicles, life was also grim. They had to be on the job very early in the morning, to attend to their charges, grooming and feeding, and most importantly cleaning and polishing the leather harnesses and brass work which the Clydesdales particularly, were dressed up in. The horses employed by the breweries, bakeries, and even the Corporation Cleansing Department, were always beautifully presented.

A big advantage with a horse or a team of horses was their ability to carry out deliveries and collections, by starting and stopping at the relevant spot, whilst the driver talked to them from the pavement, or the rear of the larrie, without having to climb up and down from the high driver's seat. Auntie Bella's husband worked for the Cleansing Department, collecting garbage from greengrocers. Alec Dorans was a diminutive man, even by Glasgow standards, a lot less than five feet tall, but wiry and tough, and always full of wisecracks, for all that. His working day started at six am, when he unstabled his Clydesdale, 'Bobby', groomed him, and polished the elaborate harness and brasses.

By eight o'clock Bobby and his cart looked a million dollars, and ready for a long day on the streets. It was only then that Uncle Alec's pay started, for carters were expected to carry out the necessary horse and harness preparation work in their own time, morning and night. This meant that they worked from two to four hours per day without pay. Bobby was as smart as a tack and knew his way around his daily collection route by heart, stopping and starting with minimal interference from Uncle Alec.

We lived almost directly above Hutcheson's fruit shop and were on Bobby's route. As a morning ritual, we would take two slices of stale bread with treacle filling, down to the close-mouth, ready for Bobby, who was always punctual. When he saw his treat coming, he would snort in anticipation. As a treat for me, I was helped up onto Bobby's very broad back, clinging tightly to his decorative harness, and allowed to ride to the next greengrocers which was not far away, in Florence Street.

I always tried to stay on but being threatened by the promise of no more rides, would be lifted off to walk home with Mammy. However, difficulties were experienced when one day we were not able to be there. Bobby would not budge without his treat, ignoring all instructions, until Uncle Alec gave in and bought him a sugary bun from the nearest bakery shop. Shortly after this incident, Uncle Alec and Bobby were transferred to another collection route, so my daily worship of the beautiful Bobby came to an end.

Another feature of tenement life was the street vendors, usually pushing handcarts, and advertising their wares at the top their voice in a jargon which was unintelligible, even to us. Whelks, mussels, cockles, and dulse (edible seaweed) were sold by separate vendors.

If we could inveigle sixpence, or even thruppence, from Mammy we would queue up eagerly for a paper poke of whatever was being sold. Unfortunately this was seldom possible, as Mammy rarely had a spare penny, never mind sixpence. We were usually confined to watching others scoff these treats. Other hawkers sold fresh Loch Fyne herrings, which we loved; others sold such disgusting things as tripe and other offal, from which we steered well clear.

The ragman was another daily hawker, pushing his handcart. He would give weans a tawdry trifle in exchange for a bundle of rags. Mammy would never allow us to take rags to the ragman, as she regarded him as a thieving swine. Our rags were saved up until we had a sufficient bundle to take to the rag store, where they weighed them properly and gave the going rate without any nonsense.

The horse-drawn coal larry was another fixture, with each vendor having his own regular customers. Mammy would only buy our coal from Earnoch's, as she trusted them to supply clean coal without the useless stones which other coalmen regularly mixed in to make up the hundredweight (50kg), which each sack should contain. The climate was so cold and damp that our coal fire was kept burning all year round.

Each household stored the coal in a coal bunker just inside the entry door. You can imagine the amount of black dust which was raised when the coalman dumped the contents of the coal bag from shoulder height into the bunker, settling inside the house and adding to the grime which was a constant enemy of every family. Some fought the battle against filth and grime with stolid determination on a daily basis, against the considerable odds, whilst many others lived with a fatalistic acceptance of the hostile environment.

Another source of grime was the communal open middens, located in each back court where all tenants dumped their daily waste. A large proportion of this consisted of ashes from the coal fires. Each day the middens would be filled to overflowing.

Every night, horsedrawn carts, each accompanied by about six men wearing miner's helmets, complete with an acetylene lamp and studded leather shoulder shields just like the coalmen wore, arrived, each carrying on his back a large wickerwork basket, and a large shovel. Working in pairs, the middenmen would shovel the contents of the midden into each other's baskets until full, despite the presence of the large rats which were disturbed during the process. They would then return to the cart, climbing up onto the tailboard step, and leaning over bent double, tip the stinking contents of the basket behind their own heads into the cart.

The majority of this refuse consisted of ashes, choking clouds of which floated everywhere, not least onto the middenmen, who looked absolutely ghastly and white all over. You might think that they must have been well paid to do such a health-threatening and physically demanding job, with a permanent night shift, but they were only paid a pittance, as most unskilled labour was. Remember also that no employers, at that time, provided such luxuries as basic washing or changing facilities for workers.

Everybody went home covered in whatever grease or grime they had accumulated during the course of their working day, travelling on public transport, to a tenement which lacked hot water or a bath (showers were not even dreamt of). The characters that went to the pub on the way home would eventually arrive home filthy and drunk. You can imagine what a middenman looked like when he got home. Only the desperate need apply! During the war, women took over a multitude of jobs normally done by men, but being a middenwoman was definitely not one of these.

Air raid shelters were a feature of the local landscape, being built wherever there was an available site, such as back courts, or school playgrounds, or even in the middle of the street. In front of each close mouth a steel reinforced galvanised iron structure was erected which was then packed with sand. These baffles were intended to prevent a bomb blast from directly entering the close mouth. But they were not fitted with a roof, the sand being exposed to the elements and the street urchins, who normally had only filthy muck to play in.

This was a major error, as the kids from each close soon discovered ways of removing the sand, and carting it into the backs, to be converted into sandcastles or deserts, eventually leaving an empty blast baffle shell, which would have been easily blown away if a Clydesdale had farted sideways.

The close itself was reinforced with a substantial timber bracing structure, just like an underground mine shaft, to resist caving in of masonry. In practice this structure was used as a type of jungle gym by the older weans, especially at night when the blackout was in force, when they would wait until someone was coming through the close then unleashing a cacophony of shrieks and moans, frightening the holy crap out of the poor victim. If we had to come home after dark, we would stand in the middle of the street, and call out "Mammy, Mammy I'm coming up the noo, open the door". When we saw the faint glimmer of light on the first landing caused by our door being opened, we ran in through the close and up the stairs like greased lightning.

The design of the main air raid shelters was very basic, consisting of walls of brick, forming a rectangle, conforming to the amount of space available, a brick blast wall shielding the dual exit/entrance, and the whole topped off with a massive concrete roof slab. Even we weans could figure out that the design of these shelters was not as good as it should be, and would be a likely death trap if a German bomb dropped anywhere in the vicinity. We could imagine the flimsy walls caving in and the concrete roof slab collapsing, crushing the sheltering occupants.

Consequently, the majority of tenement dwellers preferred to take their chances in their own homes, or with neighbours, sharing the risk. The people who lived up our stair all crammed into the 'back shop' of the ground floor greengrocers, owned by old Jock Hutcheson, as soon as the dreaded air raid sirens sounded. He was the most prominent local character and the owner of several large stable and horse cart establishments. Despite his obvious assets, he still lived by himself in the back shop which contained a bed, small table and little else.

As soon as the nearest pub opened, old Jock was swiftly inside, not to emerge until he was only just barely able to stagger across the street, taking ages of fumbling to unlock the door of his back shop. We kids would hang around, for he would always produce a two-shilling coin from a pocket, press this into the nearest grimy outstretched hand, and mumble "get me a fish supper, son" before reeling in through the door, and slamming it behind him. We knew that we were on to a winner regardless, for if he was still awake when we returned with the fish supper -- he never asked for the sixpence change, he just grabbed the newspaper parcel and slammed the door.

We would race back to the chip shop and get sixpence worth of chips, which was enough to satiate the semi-permanent hunger of three or four kids. If our hammering on his door failed to rouse him from his drunken stupor, then we would eat the fish supper, and keep the sixpence for the morrow, to spend on some item of food to share, such as tottie scones, hot buttered rolls, or Vienna rolls, topped off by a penny's worth of broken biscuits.

Chapter 2

A total night-time blackout was enforced for the duration of the war, with no vehicle lights allowed, except for dimmed lights on tramcars, buses, and trains. No lights were allowed, unless in the case of shops, offices, factories, and dwellings the already dim lights were blocked completely by thick blackout blinds. Any transgressors were sure to receive a swift visit from the Air Raid Precautions (ARP) people or the regular constabulary, and forced to comply immediately, or else.

In our neighbourhood, these precautions in not assisting the Luftwaffe night bombers were totally negated by an inescapable factor. The next-door Govan Ironworks were not known as 'Dixons Blazes' without due cause.

The ironworks sprawled over a large area and were very old, using technology of a previous era or two. Three enormous Open Hearth Furnaces formed the core of iron smelting operations. From these furnaces, twenty-four hours a day, three hundred and sixty-five days a year, belched great columns of smoke and flames high into the sky. The sky at night was dominated for many miles around by this bright red glow. The actual night sky, complete with stars and moon, was completely unknown to us, being permanently obscured by the light emanating from Dixons Blazes.

The Luftwaffe bomber squadrons which regularly bombed Glasgow and Clydebank were based in Norway. I am sure that they were able to spot Dixons Blazes from halfway across the North Sea, if not from Norway, on most nights. Yet we continued, for the duration of the war, to fumble around in the dark like troglodytes. We listened, our mouths agape with wonder as our older cousins, and our grownups, told us of the days before the war, when street gaslights were lit at night, and nobody used blackout curtains, or cared about bombers at all.

'Before The War', became a phrase which inevitably preceded a story of some kind, which we listened to with intense concentration, even when we had been told the same story many times before, just in case the storyteller got something wrong, or missed something out.

We became juvenile authorities on 'Before the War' folklore, being able to argue fine points with anyone who had the misfortune to tell a story which deviated from the version which we had consigned to cast-iron memories, within which the filing system was absolutely infallible. "How can youse weans mind a' thae things when yese wurnae even boarn?" my aunties would exclaim with frustration, when we would butt in with a correction when they were telling someone a familiar story. My mother was used to being corrected regularly from below waist level, and would take it in her stride, with hardly a pause for breath, incorporating the correction into her conversation.

Our single end was tiny, with our scrubbed kitchen table taking up almost all the spare space. Some of my favourite memories are of my mother's sisters congregating round the table with cups of tea. As there was literally no room for us, we were pushed under the table to sit on the floor, being told that weans should be seen and not heard. "Mammy", we would call out, "naebody kin see us alow the table oneywey". Our aunties would roar with mirth and give us a sly kick at the same time. Although we did our best to listen to the ribald gossip, it was very difficult as they all spoke at the same time, at the tops of their voices, interspersed with peals of raucous laughter.

Auntie Jean swore like a trooper at all times, not caring who was present, and embarrassing her sisters, who neither smoked nor swore, or drank. Auntie Jean did all three, in an environment which frowned upon these habits. She didn't give a bugger about anyone's opinion, but we could not help loving her regardless.

When I was about three years old, she taught me a little song and dance routine, whilst she was babysitting us. The title of this piece was 'Flooers fur the Hoors'. I knew what flooers were but had no idea what a hoor was. I had a vague feeling that it had something to do with telling the time, which I was just learning to do. I soon had the whole routine off pat.

The next time Mammy and her sisters were having one of their get togethers, this time at Auntie Bella's hoose in Caledonia Road, we were parked under the table as usual. Halfway through proceedings Auntie Jean leant down and whispered, "Hey Allan, hoo about daen the wee turn Ah showed ye", at the same time pulling me out from under the table. I was lifted onto the table. At a nod from Auntie Jean, I proceeded to sing and dance. After a brief period of stunned silence, everybody started to giggle, then burst into uncontrolled laughter. Tears were running down faces. When I finished and bowed, as I had been taught, the laughter carried on unabated.

Gradually my Aunties gained control and wiped the tears from their flushed faces. “Dae ye know whit a hoor is, Allan?” someone asked.” I think it’s part of a clock” I replied, now feeling very embarrassed, as I couldn’t really understand what was so funny. My reply caused another outbreak of hysterical laughter. I crept back under the table and rejoined Bobby, who was still playing with some discarded cotton reels and elastic bands, which we imagined as tanks. It was many years later that I learnt what a hoor was. Auntie Jean was a right bugger!

As pre-schoolers, we were expected to look after ourselves, and each other, to a far greater degree than would be expected today. Although we lived in what was probably one of the toughest neighbourhoods in the western world, if not the toughest at that point in time, the majority of tenement dwellers were decent folk, who lived a blameless and industrious life, fighting hard to keep their homes clean, despite major difficulties, and doing their best to ensure that their families grew up, as untainted as possible by the awful living conditions, which everyone had to contend with on a daily basis.

For self-protection, it was necessary for kids to belong to a group which functioned loosely as a gang. This consisted of kids who lived within an area of half a block or so, who played together, went to the pictures together, to the parks together, and patrolled the unmarked but accepted territorial boundaries, which nobody crossed without expecting trouble to erupt. It was, in many ways, a tribal society. For those kids who did not win acceptance into a group, life was tough, as they were forced to stay indoors, or risk getting roughed up if they ventured into the street without the protection of an adult.

The gangs were based on a matrix system, which just happened naturally. The overall governing factor was territory, within which the members arranged themselves in age groups, at roughly two-year intervals. This meant that each territory was occupied by approximately four or five gangs at once, without friction. A typical territory consisted of a section of street, in our case Kidston Street, from the junction with Crown Street, which was a major thoroughfare, round the corner into Florence Street, and up to the corner of Caledonia Road.

The streets were surfaced with very smooth asphalt, suitable for horse-drawn traffic. They were also ideal for a playing area. We had to be totally reliant on our collective imaginations, ignoring our grim and grimy reality, to turn our street into the Wild West, pretending to be Roy Rogers, Jee Notry (Gene Autry), Geronimo or Buffalo Bill one day, or the Martian landscape occupied by Flash Gordon and his various evil enemies such as the Clay Men, the next. The street could instantly become the ocean, with the pavements dry land, whilst we acted out the latest pirate picture. In effect we invented our own version of virtual reality, long before the computer age. We took turns at playing the goodies and baddies.

Any film which had grabbed our collective imagination would be played out in the street and backs, until we tired of it or saw another film. All it took to create the scene for any scenario was some chalk and a large dollop of imagination. To play pirates we drew a large pirate ship on the smooth street surface and, alongside, another ship to be manned by the 'goodies'. The system was open-ended, and totally flexible. We could be anything we fancied just by drawing the required objects on the surface of the street and stepping on them.

The side streets like ours were pretty safe to play on. There was minimal traffic, which was largely horse drawn anyway. Horses understood weans, and would stop of their own volition, rather than run over them, even if the driver was unaware of the weans in front. Nobody local owned motorcycles or cars, so the streets were clear of parked vehicles at all times. On the downside, there was horseshit to spare. As nobody had gardens, the shit accumulated until the Corporation streetsweepers, with stiff brooms and shovels, and accompanied by the usual horse and cart, swept it up.

About once a month, another horse-drawn cart would arrive late at night, equipped with large reels containing fire hoses. We waited in high excitement for the men to unlock the nearest fire hydrant, connect the hoses and run them out to their full length. When this was done, the men took a hose each, and proceeded to methodically blast the filth and grime from the street and pavement into the nearest 'stank', as the drains were known. We kept well clear otherwise the men would turn the high-pressure hose on us. We would have perished from exposure if that had happened, and of course there would have been the hammering we would get when we arrived home.

Our local cinema, or 'picturhoose', was the Crown Cinema, or 'the Crownie' which was mainly patronised by weans. It wasn't the worst dive in town, but it was well up in the league table.

Pictures were shown continuously from 3pm until 1030 in the evening. B grade pictures were interspersed with 'Chapters', which were serials which changed twice per week. Samples of these Chapters were Flash Gordon, The Clutching Hand, Charlie Chan, the Chinese master detective, and many others. If you wanted to keep abreast of the Chapters, you had to go twice a week. There was no fixed session, you went in at any stage of the programme, and stayed until the part of the picture where you came in arrived, then you would leave and go home. On the other hand, you could stay as long as you liked.

The fact that 99% of the audience were weans, and usually in excitable groups, caused the theatre to exist in a state of semi-permanent anarchy. Everybody smuggled in stones, tin cans, paper bags full of rubbish, 'screwtap' beer bottle tops, and any other potential ammunition which could be hidden in our clothes.

Whenever the action hotted up, and the baddies looked to have the upper hand, the rowdy audience howled encouragement to the goodies, at the same time hurling showers of missiles at the baddies on the screen. The noise was unbelievable, with everybody vigorously drumming their heavy tackety boots on the floor and yelling loudly. The more aggressive boys would rush down to the stage, climb up, and punch and kick the baddies on the screen repeatedly, whilst the audience cheered madly and egged them on. The management was long suffering, but the screen punchers were inevitably grabbed by the scruff of their jerseys, dragged to the fire escape door, and energetically slung out into the alley.

We were allowed to go to the Crownie straight after school for years, because our parents had absolutely no idea what went on inside. Our trips to this establishment came to a sudden and definite end one day when Daddy warned us to come home straight after the Chapters finished, as he and Mammy were going visiting. Our older cousin Isa Dorans would be 'watching' us and putting us to bed. Unfortunately, we went to the Crownie with other boys, who jeered and sneered at Bobby and me when we said that we had to go home.

Not wanting to be regarded as 'fearties', we stayed on right through the whole programme again. We thought that we would get away with it, as our parents had gone out, and Isa would not tell tales.

When we arrived home at ten o'clock, the door was wrenched open, with a furious Daddy glaring at us with bulging eyes. "Where the bloody hell have you two been?" he yelled. "At the C-c-crownie," we stuttered. "I'll gie ye bloody Crownie," he screeched, "we couldnae go oot with you buggers no' hame yet." He put us in turn across his knee and gave us the most thorough tanning with his leather belt that we ever had up to that time.

I was first for treatment, and took the brunt of his fury, as I always refused to greet (cry!), which only made him even angrier, and he prolonged the belting until Mammy intervened. Bobby was always much smarter than I was when he was being belted. He would start howling at the top of his voice before the belt even hit, so he would get off more lightly than I did. We retired to bed with our well wealed behinds. It was the next day before Mammy told us what had happened.

When we failed to come home at the expected time, Daddy had walked down to the Crownie hoping to hurry us up home. When he got there without meeting us, he returned home. Finding that we were still not home, he sped back to the Crownie, bought a ticket, and went inside to look for us. Once inside, he couldn't believe the uproar and missile throwing that was going on without a stop. He spent a whole hour inside combing the rows of seats, one by one, but couldn't find us.

From that day onwards we were banned from even mentioning the Crownie, never mind going there. We had to rely on other weans to keep us up to date with the Chapters. Many years later the Crownie was totally refurbished and reopened as a perfectly respectable cinema catering for upmarket adults who preferred European films. However, it was a long time before the Crown Cinema lost its previous reputation with the locals as a 'right den'.

Chapter 3

I don't remember a lot of details about events before I reached the age of four, but a few seem to stick in my mind. We never used any of the regular air raid shelters. When the air raid sirens sounded with a terrible moaning wail, which frightened the hell out of adults, you can imagine how the weans felt. I can still remember the sheer terror, as we were bundled up quickly in our blankets, and hurried downstairs to old Jock Hutcheson's back shop where we crammed in with all the other neighbours.

Nobody said very much whilst the bombs were falling, most probably around Dixon's Blazes, which must have been easier to hit than to miss. The noise of the anti-aircraft batteries only added to our discomfort. We looked to Mammy and the other women for reassurance. Despite the white faces, nobody let the side down by snivelling or showing any sign of distress. When the all clear eventually sounded however, all the usual wisecracks flowed like a torrent, due to the relief of still being alive.

Most of these were above our heads, but we got the gist of the ribald jokes, nevertheless. As successive raids occurred, our terror diminished, and the jokes and laughter, carried on whilst the Luftwaffe tried its best to level the neighbourhood. All I can say is that their bombing skills were rubbish. When we went out the next morning we looked all around, expecting to see colossal damage from the night before. We were always to be disappointed. Life was going on as normal, as if the previous night's air raid had been just a bad dream.

We got very blasé about the air raids, to the extent that we stayed in bed throughout, wide awake, but ready to scoot down the stair, if we thought that the bombing was getting too close for comfort. This attitude changed dramatically one night. The moaning sirens had sounded, and we were sitting up in bed, playing with our cotton reels, which were just about the only toys we had.

The very first bomb must have scored a direct hit on our side of Dixons Blazes. The blast hit our building, shaking it violently to the foundations. Our iron bedstead collapsed onto the floor, knocking the breath out of us, whilst the plaster ceiling above the bed came down, luckily in pieces. We, that is, Mammy, Bobby and I, were left looking up at the exposed laths of the ceiling. We scrambled out of our flattened bed, covered in plaster and the horsehair which was used by plasterers as reinforcement.

We grabbed our blankets, without stopping to shake the plaster out, and ran down the stairs like linties, banging on the back door of the fruit shop to be let in. We dived through the doorway, even faster than Flash Gordon could have managed. We, like all native Glaswegians, were of a white pallid complexion, due to a lack of exposure to natural sunlight. Now we were even whiter than white, from sheer fright, and thoroughly covered with white plaster and horsehair.

When the all clear sounded, we cautiously returned to our single end. The door was wide open, as we had fled without locking it. The hoose was shambolic -- the rest of the ceiling must have collapsed after we abandoned ship. "Never mind," said Mammy, "we're still here, and no' deid," as she grabbed the dustpan and brush. As was expected of weans, we helped to clear up the mess, using buckets borrowed from the neighbours, to ferry the fallen plaster down to the midden.

The clean-up was accomplished by noontime, as the hoose was very tiny anyway. We then had to join a long queue at the Factor's office in Crown Street to report the bomb damage. It turned out, as Mammy talked to others waiting, that we were relatively lucky. Most had suffered more severe damage than we had. Waiting in the long queue took far more time than the cleaning up operation did.

We had to wait for months before a couple of plasterers turned up to effect our ceiling repairs. They lugged all the necessary materials up the stairs. We had to shift the pram and the kitchen table out to the landing. The clothes pulley had to come down and be laid down the stairs. Once this was done the plasterers laid a large sheet of plywood on the floor. This was used to mix the plaster on. We were very keen spectators and were allowed to pour the water into the middle crater of the mixed ingredients. The finished stiff mix was bright pink in colour.

The skill which the men displayed in transferring the plaster from the 'howk', held in the left hand, to the trowel in the right, then slapped overhead onto the ceiling, was marvellous to watch. When the job was finished, we had to clear up the mess, and bring our stuff back inside. Standing on top of the kitchen table, Mammy somehow managed with the help of our older cousin, Nancy Patterson, to rehang the pulley above the table.

Another incident, which took place when I must have been about three years old, has lodged in my memory. Daddy was home on leave. For some reason, we were staying at Granny Cunningham's hoose. He was dressed in his army uniform and took me on the tramcar into the city. The reason for the trip was to have our photograph taken together, at a studio in Argyle Street. When we were finished, we walked along the street, towards the Central Station overbridge, known locally as 'The Heilan'man's Umbrella'.

At that time, believe it or not, Glasgow Zoo was located within a large building on Argyle Street, right in the centre of the city. Daddy sprung a surprise by taking me through the turnstile into the zoo. I was delighted. We had a look at some monkeys, and some camels. "Dae ye want to see the lions?" asked Daddy. "Aye", I said, not knowing what a lion was. We were just nearing the lion's cages, when one of the lions roared. The noise was greatly magnified by being inside the building. I stopped dead, terrified, tearing my hand from Daddy's, and taking off for the exit. I didn't dare look back, as I was convinced that the lion was right on my tail.

I was outside, and well down the street, despite my little legs, before Daddy caught up with me. It was a long time before he managed to calm me down, as I was convinced that the lion had escaped and was somewhere close around. As we waited at the tram stop for a number 9 Auchenshuggle tram, I continued to look in every direction, for I wasn't convinced that the lion was not loose and would not appear suddenly and eat me.

Not until we were safely on board the tramcar, and well down London Road, did I even start to relax. Even then, I thought that anything that could roar like that must be able to run much faster than a tramcar. I kept my eyes fixed firmly back down London Road, praying that Daddy was right, and the lion was still locked up in his cage.

Getting off at the tram stop opposite Belvedere Hospital, we walked up McDuff Street to Big Granny's hoose in Glamis Road. As we approached, I stopped dead in total horror. The decorative cast iron railings which had surrounded the front gardens, and which were still there when we left for town, were gone. Only little stumps were left, embedded in the low sandstone wall.

I took one look and locked my arms firmly around one of Daddy's legs. "Whit's wrang wi ye?" he said. "The lion must have beaten us hame an' eaten a' thae railins" I said. "Don't be bloody daft" he said, "Lions cannae eat railins, they wid break their teeth aff, ye silly wee bugger, then whit they dae fur eatin their dinner?" Even to a terrified three-year-old, this seemed like a reasonable proposition.

Despite this I still retained my death grip on his leg, until we were safely inside Granny's hoose, with the door firmly locked at my insistence. Only then did I realise that I had not even seen the lion, having only heard one almighty roar before bolting for the Zoo doorway. I never found out what a lion looked like until I came across a picture of one in a library book, years afterwards. By the look of the lion in the picture, bolting from the zoo had been the right course of action to follow.

It turned out that the Government had in their wisdom decreed that, because of the shortage of raw materials required for the war effort, all unessential indulgences, such as garden railings, would contribute far more to the general good by being removed and melted down to be reincarnated as tanks, warships, fighter planes and bombers. That morning, whilst Daddy and I were in town, trucks and a work gang had arrived, equipped with hydraulic cutters, and systematically removed every railing from the entire district. This was done so quickly that our railings were probably being melted down at Dixons Blazes, whilst we were still fleeing from that terrible roaring lion.

Mammy and Daddy were not, in any way, religious. (It was not until I was fourteen years old that I found out that my father had been brought up in the Catholic faith.) Despite that, we were packed off to Sunday school, from the earliest age possible. The Wynd Church was located right next door to our close. Mammy would scrub us up (literally) on Sunday morning, and escort us next door, handing us over to the bucktoothed biddy who ran the Sunday School. Her teeth were so prominent that the older weans said that she could eat her dinner through a tennis bat. What a tennis bat was, we had no idea, but it sounded like a good joke anyway, so we laughed on cue.

We were each given a penny to put into the collection bag. This was a red velvet cone shaped bag which was carried on a long pole by a smarmy looking character who went along the rows of pews, thrusting the bag at everyone in turn. When we first attended, we dutifully dropped our penny in the bag, albeit regretfully. "Yir mugs, yese ur", the older weans told us on the way out, showing us their pennies retrieved from their pockets. "Ye don't drap the penny, ye put yer haun in an' make a noise, but haud on tae yir money".

The next week, we followed their advice, blushing red, as we held tightly on to our penny, sure that we would get caught in the act and give Mammy a right showing up. Nobody seemed to notice, so we always kept our pennies from that Sunday onwards. From listening to adults such as Auntie Jean, we knew that Jesus Christ was a swear word. We were very confused by people in church seemingly swearing a lot, even during the singing of hymns. This gave us even more reason to hold on to our pennies.

As time passed, we graduated to joining the 'naughty boys' at Sunday School. We were shown how to dodge the awful dreary hymn singing sessions, by sneaking into the boiler room, climbing down a steel ladder into the coal cellar. Once there we could prise open the loading chute, clamber out into the street, and scamper off to spend our pennies. When we arrived home, as if we had just left Sunday School at the correct time, Mammy would say "Jist look it the state o' yese, ye look mair like ye were dragged heid furst through a coal yaird, instead of being at the Sunday School, where did a' that glaur come fae?" Poor Mammy, she was so trusting at that time.

Once, when we were visiting Granny Cunningham, I was totally engrossed, playing in the bedroom with some rare treasure in the form of coloured glass jauries (marbles) which had belonged to my Uncle Rab when he was young. Mammy came into the room with a brown paper parcel tucked under her arm. "Just look at what Auntie Annie has goat for ye," she said, with a beaming smile on her face. I was immediately excited, as presents were few and far between. What could it be, I thought? An aeroplane, a battleship, a boax o' wee sodgers (toy soldiers)?

Mammy unwrapped the parcel and held up the contents. "Jist look at that," she said, "a lovely wee kilt for ye tae weer tae the Sunday School." I recoiled in horror. "Naw, ah'm no' weerin that". "But ye huv tae" said Mammy. "Yer Auntie Annie hid a right joab getting wan the right size". This stumped me, as I would rather die than offend my Auntie Annie. I knew two definite things about kilts. The first was that nothing but a bare bum was worn underneath. The second was that a' the lassies in the street would troop behind the kilted boys singing "Kiltie, Kiltie Cauld Bum!" over and over, and lifting the kilt to prove it.

They did this to grown up soldiers in the street too. What chance would I have of escaping this ignominy? Mammy removed my shorts, whilst I struggled, and buckled on the kilt. "There ye ur, ye look like a proper wee sodger, ah'll jist go an' get Nellie an' Granny tae hiv a wee look at ye". As soon as she left I whipped off the kilt, ran to the window, opened it with a strength born of desperation, and hurled the kilt out of the three-storey window as far as I could, and shut the window again. I was just buttoning up my shorts, when Mammy returned with Granny and Auntie Nellie.

"Whit hiv ye done wi' the kilt?" Mammy demanded. "Ah've loast it" I mumbled. "Loast it," Mammy yelled, "Hoo cuid ye hiv loast it? Where the hell is it?" "Ah threw it oot the windae, Mammy." "Mah goad almighty, ye wee rascal, whit ahm ah gonnae tell oor Annie, she'll want to kill ye!" shouted Mammy. "Ah'll run doon the sterrs and get it back the noo". As she ran out of the door both Granny and Auntie Nellie glared at me. "Ye're a right wee bugger," said Granny, "whit ur ye gonny dae next". I hung my head in embarrassment. It was hard to take such a telling off from Granny.

Mammy returned from the street after about ten minutes. "It's no therr, somebody must hiv stolen it already, kin ye credit that?" she said. "Who wid be so low, as to steal a wee boy's kilt?" I didn't know either but thanked the low life from the bottom of my heart.

"Whit ur we gonnae tell oor Annie?" asked Mammy again. Granny thought for a while then said, "We'll just tell her that you washed the kilt and were drying it in front of the fire. When you goat back from goin' fur yer messages, you foun' that the wee kilt had fa'en intae the fire an goat a' burnt up". I was lucky that Auntie Annie believed the story, but I was so ashamed of what I had done it was a long time before I could look at her without feeling guilty.

Another event which left an indelible memory in my mind was the time that we went on a camping holiday on the banks of Loch Lomond, when I was four years old. I suppose that the memory was so embedded because I never ever had another holiday until I was working on the railway and qualified for a free rail ticket.

When we were told that we were going on a camping holiday, we spent each day counting down, from two weeks before we actually travelled, until the great day arrived. Somehow or other, Big Granny had the use of a large ex-army bell tent. Granny cajoled her coalman to transport her and the tent, plus all the poles and paraphernalia, on his lorry from Glasgow to Luss on the shores of Loch Lomond, where she had booked a camp site for a month.

During the month, everyone in the extended family group would have a holiday in turn. Granny travelled ahead in the coal lorry, to set up the tent ready for our arrival. We were in the first batch to travel to Luss. The group was made up of us, the McLachlans, and the Duncans, Auntie Jean's family, Jean, Gilmour, Robert, Grace, and young Jean, who was the same age as me.

We all met in the city at the SMT bus terminal and went down to Luss on the bus. We travelled light as we owned practically nothing to pack anyway -- the main items carried consisted of food, blankets, pots and pans, and home-made 'tinnies' with wire handles for boiling over the fire. None of us had ever been outside the city so we were totally agog all the way, as we passed through unfamiliar parts of the city, then affluent suburbs with real houses and gardens which were not blackened and grimy. We were so excited that we found it impossible to sit still.

It was a cloudless sunny day, which was very unusual. God, it was brilliant, and way beyond adequate description. When we eventually drove around a sharp bend in the road and got our first glimpse of Loch Lomond shimmering in the sunshine, we were totally awestruck. As we drove along the winding road which closely skirted the lochside we were presented with fresh vistas every few minutes, prompting continual "oohs" and "aahs" from our wide-open mouths. I remember a small bay, with a large rock projecting from the loch, about fifty yards from the shore. Some young men were diving from the rock into the crystal clear water. It was all so far removed from our grim, grimy world of the Gorbals, and of Bridgeton where the Duncans lived.

We pulled into the small town of Balloch, where everybody except us got off. After a few minutes the bus carried on towards Luss. We had only driven a few miles when the bus screeched to a sudden halt, tipping us out of our seats. We all stood up, wondering what the driver had stopped for so abruptly. We looked out of the front window of the bus. About ten yards in front of us stood an enormous shaggy red stag, which must have emerged from the dense forest to our left.

It was pawing at the road with its front hooves, rolling its eyes, and making an awful roaring noise. When the bus didn't run away in terror, the stag charged head on into the bonnet of the bus, with a loud bang shaking the bus from front to rear. It shook its massive antlers, as if he had just run headfirst into a giant marshmallow and charged again with the same result. After two more charges at the fearless bus, the stag shook his head, snorted loudly, as if to say, "what a bum fighter you turned out to be, you'll never attract a harem of hinds," and slowly ambled off into the forest in presumed disgust. The driver tentatively got out to inspect the damage. He found that, apart from some severely dented metal work, no critical damage had been done. The driver would not drive on until he had filled in a damage incident report sheet which Mammy and Auntie Jean signed as witnesses. Only then would he continue on to Luss.

Arriving at the bus stop at Luss we all piled out and unloaded our possessions. Each of us was then loaded up in accordance with our age. Mammy had the instructions of how to get to the campground. Rocket science was not required, as there was only one narrow road anyway. We trudged in single file northwards along the lochside for a mile or so, until we rounded a bend, and saw the huts and tents of our final destination, with smoke rising from the cooking fires.

This was not the acrid nose pinching smell of our familiar coal fires and factory chimneys, but a new smell to us, the wonderfully invigorating smell of fresh wood from the forest burning. We all rushed forward when we spotted Big Granny standing outside the biggest bell tent on the site. As soon as we were allowed, we rushed down to the lochside. "Can we take aff oor buits?", we asked, in a state of high excitement. "Ach, ye dinnae need buits or shoes here," said Granny "unless yir feet ur cauld, mind". We ran back to the tent, and unlaced our heavy boots, then ran down to the water and splashed in. The water was crystal clear, but breath-snatchingly cold. My agile little testicles disappeared back to where they had come from before I got even knee deep, having been previously well trained in the filthy duckpond in Richmond Park.

We ignored the cold as best we could and played in the loch as deep as we dared. Mammy should have known better, as our clothes were all too soon dripping wet from head to toe. Not until we were unable to cope with any more shivering did we leave the water and run back to our tent. “My Goad, look at the state o’ thae weans, they’ll catch their death o’ cauld, get their claes aff and hap them up in a blanket,” said Granny. Mammy and Auntie Jean did the necessary unpeeling of the whole tribe.

In no time at all we were all sitting around a roaring fire each wrapped up in a dry blanket, gripping a hot tinnie of OXO with our numbed fingers. As soon as we had finished our tinnies, we were laid out in a circle around the massive centre tent pole, to swiftly fall asleep. We were far too weary to engage in any horseplay anyway, and slept the sleep of the dead, at least for the first night. With Granny, there were nine of us of all ages sharing the one tent. The tent was large and roomy, so we all fitted in very comfortably.

I don’t remember a lot of detail of day-to-day activities, but a few things come to mind, apart from the weather, which was unusually hot and dry for the entire fortnight. My cousin Jean Duncan and I were given a cardboard box and sent off to the thick woods on the hillside to gather twigs for kindling the campfire. We set off, crossing the deserted road, climbing over the drystone wall and into the woods beyond.

We found plenty of twigs and started to load these into the cardboard box. As we were picking up twigs, I noticed that one of the twigs was speedily wriggling away from us. I grabbed it at one end, which made it wriggle even more. "It's a snake!" I said, handing it over to Jean, who was a fully paid-up tomboy and frightened of nothing. She held the snake at both ends, stopping it wriggling. I tipped the gathered twigs out of the box, to make room for our newly found treasure.

We forgot all about gathering twigs and looked for more snakes. Within an hour we had caught three more. "Dae ye think they cuid bite us deid? asked Jean, "Naw dafty, this is Scoatland, no' Africa". "Jist you wait tae oor mammies see these things". Full of pride and bubbling over with excitement, we hurried back to our campsite. "Hoo much wid did yese get?" asked Auntie Jean, who was sitting just inside the tent, enjoying a cigarette, whilst Mammy was peeling potatoes. "See for yirsel", I said, hoping to give them a big surprise. Auntie Jean looked into the box, as I proudly held it out for inspection.

"Fuuuuuuck!!!" shrieked Auntie Jean, dropping her cigarette and falling over backwards as her shaky camp chair collapsed under her, before recovering instantly and leaping to her feet. Mammy screamed in sympathy, without knowing what was so frightening but figuring that it must be something unbelievably dreadful to frighten Auntie Jean. Shattered by the reaction, I dropped the box on the ground as if it was on fire. "Snaaaakes! Snaaaaaakes! Bliddy Snaaaaaaaaaakes!" yelled Auntie Jean, kicking the box violently but accurately, booting it straight through the tent door and tipping it over. By this time quite a crowd of curious campers was racing over to see what all the screaming was about. Our poor snakes were wriggling off as fast as they could in four different directions.

One of the adult male campers, on seeing the snakes, fetched a spade from his tent, and proceeded to whack the poor wee snakes until they were limp and totally lifeless. "See youse two, you gave us a helluva fright, right enough," yelled Auntie Jean. "Ye wee bastarts, ah hiv a good mind tae kick yer erses, so ah dae." Then she burst out laughing. "Whit a terr, eh? Jessie, we better go and chainge oor knickers."

Granny then arrived back from Luss, where she had been hoping to buy some fresh eggs from one of the local cottagers, but with no luck. "Ye fair missed yersel', Maw," said Mammy, "Jean and I hiv been hivin a great time dodging a cardboard boax o' snakes that the weans broat back fae the wids. Whit a cairry oan we've hud !"

Without the twigs we had to start the supper fire with screwed up newspaper. The subject of the snakes kept everyone chuckling for the rest of the holiday and passed into family folklore.

Another daily chore was walking to the nearest ferm (farm) with a couple of big cans, to buy fresh milk from the dairy, run by the farmer's wife. Auntie Jean had been before, and knew the way, so Mammy decided to go along, in order to learn the route. I was allowed to accompany her, as I liked to explore new territory and was dead keen to see a real ferm wi' chickens, hoarses, sheep, and coos. We walked along the grass verge, a drystone wall between us and the narrow green strath bordering the loch. For a four-year-old boy it seemed to take forever, but eventually we got there.

We went into the ferm dairy, where the fermer's wifie poured milk from a pail into our cans. "Wid ye like tae see where the mulk comes fae", asked the wifie." Aye, missus", I replied. She took my hand and led me into the next-door barn, with Mammy and Auntie Jean following behind. Opening a stall, she showed us the hoose coo. "Is she no' a beauty", she asked, as if we knew a coo from a donkey's uncle. "Just look, while ah get some mulk intae this pail", said the wifie. I couldn't believe my eyes, when milk spurted from the coo's teats. "Imagine hivin yer tits pulled like that every day, Jessie," exclaimed Auntie Jean. "It wid be murder in the wintertime wi' cauld hauns grabbing it ye first thing in the moarnin, afore ye've hid time tae light yer furst fag even".

The fermer's wife dipped a mug into the pail and handed it to me to drink. I gulped down a large mouthful, then refused to drink any more, as it was unexpectedly and unpleasantly warm, which put me right off. "Ye doant know whit's good fur ye, son," said the wifie, "ye'll never grow up tae be a big man an' grow herrs oan yir chist, if ye dinnae drink yer mulk". We lifted our cans, whilst Mammy paid the wifie sixpence for the milk.

"I know a better wey back", said Auntie Jean. "It's a wee bit longer, bit there's faur mair tae see". We headed down a narrow lane towards the loch, until it turned right, following the shoreline. Half a mile along the lane we unexpectedly came to a large army encampment, complete with vehicles, tanks, and artillery pieces.

I was dead keen on military things, and wanted to stay where we were, as seeing real soldiers was a revelation for me. "It's the training camp o' the Polish Division", explained Auntie Jean. I was totally mystified, as to why soldiers were called the same name as the stuff that we cleaned our boots with. The camp was spread out for at least a mile along the lochside. I was mesmerised by the whole thing. "Come alang, Allan, or we'll niver get hame the day", said Mammy. We eventually reached the end of the encampment, where we saw a large group of men frolicking in the loch, buck naked.

Mammy was highly embarrassed, and wanted to hurry along with her eyes averted, pulling me along with her. Not so Auntie Jean, who stopped and leaned over the wall to get a better look.

Seeing her, the Poles started to leap higher out of the water, showing off their credentials. Auntie Jean cupped her hands around her mouth and yelled at the swimmers at the top of her voice, "Ah've seen faur bigger wullies oan wee wally (china) dugs". Mammy was blushing furiously and pulling at my hand.

"Krasnik Karppuki Fuckofski", yelled the Poles, not understanding a single word of what she was yelling. "Poles ur only good for haudin' up bliddy claes lines", she yelled. "Beerski Wisski Runski Getski Thepoliski", yelled the Poles. "Ach away wi' the loat o' yese, yer drawers are full o' mince", shouted Auntie Jean, which was a terrible insult in Glaswegian terms. The Poles thought this was some sort of invitation and left the freezing loch en masse, running towards us. "C'maon, Jean, fur Goad's sake, start runnin the noo, ur they'll catch us up in a minute".

We all started running with me being dragged along between them. Luckily for us, the Poles stopped dead at the stone wall and just milled around, for they would have caught us easily.

"Mah goad Jean, ye're jist terrible, they might've coat us", wheezed Mammy when we were far enough down the road to slow to a walking pace. "Naw, I knew they widnae, they're no allowed tae go ower the wa' or they'll get the jile". "How dae ye know that" asked Mammy. "Ah've been daen this every time ah've goat the mulk", replied Auntie Jean, laughing her head off.

When we got back to the tent Mammy was still annoyed with Auntie Jean and relayed the whole story to Big Granny. "Oor Jean's a right heidbanger right enough, she'll get us a' shot wan day, so she wull". Granny gave Auntie Jean a right roasting, when she got her by herself, and banned her from going anywhere near the Polish camp. I was still mystified however, as to why they were called

Poles. As far as I could figure out, poles were long wooden things that held up washing lines, and polish is what we put on our boots every night. I quizzed Mammy at length, on this perplexing matter, but was no wiser at the finish, as Mammy was as mystified as I was.

We thought we were in heaven. Camping was what we wanted to do for the rest of our lives. Nothing could be better than this. We did something different every day, with Mammy and Auntie Jean always accompanying us. We didn't really think about it at the time, but it must have been every bit as good for them as it was for us, if not better. When at last the dreaded day came around when the next family group would arrive, we would be forced to return home.

We were duly loaded up, and tramped into Luss to meet the bus that would drop off the next batch of families. We were surprised when only the Dorans family disembarked, Auntie Bella, and our big cousins, Grace, Cathy, and Isa. "Phamie could'ny manage it, Maw!" explained Auntie Bella to Granny, who had walked in with us to meet the bus. "She jist could'ny afford the bus fare for hur an' a' thae weans".

"Whit dae ye think, wee yin?" asked Granny, "dae ye want to stey fur anither foartnight?" "Nae bother", said Mammy, "ahm sure that Allan and Bobby wullnae complain aboot tha'". We said cheerio to the Duncan clan and walked back to the campsite with a spring in our steps.

The rest of our extended holiday was okay, and Bobby and I enjoyed playing in the loch shallows. It just wasn't the same without the wild tearaways of the Duncan clan, not least Auntie Jean, who was always good for a laugh, whatever the circumstances.

The Dorans family were all very nice, but very sedate in their habits. The only real laughing matter occurred when Auntie Bella produced brand new swimming costumes for herself and the girls, which she had managed to buy on the black market. Incidentally, the term 'Black Market' was something else that continually puzzled me. Everybody talked about it, but despite being constantly on alert, I was still waiting to see this marvellous mysterious place where you could buy anything if you had the money. Why was it black? It must be only open after the blackout started at night, so it was no wonder we never saw it!

Auntie Bella and the Dorans girls changed into the all white swimming costumes after we had been banished from the tent and, emerging with pride, minced down to the loch. Inch by inch, they took ages to get waist deep. They dog paddled and splashed around for a few minutes. The chilling water soon got to them, however, and they stood up, struggling to reach the shore, as fast as they could, shivering visibly. When I say visibly, I mean it literally. The glamorous swimsuits had somehow become transparent, and even worse, were disintegrating as they struggled towards the shore.

There was quite a crowd of bathers around at the time, who had enviously watched the white swimsuit brigade enter the water. When Auntie Bella realised what was happening, she was mortified, and laid down in the water, whilst pushing herself back into deeper water with outstretched arms, with my cousins following suit. "Allan, Allan!" she screamed in desperation, "Rin tae the tent and get yir Mammy and blankets, an' rin like hell afore we catch oor death o' cauld".

I did as I was bidden but had great difficulty in explaining to Mammy what the problem was. After some minutes had passed, both Granny and Mammy gathered up an armful of blankets and followed me down to the lochside. By this time a large crowd had gathered at the spot. Neither Mammy nor Granny could swim, and were frightened to even paddle, in case they were swept away and drowned. The only solution was to ask some girl swimmers to wade out with the blankets to Auntie Bella and the girls.

When the soaking wet, blanket wrapped unfortunates reached the beach, the crowd roared its appreciation, and clapped loudly. Auntie Bella was mortified, saying loudly "Bliddy black market rubbish, jist wait untae ah git ma' hauns oan him, the flyman, the lousy bugger." Salvaging the remnants of the swimsuits, which Bobby and I couldn't wait to do, we found that the material was some type of tough paper, which would have been okay if Auntie Bella and the girls hadn't had the brazen effrontery to use them for swimming.

Unfortunately, this set the tone for the remainder of the holiday, as Auntie Bella wouldn't leave the tent in daylight, due to the embarrassment of it all. My cousins were not much better, and proved to be no company at all, to our disappointment. Mammy, Bobby, and I were left to our own devices, which was pleasant enough, but without the daily dramas which we had grown accustomed to.

When we went for the milk in the mornings, Mammy point blank refused to go back via the camp of the Polish Division, despite our tearful entreaties. We were denied the chance of finding out why they were called Poles, or Polish, leaving us to wonder for many years.

(At this point it should be mentioned that the Polish Division embarked in Glasgow and sailed to become part of the famous 8th Army which participated in the invasion of mainland Italy). The Poles soon earned themselves a reputation as stubborn fighters, especially at the grim and drawn-out battle to take Monte Cassino from the determined German parachute troops who defied every effort to dislodge them for months.

When our sojourn ended, we travelled home with a feeling of great loss, which increased dramatically when we walked home through the gloomy and dirty Gorbals streets, suntanned and proudly carrying our camping stuff and blankets. It was difficult to even imagine Luss and Loch Lomond when we, for the very first time in our young lives, realised the degree of mind-numbing squalor that we had to contend with every day of the week.

It was depressing, and it took us months to settle back into the slum environment. I never saw Loch Lomond again, until well into my teens, when I was earning enough money to put a small deposit on a racing bike at Andy McNeil's cycle shop in Govan and was able to join the Scottish Youth Hostels Association. Andy was a dwarf, but he ran a small well-equipped workshop where every single bike was made to measure for the customer. When you saw the name Andy McNeil on a bike, you knew it was something special. He was one of the great characters with which Glasgow has always been well endowed.

Chapter 4

When I was four years old, brother Alexander (Alex or Alec) was born. I don't remember being aware that Mammy was pregnant. In many ways our environment made us old beyond our years, but in other ways we were incredibly naïve. This meant that we had to cram a large, old-fashioned pram into the tiny single-end again, as well as the table and chairs. This was somehow managed, but I can't remember how.

The other battle was getting the large-wheeled pram up and down the stairs several times a day. We were lucky in living only 'one stair up', on the first floor. Only two flights of stairs had to be negotiated. Those who lived three stairs up had a much greater problem, as did the poor coalmen who had to hump dirty and wet hundredweight sacks of coal up six flights of stairs on a regular basis. One can only imagine how a coalman felt when he saw a housewife waving from a top floor window, holding three fingers up in the air, when she had got his attention. This meant that she wanted three bags of coal delivered.

Handling a heavy pram up and down the stairs was a well-practised art. Mammy had to do this by herself, as I was too small at that time to manage it. The pram was turned in reverse, with the push bar facing the stairs. The pram was balanced on the back wheels only, with Mammy climbing the stairs backwards, and bumping the pram up, step by step. The pram was parked in the short lobby between our door and the single end proper, sharing this space with the coal bunker. The pram had to double as a cot, until Alec was old enough to share the recess bed with Mammy, Bobby, and myself. The pram itself was passed around the various related families, as weans were born. What would have happened if a wean was born whilst another was still occupying the communal family pram, I don't know.

The arrival of Alec meant that I had to be become a lot more independent at the age of four, more or less overnight, and to take some of the weight off Mammy's shoulders. This meant looking after Bobby when we were playing outside, running errands on demand, and doing things like chopping the kindling wood with the hatchet inside the coal bunker, and lighting the fire every morning. The fire was allowed to die down at nights, not because the room was warm, but to conserve coal. We huddled together under the blankets and a couple of army greatcoats to keep warm. The greatcoats were much cheaper to buy than blankets. Even these coats came with a type of pecking order and stigma which was implicitly recognised and observed. Army greatcoats were the least desirable, with those who had more money than sense paying a premium for ex naval coats. The upwardly mobile splashed out on ex Royal Air Force coats, preferably with an officer's insignia still attached, to impress visitors. We had no luxuries such as pyjamas, and slept in our shirts, which we wore every day. Because of the difficulty of washing and drying clothes, not to mention the lack of money, we only had two of anything, at best, at any one time.

Our clothes were changed on Sunday nights after we had our weekly bath, standing up in a tin tub, in front of the fire. The only source of hot water was a kettle boiled on the gas ring on the floor. This meant that the bathwater was only just warm, not hot. Mammy kept topping up with successive kettleful's to keep the bathwater warm. We stood up in the galvanised tub whilst Mammy scrubbed us with carbolic soap and a stiff brush, then dipped a small pot into the water, pouring this over our heads to rinse us off. This was always the best part, as we had been shivering with cold until then.

The next candidate now squatted down in the tub, whilst Mammy hurriedly dried the last bather with a dry rough towel. We enjoyed standing as close as possible to the fire naked and relished the delicious feeling of the heat on our bare skin. When all were finished Mammy pulled next week's shirt over our heads and tucked us up in bed. There was no doubt that the Sunday night bath was a highlight of our week. We were accustomed to these conditions and knew that other kids were much worse off than we were.

Being in charge of kindling the fire, and getting the fire to draw properly, meant that I had to be first out of bed in the chilly dark mornings, and had to light the single gas mantle, which was the only source of illumination. Mammy got up as soon as the gas mantle was lit, and started preparing breakfast, which was always porridge (pronounced purritch), and freshly baked rolls. The rolls were bought fresh every morning, from a little shop straight across Crown Street from our street, run by a woman and her adult daughter.

They were universally disliked, being invariably sour-faced and abrupt in manner. If they took a dislike to anyone, they would point blank refuse to sell them anything. Mammy preferred to send us to buy the rolls. It was unlikely that the sour old biddy would manage to refuse to serve innocent wee boys, even if she would like to. "Where's yer Mammy, son?" she would ask. "She's no' well," we would reply. This was wartime, with rationing and incessant shortages of basic foodstuffs. The sour old biddy could pick and choose her customers with impunity, and still be sold out of bread and rolls by noontime. We liked rolls which had been overbaked, with a lovely chewy black crust.

When we asked to buy burnt rolls, she would try to pretend that she had none. "Missus, we can see some from here," we would say, hoping to shame her into giving us what we wanted. She might then reluctantly mix a couple of burnt rolls in with our half dozen order. When we got home, we would argue over who got the burnt rolls. Being the eldest, and being totally ruthless when it came to food, I always got one. If we were flush, we had jam on our rolls; if not, we had margarine.

Although I was only four years old, I was intensely interested in learning to read. Mammy was no help at all, as she had left school at the age of twelve to start work in the cotton mills operated by Coats. She wasn't that literate herself, and never read anything at all, during that period of her life. "Whit dae ye want tae read fur, ye'll get plenty o' that when ye get tae the school", she would say in good humour. Despite this I carried on with my single-handed attempts to decipher written text. There was nothing to read in the house, so I had to confine my efforts to trying to read the large print on shopfronts, cardboard cartons, and on wooden crates.

Having always accompanied Mammy on the constant round of shopping, I knew what a keg of butter was, and what all the bulk merchandise was that was stored behind the shop counters, with the description of the contents stencilled in large letters on the outside. By trial and error, I started to learn the letters of the alphabet, in the process causing much laughter when I got things wrong. The task was made more difficult than it should have been, as the wording was in English, whilst we spoke broad Glaswegian, which in effect was a different language.

Nevertheless, I persevered. In a relatively short time, I was astounding Mammy and everyone else in the family by reading out loud the names above shops, and the descriptions on cartons and boxes. The next task was to learn longhand, or joined up writing, as we called it. This was much more difficult. The best that I could do was to scribble on a piece of paper, and pretend that it meant something, as it looked the same to me as longhand did.

My Auntie Mary, Daddy's elder sister, was working as a bus conductress down in Dumfries, in the Scottish border country. When Mary was twelve years old, she had been taken out of school and packed off to work in a series of large country houses, as a skivvy. The polite term used was that she was 'in service'. During her time 'in service', she had learned to speak 'proper' English, albeit with a Scottish accent.

At some time, she had met, and married, a sergeant pilot, who was flying Hurricane fighter planes. His airfield was located near Dumfries, and Mary had moved there so that they could be together, renting a small apartment and getting herself a job as a bus conductress. Unfortunately, her husband was killed in action about two months afterwards, in the spring of 1942, leaving her disconsolate. She had arranged for Wee Granny to visit her for a week, in July of 1942. Granny, despite her age, had never been outside the confines of her very limited environment.

She arrived one day to ask Mammy if she could take me with her for company. Mammy, with some reservations, agreed. I was very excited at the prospect of getting out of the slums, and travelling a long way on the bus, remembering our holiday at Luss. On the day of travel, we all went into the city on the tramcar, and walked to the SMT bus terminus.

We met Granny at the bus terminus, where we eventually found her clutching her luggage, consisting of a large message bag. I was carrying my stuff in a small compressed carboard suitcase, that Mammy had borrowed from Auntie Annie for the occasion, with a great deal of pride. Mammy eventually located the proper bus, and Granny and I climbed aboard, sitting right up front behind the driver's cab. We waved goodbye to Mammy and the boys, as the bus pulled out of the terminus. As the bus travelled through the southeast suburbs, Granny kept asking "Ur we oot o' the toon yet?" as if I, a four-year-old, would know where the city boundaries were.

When the houses were thinning out, and some grassy fields appearing, I told Granny that we were getting close to leaving the city and were entering the countryside proper. Granny showed some interest in our surroundings as we progressed further. "Ahv'e niver been oot in the country in mah hale life," said Granny.

"Remind me tae buy some postcairds tae sen' tae a'body richt away, they'll be that jealous o' us so they wull".

It seemed to take forever to reach Dumfries, but we eventually reached the sparkling clean town, to find Auntie Mary waiting for us at the little bus terminal dressed in her conductress's uniform. Without fuss, she welcomed us. Kissing, hugging, or any other form of affection displayed in public was foreign to us and would have been regarded as unseemly and embarrassing in the extreme. We walked for some time until we reached Auntie Mary's little upstairs flat, which was reached by climbing up three flights of wooden stairs, attached to the outside of the building.

"Michty me, Merry, Ah don't know hoo ye kin climb these sterrs a' the time", wheezed Granny, grimly hanging on to the banister for support as she tried to get her breath back. I was surprised by her distress, as I had been used to climbing up and down stairs many times a day for all of my short life. "C'moan Granny," I bellowed into her better ear, "it's nae bother a' ta' ". We reached the flat eventually, with Granny puffing like a Grampus, all the way. I had no idea what a Grampus was, or what one looked like, but I knew from listening to stories that they puffed a lot.

Granny collapsed into the nearest chair, gasping for breath, and wiping her sweating brow with a large hanky. "Ah kid go a nice wee cup o' tea wae some biscuits, an' wae a wee gless o' whusky," Granny added hopefully. "There's not a drop of whisky in my house, and never will be," snapped Auntie Mary, "you're here to get some fresh air, and improve your health, not to sit on your behind drinking whisky." Granny got her tea and biscuits, which I shared in case I got offered nothing. Auntie Mary changed out of her uniform in her room, emerging in a neat summer dress, and carrying a handbag.

"Come on mother, we are going for a nice walk around town, so that you can see where we are, and how to get around."

Granny groaned "Kin ye no' jist take wee Allan, he's richt smairt ye know an' wullnae forget the wey aroon the toon, he kin show me the wey aboot the moara'." "Don't be lazy mother, you have to come with me now as I'm working a double shift tomorrow to make up some time, so that I can have the rest of the week off". Granny reluctantly groaned to her feet. "Kin we no' wait a wee while, jist tae ah get mah breath back?" Auntie Mary ignored her entreaties and ushered us out of the door. Granny found that walking down the stairs was nearly as bad as climbing up, grumbling to herself all the way down to the street.

We walked slowly through the quiet country streets, taking in all the lovely little houses, hedges and gardens. We eventually came to a stone bridge right in the middle of the town, spanning the river. This river looked nothing like the turgid smelly polluted Clyde, which was at that time the only river that I had seen. Under the bridge was a series of rocky cataracts with white water cascading down the waterfalls, with stiller pools between. A group of men dressed in rubber waders up to their armpits were using nets to fish. As we were watching, huge salmon were being netted. I was fascinated and had to be pulled away forcibly when Auntie Mary wanted to move on. I clung to some railings, whilst Auntie Mary, using both hands, prised my little fingers open. "Come on Allan, we can see them fishing another day", she said in an irritated voice.

We spent the late afternoon walking around the rest of the town, before heading homewards. Granny started to mutter to herself as the dreaded stairway hove into sight. "Ye'll hiv tae gi'e me a haun' up, fur ah dinnae think that ah kin manage by masel'." With Auntie

Mary pulling, and me pushing ineffectually from the rear, Granny eventually, puffing and blowing, made it to the top holding on to the handrail like grim death.

I can't remember that much about the remainder of our holiday, except that Granny wouldn't walk a step without holding firmly on to my hand at all times, not for my safety, but for her own. The woman who was quite at home negotiating busy city streets, even when drunk, was terrified to cross the quiet Dumfries thoroughfares by herself. Despite Auntie Mary's assurances, the salmon fishermen didn't appear again whilst we were there.

The remainder of the week was taken up with Auntie Mary showing us all around the district, using her SMT bus pass, and getting nominal fares for us. Granny wasn't able to sneak into a pub, either, which must have been a great irritation to her, but she knew better to even try if Auntie Mary was within miles of her. At the end of the visit, Auntie Mary put us on the bus to Glasgow, for the long journey back home.

Mammy and the boys met us at the terminal. "Did yese hiv a good time?" asked Mammy, shouting into Granny's ear. "Aye, we did that, bit ah' dinnae know whit ah wid hiv done withoot wee Allan tae get me acroass the streets, an' roond the toon. Ye've nae idea Jessie, whit the traffic's like, an' thir's nae traffic lights a' ta'". We saw Granny on to a number 9 Auchenshuggle tramcar and crossed over Argyle Street to catch a tramcar along Crown Street to home. Once again, I experienced the same sense of desolation and grey gloom that I had felt when we returned from Luss.

Chapter 5

At last, the great day arrived, my fifth birthday. I was now a big schoolboy, for the system was such that children started school on the very day that they turned five.

Mammy dressed me in brand new shorts and jersey, complete with a matching woollen tie and a tweed jacket. The nearest Protestant school was Camden Street primary school, which was less than a hundred yards from our close mouth. As was common during the war, a large part of the school had been taken over by the air raid precautions (ARP), and the Emergency Fire Brigade (EFB). This meant that all pupils were crammed into the junior part of the school, which normally housed the five- to eight-year-olds.

Mammy took me to the office of the junior school Headmistress, and the Headmistress entered my particulars into the school roll. Mammy left as quickly as possible so that she wasn't seen having a wee greet. The Headmistress then led me down a long corridor, to the junior classroom where the new entrants began.

This class was known locally as 'The Penny Buff.' I was handed over to the teacher and led to a miniature wooden desk at the front of the class, sharing this with a little girl wearing thick wire framed spectacles. I was issued with the standard learning kit, of a wooden bordered slab of black slate, a piece of white chalk, and a small box containing tiny seashells.

The chalk was for writing, and the seashells for counting. The first instruction from the teacher was to raise my right hand if I wanted to go to the toilet. The lesson in progress was reading a very elementary group of words printed on a large oilcloth scroll suspended from a hook at the top of the blackboard. The teacher was using a wooden pointer to point to words in turn, asking the class to read the three letter words out loud. She was having a difficult time, with the great majority of pupils blushing and shaking their heads. After some considerable time had passed with little success, the teacher berated the class.

"We've been learning these words for months, and I must say that I am very disappointed in you all," she said in an exasperated voice. "Is there anyone in the class who can say any of these words?" Nobody stirred. I realised that I could read the whole text, no bother. I very tentatively raised my hand. "Do you want to go to the toilet?" she asked. "Naw miss," I mumbled in total embarrassment. "Ah kin read a' the words okay". "But you're a new entrant, how can you read?" she said. "Ah learnt masel' miss", I said in a low voice. "Okay ", said the teacher, "read the words out as I point to them".

She started to point to the words in turn, from beginning to end. I only made one mistake, pronouncing the word 'one' as 'onney' as I hadn't seen it before. The teacher was totally silent. "Once more", she said. I read the words again, with the same mistake, as she hadn't corrected me. "Class, sit still, I'm just going to get the

Headmistress". I was totally embarrassed, and blushingly crouched low over my slate, whilst the class buzzed with chatter.

The teacher returned with the Headmistress in tow. "What's your name, I've forgotten already?" asked the teacher. "Allan", I replied. "Right Allan", just read those words out again for the Headmistress." I repeated the reading of the words. The Headmistress was obviously impressed and pointed out my mistake." "Oh, En, Ee, is pronounced Wun", said the Headmistress. I had never heard the word 'pronounce' before but could guess what it meant. "Okay Allan," said the Headmistress, "just gather up your things, I'm going to put you into the next class up, just follow me." Very apprehensively, I gathered up my new leather schoolbag, the slate and the little wooden box of seashells, and followed her down the corridor, to the next classroom.

As we entered, my heart sank. The kids in this class were big six-year-olds and were all bent over their desks in diligent concentration. Not one child looked up to see what was happening. I was led to the front of the class. Ahead of us stood a very large old lady clothed in a voluminous black traditional teacher's gown, with her white hair in a bun, and with a ferocious expression on her pug-ugly piggy face. "This is Allan McLachlan, Mrs Campbell," said the Headmistress. "He has only started school this morning, and I have just heard him reading aloud. He is up to the standard of your class, so I would like to start him off here."

Mrs Campbell just grunted. I looked up at her and felt real fear for the first time in my young life. Her little gimlet eyes glittered in her piggy face, which was liberally endowed with long white whiskers. I had never met anyone who projected such a frightening aura. The Headmistress left the room without a backwards glance.

"McLachlan, sit here at the front of the class, where I can reach you easily", grunted Mrs Campbell, pointing at a vacant half desk.

I slid into the seat as quietly as I could, but getting my schoolbag and slate tangled up. "Quiet, you stupid boy," thundered Mrs Campbell. "I can see that you've got a lot to learn!" I squirmed in my seat with embarrassment. I thought that everyone would be looking at me and sneaked a glance around. Not one face was looking at me, all were silently bent over their desks in total concentration. I soon learnt to my cost that Mrs Campbell detested teaching and would vent her spleen on any child who crossed her in any way.

Because of the wartime requirements of the armed forces, many teachers of both sexes had been called up for active service in the armed forces. To fill the gap, retired teachers had been press ganged to fill the vacant positions. Mrs Campbell was one of these very unhappy recruits. Her teaching armoury consisted of a yard long pointer for close range work, a much longer pointer for longer range engagements, and a heavy wood backed blackboard duster to act as a guided missile.

In her classroom nobody even whispered or did anything at all which might attract her baleful attention. I had upset her routine and was constantly the subject of her ire. As she well knew, I had an awful lot of catching up to do. Rather than helping me she would hold me up to ridicule at the slightest excuse. She taught from the back of the class, so that she could watch us unseen. If the slightest move was made, or the wrong answer given to a question, the unfortunate pupil would receive a violent blow to the back of the head without any warning. The pointers were painful enough, but the wooden duster was lethal. She was unaffected by the recipient bursting into tears, yelling "Stop snivelling, boy!" It was always boy, as she never hit the girls with anything but the regulation tawse, a long leather strap ending in three fingers, and rarely did she do that.

I received so many blows to the head that I was suffering from semi-permanent headaches. I had more lumps on my head than could be found in a restaurant sugar bowl. When I told Mammy what was going on, she complained directly to the headmistress. The only result of this was that Mrs Campbell was even more vindictive towards me than before. I decided to just put up with the frequent bangs to the head, as it obviously wasn't worth it to complain. This unpleasant classroom atmosphere carried on for the rest of the school year. Instead of the marvellous chance to learn that I had been so looking forward to, school was absolute hell, and I hated going there.

Unbeknown to me, other parents had also been lodging complaints with the headmistress, as I was by no means the only boy who was being battered about the head on a regular basis. Salvation arrived, in the form of Jimmy Boyle's mother. One day we heard a terrific commotion in the corridor outside but kept our heads down in case we gave Mrs Campbell an excuse to launch one of her attacks from the rear. The classroom door, which was located at the back of the class, burst open with a crash. We still kept our heads down, looking to the front. "Ur yoo Mrs Campbell?" a woman's voice roared. Mrs Campbell retreated to the front of the class, where we could see her for a change. We looked back to the doorway where a youngish woman was poised. I recognised her as the mother of one of my classmates, Jimmy Boyle. "Yere nothin' but a vicious bad auld besom, that's whit ye ur. Ah'll gie ye a taste of yerr ain fuckin' medicine, ye nasty auld bastart", she shrieked at the top of her voice.

With that Mrs Boyle grabbed the long pointer which was leaning in the back corner of the classroom, and raced towards the front of the classroom, yelling “Ye’ll no’ git away fae me, ye bliddy auld bastart, Ah’ll shove yer bliddy pointer right up yer erse”. Mrs Campbell was no match for her much younger attacker. Mrs Boyle soon caught up with her and started raining angry blows about her head and shoulders, raising large puffs of chalk dust as Mrs Campbell ran out of the door and down the corridor. The commotion quickly faded into the distance.

We looked at each other in delighted amazement. “Yir Mammy’s great, she’s a right champion”, we shouted at Jimmy. The school janitor arrived shortly afterwards, with the good news that we could go home for the day. Mammy laughed for a long time, when I told her what had happened. We never saw or heard of Mrs Campbell again. The next morning the Headmistress, without mentioning a word about Mrs Campbell, introduced us to Miss Logan who would be our teacher until the beginning of the school holidays. She was the opposite of our late departed teacher, being pleasant and helpful, so school was okay after all.

Another aspect of the slum environment, combined with food rationing, was that school dinners – which is what we called lunches -were provided free to those children most in need, being those who could not afford to pay even the nominal sum charged for a weekly book of tickets. For a lot of children, this two-course meal was the only meal that they got in the day. We didn’t qualify for free meals, but Mammy decided that I should be better nourished if I got a square meal at lunchtime, so she enrolled me for school dinners. Only a few schools in each area were set up with a large dining hall and catering staff, with the meals delivered in bulk from a central kitchen in Polmadie. The nearest dinner hall to us was at the Oatlands school, about half a mile away down Caledonia Road. Mammy arranged with an older boy, Jimmy Hutton, to take me to the dinner school and back, on a daily basis.

On the first day of dinner school, Jimmy and I walked down the length of Caledonia Road, until we came to the Oatlands school. As we approached the front door of the dining hall, he said to me, "tell the wumman at the door, Nae Figs". "Whit ur figs?" I asked. "Never mind whit they ur, jist say Nae Figs", he said. We filed past the pleasant woman at the door, who clipped our coupons and made a note in her book about the figs, when we both said, "Nae Figs". The first course was a very tasty stew, with potatoes, peas and carrots. When the waitresses cleared away the empty plates, they started dishing out big bowls of custard and stewed fruit. I had been told about custard, knew what it looked like, but had never tasted it as our budget didn't run to puddings. I couldn't wait to get stuck right into my pudding. The ladies served everybody except me and Jimmy Hutton.

When I began to realise that I was not going to get any pudding, I burst into tears. The kindly woman who had been manning the doorway asked why I was crying. "I didnae get any puddin", I howled. She consulted her notebook. "But ye said Nae Figs at the door son", she replied. "Bit ah didnae know whit figs wur," I sobbed through my tears. "Ye'll know better the next time son", said the lady. "Ah cannae gie ye any the day, fur there's nane left an' greetin' wull get ye naywhere here."

I was inconsolable and cried all the way back to school. If I was three or four years older, I would have given Jimmy a right good hammering, but he was far too big for me. The best I could do was to 'accidentally' keep stepping on the back of his shoes, causing him to stumble a few times, cursing. From that day onwards, I never said no to anything. The meals were invariably excellent in quality for the ten years that I ate them, considering that food supplies were so scarce across the board, especially during the war.

Another little episode concerning Jimmy Hutton, comes to mind. Mammy came up the stairs one late afternoon. She knew that I was crazy about all things military. "Ah've jist been talking to Mrs Hutton", she said. "Jimmy's uncle is visiting, an' he's goat some things that ye wid love tae hiv". "Dae ye want tae come doon and see thim?" I needed no prompting and galloped down the stairs. Knocking on Jimmy's door, I was ushered inside. On the kitchen table were large metal models of aeroplanes. One in particular attracted my attention. This was a large Italian bomber, painted in full desert camouflage. Seeing my eyes widening, Jimmy's uncle handed me the bomber for closer inspection. I couldn't believe my luck.

By this time Mammy had joined us. "Whit dae ye say, Allan?" asked Mammy. Taking this as a cue to show off my good manners, I said, "thank you very much", holding the bomber tightly to my chest. They all laughed loudly. "He's no' geein' it tae ye, Allan", said Mammy, "ye're only supposed to be lookin' at it". Having held the bomber, I wasn't going to give it up. It took Mammy a long time to prise the model from my grip, without losing her temper in front of strangers. Going back upstairs Mammy was very embarrassed by my behaviour, and holding my left arm firmly, proceeded to skelp my backside until we were well inside our house. "Ah wis black affronted", said Mammy, "that's the last time ye'll get yer hauns on somebody else's guid stuff ye wee rascal. Ah'll gie ye 'thank you very much', ma boy".

Chapter 6

One day I came home from school as usual, at three o' clock. I banged on the single end door, to be let in. As I stood there, wondering what was causing the delay, the door of the next-door room and kitchen opened, and old Mrs Maloney appeared. "C'mon in, Allan," she said. I followed her into the house where old Mr Maloney was sitting with his bonnet on, puffing on his old clay pipe and reading a newspaper. I had never seen him ever do anything else.

The Maloney's were Irish, and a lovely old couple who shared their house with their grown son John, who was a truck driver. "There has been a wee bit o' an accident, son", she murmured, in her quiet Irish accent. "Yer wee brither Alec burnt his fit, an' yer Mammy his took him to the hoastipal". I was instantly frightened. I didn't know what a hoastipal was, but it sounded very ominous. Never had Mammy not been home for me, never ever. I was totally at a loss. "Jist sit ye doon, an' I'll get ye a nice cup o' tea and a big slice o' soady scoan," said Mrs Maloney. I would normally have drooled over the prospect of this treat, as Mrs Maloney's soda scones were just fantastic. I was too upset to even think about eating or drinking. "Ye can stey here, until yir Auntie Annie comes hame wi' hir messages".

I couldn't concentrate on anything, as my mind was in real whirl. The soda scone and tea sat on the sideboard, untouched. After what seemed to be an interminable wait, a knock came to the door. There was Auntie Annie, looking worried. "C'mon upsterrs, wi' me Allan, ye kin listen tae the wireless, the McFlannels wull be oan in a minute, ye aywis like thim don't ye? she said. I trudged upstairs with leaden feet and heavy heart. I sat next to the wireless cabinet but I couldn't concentrate on anything. Auntie Annie tried her best to cheer me up, but nothing worked.

About eight o' clock there was a knock on the door. I rushed to open it. There stood Mammy, with Bobby holding on to her arm. Both looked utterly exhausted. "Ah'll make ye a nice cup of tea'", offered Auntie Annie as Mammy slumped into the fireside chair, her face white and drawn. Bobby instantly fell asleep leaning across Mammy's lap, as we watched. "How's wee Alex, Jessie?" asked Auntie Annie. Mammy burst into tears and sobbed, with her shoulders heaving. "Oh, Annie, it was jist awfy. Ah hid tae haud him oan ma knee, while the Sister took a great big pair o' scissors, an' peeled a' the skin an' meat aff his puir wee fit."

It took a long time for Auntie Annie to comfort Mammy to the stage where she stopped crying. It was some days before Mammy was able to tell me what had happened. Alec had started to walk with confidence and was toddling around whilst Mammy was washing some clothes in the sink. In the process she was boiling water in the kettle on the floor mounted gas ring. She had turned away for a moment. During that brief period, Alec, with childish curiosity, put a foot straight into the kettle. He screamed in agony, not being able to withdraw his scalded foot.

Mammy looked round to see what the noise was all about and was horrified when she realised what had happened. She tried to extract Alec's foot from the kettle, but his tiny foot had already swollen up like a balloon. She picked up Alec, and the kettle, and turned on the sink tap to cool the kettle water. Alec was screaming with the extreme pain. She managed to get his foot out of the kettle and wrapped it in a tea towel. She ran with Bobby running at her heels, down Crown Street to the nearest doctor's surgery in total panic.

Dashing into the surgery, the screaming brought the doctor running from his room. Mammy was in shock, and incoherent. The doctor took one look at the scalded foot and telephoned for an emergency ambulance, which arrived with little delay. He instructed the ambulance men to get Mammy and Alec, with Bobby, to Belvedere Hospital at Parkhead as quickly as was humanly possible. On arrival, a nursing Sister took total charge. Mammy assisted by holding the screaming Alec on her lap whilst the nurse carried out her grisly work paring away the parboiled skin and flesh. I have no idea what painkilling medication was available then, or what treatment was given. All I know is that Alec was in hospital for months.

We visited about twice a week, but we were only allowed to look through a window placed high up in the ward wall, with Mammy holding us up in turn to try to spot Alex. The strict hospital regulations at the time decreed that children did not receive visits from anyone, including parents and siblings. The official rationale was that visits caused children to get upset and homesick when the visitors left. The day eventually came when we were allowed to collect Alec and take him home on the tramcar. Despite his lengthy treatment, his foot was very badly scarred, taking many years to gradually regain a reasonable semblance of normality. From that point in time, Mammy kept a very close eye on Alex at all times.

We were allowed out to play unsupervised in the streets, much later at night than responsible parents would allow today. Mammy knew, because she had tried, that to try to keep us inside, and to get us into bed before nine or ten o' clock, was a no-win situation. The noise of kids playing in the streets penetrated the thick sandstone walls and windows as if they weren't there.

Every kid knew only one level of vocal volume, which was to conduct every conversation and game playing, by shrieking loudly to be heard above the high decibel background hubbub of tramcar bells clattering, and of other kids screeching, also at the tops of their voices. Mammy also realised that if she called us in early, by calling out of the window, or even more embarrassingly by coming downstairs to drag us inside, we would be called 'Mammies' boys' by the rest of the street urchins, and get a hard time forever, and not be allowed to play the street games as equals.

One night Bobby and I were playing in the street, when some kids emerged from the nearby Wynd Church clutching brown paper bags. As we watched, they opened the bags, pulling out sugary Paris buns, which they greedily scoffed as we looked on salivating. "Where did yese get thae Paris buns?" we asked. "Fae the Bandy Hope," they replied. "Whit's the Bandy Hope?" we asked. "It's upsterrs in the church, a' ye hiv tae dae is sing stupit hims an' ither daft songs aboot Jesus'n stuff." "Dae they gie ye a Paris bun fur jist daen tha'?" we asked. "An' they've goat a loat o' pictures tae," said the boys. "Its oan Tuesday an' Thursday nights at six o'cloak." "How dae we jine?" was our next question. "Ye dinnae hiv tae jine, ye jist turn up, they let anybuddy in, aw' ye hiv tae dae is queue up it the door before they open it." We went home to ask Mammy if we could attend the Bandy Hope. "As long as it's oan at the church it will be fine, ah'm sure that it'll dae ye the world o' good since yev'e stoapped goin' tae Sunday School."

At six o' clock the next Tuesday night we joined the queue outside the church door. We didn't know what to expect, but the remark about the lots of pictures had struck a chord. I imagined that they had some sort of art gallery, with rows of paintings hung along the walls. The door was opened from the inside, and the crowd of weans poured inside as if it was the Crownie. The door was immediately locked behind us with an audible grating noise from the huge iron key. We trooped up the stairs, and entered a large room furnished with rows of long wooden benches and a lectern. On the facing wall was a big white cloth screen. On a large table beside the lectern was a huge brass contraption, with a sort of short gun barrel projecting from the front, and a little soot- blackened chimney on top.

Two serious looking men and a woman stood out in front. One of the men started his spiel by ranting on about the evils of strong drink. I had no idea what strong drink was, but imagined that it must be super strength Barrs Irn Bru, or something like that. As the first man was finishing shouting about God knows what else, the other man was opening the back of the brass contraption on the table and pouring something from a copper jug with a long spout.

Whilst this was going on I was looking around for the lots of pictures that we had been told about. Not a picture was in sight. "The lying gets!" I thought, "there's nae pictures at a'." The man working on the contraption struck a long match and poked it into the back of the contraption. This started a small fire, which the man controlled by shutting a little sliding hatch and started pumping energetically at a sliding piston.

After a few minutes smoke stopped issuing from the little chimney, and a strong white light appeared on the white cloth screen. The lecture now started in earnest. The man working the kerosene fired magic lantern (for that's what it was) inserted large glass slides into the machine whilst the other man raved on with frightening passion and bulging eyes. Each slide portrayed big heavily whiskered men holding a poor woman by the hair or throat in the midst of a howling gale, whilst a gaggle of terrified children, dressed in rags, clung to their mothers' skirts with their eyes turned up to the heavens, to where the head of Jesus Christ was peering through a gap in the raging storm clouds, as if to see what all the ranting was about.

As far as we were concerned, each picture was much the same, with only the background varying to a degree. We sat there growing progressively more alarmed, as the man in front got more frenzied with each passing slide. At long last the ranting came to an end. Now the woman took over. A tall easel was pushed into the front. The woman placed a large cardboard sheet, with the words of a religious song in large print, on the easel, "I would like you to join with me in joyous songs of worship. I will lead, just follow me." With that, she opened her mouth wide and launched into the first verse as if her very life depended on it. "Running over, running over, my cup's full and running over. As the Lord said to me, I'm as happy as can be, my cup's full and running over."

Many similar verses followed. As we joined in, the old hands on the benches started swaying their shoulders from side to side.

Everyone else joined in, giggling as we sang, with the swaying increasing in exuberance until those on the ends of the benches toppled off, falling to the floor and loudly hooting with laughter. This is more like it, I thought. The woman paid no attention; she must have been used to this behaviour. Other songs followed, until one that we knew from Sunday school: "Yes Jesus loves me, yes Jesus loves me, yes Jesus loves me, for the bible tells me so' was the chorus. She started off, "Jesus loves me, yes I know, for the bible tells me so." Our version was slightly different. "Jesus loves me, yes I know, so does Ragtime Cowboy Joe."

We thought that this was very funny, singing at the top of our voices. The woman gave no indication of hearing what we were actually singing. When we had finished singing 'Jesus loves me', the meeting was over. Now we got what we had come for. At the door we were given a hot mug of milky tea and a brown paper bag. We gulped down the tea and rushed down the stairs and out into the street clutching our paper bags tightly. We lived just next door, so we saved our Paris buns until we were safely home where nobody could steal them.

It may have seemed to be a big performance just to get a Paris bun, but we thought it was well worth it, and attended the Bandy Hope (The Band of Hope), for years. We could have a right good laugh, without the teachers seeming to notice that we were singing the wrong words most of the time. We stopped being frightened of the Magic Lantern slides and the repeated demented ranting and raving. When we became known as regular attenders, we usually got two Paris buns instead of just one. This meant that we could give Mammy and wee Alex the extra buns, which were greatly appreciated.

There were no easy everyday means of communication between family members or friends, except by face-to-face contact. Nobody had telephones, mobile phones, or the internet, to keep in touch with each other. Letters were all right for long distances but were impractical for local purposes. It was common for kids to be used on a daily basis as messengers. "Wull ye jist nip roon' tae yer Auntie Bella's, an' ask her if she kin watch yese oan Setterday moarnin' while Ah go tae the hoaspital tae see young George Patterson" was a typical errand. We started young and continued as messengers until well into our late teens. Visiting relatives in this manner allowed us to become familiar with our extended family units and get to know all family members to a far greater extent than would have been possible otherwise. Our cousins did the same in reverse, so we had a real matrix of communications.

The one exception to this was Auntie Phamie's family. The Robinsons lived on the corner of Ballater Street and Crown Street. Phamie was a gentle soul, who had married a Catholic, Bill Robinson. Bill discouraged contact with us and the rest of Mammy's family, as we were Protestants. Bill had never had a job in his entire life, living on handouts from the Bureau of Employment. (This, in typical Glaswegian fashion, was mispronounced universally as "The Brew"). Poor Phamie had to try to raise, clothe and feed a large family, on Uncle Bill's 'Brew' money. If it wasn't for the support of her sisters, who passed on food, money and clothing, during clandestine meetings on neutral ground, her family would have quickly become destitute.

Uncle Bill's daily routine consisted of lying in bed until 11am, when Auntie Phamie handed him the "Noon Record", which she had bought for him, so that he could study the racing form, and write out his street bookie's 'lines'. Getting out of bed at noon, he would saunter down to the corner where the illegal street bookie was surrounded by 'Coarner boys', who acted as bookie's runners and lookouts, in case the local constabulary were in the bookie's patch.

Having placed his lines, he would hang around the corner until all his horses had come home. If he won some money, he would retire to the nearest pub to sink pints, until his winnings ran out, then go home in a foul temper. If he didn't pick a winner, he would return home, in an even fouler frame of mind. Either way Auntie Phamie and her extensive brood had to take the brunt of his surly moods. I remember visiting their house, when Bill was in hospital for some reason. It was the gloomiest house imaginable, even for the Gorbals. The wallpaper was black, with grey and green floral designs. We left as soon as possible, with Mammy saying "Puir Phamie', over and over, as we walked home, down Crown Street.

Chapter 7

We always enjoyed visiting our other aunties, who were very houseproud, and from our perspective were rich, with offspring who were already out working and contributing to the communal family treasury. It was regarded as normal that everybody would hand over their wages on payday and would receive a relatively small sum in return as pocket money, which was also expected to cover daily expenses, such as bus fares and food consumed outside the home. The exception to our "rich" relatives was Auntie Jean, who lived in a top storey room and kitchen in Nuneaton Street, Bridgeton (pronounced Brigton). If anything, Nuneaton Street was marginally worse than the Gorbals.

The centre of the street was taken up by a large steel tank, painted black, with EWS (emergency water supply) painted in prominent white letters on the sides. The water was dark green and slimy, but nevertheless highly populated by shoals of 'baggy minnies' (Minnows). Little piles of bricks were placed at strategic intervals around the tank to allow the smaller urchins to fish for the baggy minnies. The front windows of Auntie Jean's house overlooked the street, and the kitchen window overlooked the vast expanse of a large scrap yard, containing everything from pots, pans and old bicycles to complete trucks and locomotives. Everything was rusty, and depressing to look at.

We enjoyed visiting Auntie Jean as she didn't really mind what we did, as long as we didn't kill or seriously injure ourselves. My cousin Jean was a typical tomboy of the streets and could do anything that the boys could do. When we wanted to urinate, we would run upstairs and ask Auntie Jean for the key to the outside landing toilet. "Dae ye only want tae pee?" she would ask. We would nod our heads as we hopped from foot to foot, trying not to wet ourselves.

She would raise the kitchen window as high as it would go, and lift us up onto the sink, grabbing the back of our trousers whilst we stood on the windowsill. "Away ye go, son," she would say, as we frantically unbuttoned our flies, and with a sigh of relief peed out of the open window. Not to be outdone, young Jean would remove her knickers, climb up beside us, lift her frock, arch her back, and pee out just as far as we could manage. Climbing down from the sink, she would pull her knickers back on, as if this was an everyday occurrence, which on reflection it probably was.

One day whilst we were peeing out of the window, one of Auntie Jean's neighbours wandered in through the open door. "Thae weans ur dead lucky," she said as she helped herself to a cigarette from an open packet of Woodbines on the table and lit up. "The ither day ah was jist burstin' tae hiv a pee, but the lavvy wis fu' as usual. Ah ran back up the sterrs, an' wis jist sittin' oan the sink wi' ma knickers roon ma ankles, when oor Wullie came through the door wi' a big bunch o' his pals. 'Hey youse!' he shouted, 'come quick an' see ma mammy peein' in the sink'. 'Ah hid tae sit there Jean, wi a' thae wee boys hivin a good close look. Ah couldnae finish quick enough tae jump doon, pull up ma knickers, an' kick their bliddy erses oot the door. Goad knows whit they tell t' thir mammies when they goat hame tae thir ain hooses. Ah wis that embarrassed Jean, when ah hid tae go oot fur ma messages". Auntie Jean roared with laughter. "That wull learn ye tae loack yer door when ye're peein' in the sink, Chrissie".

When we asked Mammy if we could pee out of the window the next day at home, she retorted "whit, who pit that stupit idea intae yer heids?" "Auntie Jean lets us dae it," we answered, and told her how easy it was. "Oor Jean's a right heidcase, fur learning youse tae pee oot o' a three storey windae, Ah don't know whit she wull be lettin' ye dae next, bit yer'e no daen it in ma' hoose. Jist you wait tae Ah see hur. Ah'll gie hur peein' oot o' windies." When Mammy next saw Auntie Jean, she remonstrated with her, as promised. Auntie Jean just grinned and laughed loudly, saying "thir's nae hairm in it Jessie, the weans enjoy it, an' it's faur better than thim peein' thir troosers. Oor toilet's always blocked onywey an' is mair trouble than it's worth."

Street games were our mainstay in our younger years. Playing cops and robbers, Cowboys and Indians, Flash Gordon and the Claymen, and pirates, were strictly for boys, not forgetting the ever-popular football. The girls played wall games, using up to four solid rubber balls at one time, which required a great deal of dexterity and timing, throwing them overhead, and between their legs, catching two balls at a time with alternate hands.

Another perennial favourite was skipping ropes, in very complicated sequences. The boys would supply the skipping ropes for the girls, when asked, by going to the back court of a tenement in another street, and cutting down the clotheslines, running home like the devil, with clotheslines trailing behind. If spotted and pursued, we would just drop the clothesline, and run to another tenement, through a close, and clamber over a dyke into the next backcourt, to confuse our pursuers. When we were sure that we had shaken them off, we would head home, using short cuts through backcourts, and avoiding the streets.

As the girls played, they sang traditional street songs, in time to the skipping, ball bouncing, or whatever. I can't remember many of the songs, but a couple spring to mind, such as "Mrs McGuire peed in the fire, the fire wis too hoat, so she peed in the poat, the poat wis too wide, so she peed in the Clyde, an' a' the wee fishes swam up her backside". Another was "Be baw babbity, babbity, babbity be baw babbity, ah weesh ah wis a wee laudie. If ah wis a laudie o, a laudie o, a laudie o, if ah wis a wee laudie o, ah'd weesh ah wis a wee lassie", and so on, ad infinitum. Another was "The big ship sailed through the eely ally o, the eely ally o, the eely ally o, the big ship sailed through the eely ally o". There were many verses following, but I can't remember them.

For street games, such as 'Kick the can', 'Aleevio', and Rounders, girls and boys both played, to maximise the numbers. To play 'kick the can', everyone stood in the centre of the street, and played a game of elimination, until only one kid was left, to be 'het'. There were many other games of elimination, but I can't remember any of them.

A can was placed in the middle of the street, to be guarded by the 'het'. The 'het' then held their hands over their eyes, and counted to one hundred, whilst the other kids scampered off, in different directions to hide. The 'het' then tried to find them. As kids were found, they would return to the can, to wait. The numbers found would increase, as the 'het' progressively rounded kids up. If someone who had not yet been rounded up got the opportunity, they would dash out of their hiding place, and kick the can as far as possible. This released the prisoners, who dashed off to hide again, whilst the weary 'het' would return the can to the start point, to begin all over again.

I can't remember the rules for Aleevio, but it was such a universally played game that I am sure that many do. Rounders was a game that everyone could join in. Any type of wooden bat would do, ranging from a simple slat of wood, to a slat with a carved handle. The best, and most popular, was a tennis bat, as we called it. The ball was anything like a tennis or solid rubber ball. Everybody who wasn't batting or bowling, acted as fielders. It was a combination of baseball and cricket, although we knew practically nothing about either game. The bowler stood on a chalked mark on the ground, with the batter standing on another chalked mark about twenty-five feet away. The bowler bowled underhand, without moving his or her feet. The batter would swing wildly at the ball, hitting it as far as possible, and running between the two chalk marks, with everyone chanting the batter's score. To get the batter out, the ball had to be caught before the first bounce. To stop the batter accumulating runs, the ball had to be thrown back to the bowler and caught.

Another game involving both boys and girls consisted of two teams, one team lining up on one pavement, the other on the other pavement, with the street between. In turn, a player tightly folded their arms, folded one leg up behind them, and hopped across the road. To prevent them reaching the other side, an opposing player would hop out and try to knock the first player off balance, by barging with the shoulder. If the first player was forced to put both feet on the ground, then they were out, and the successful barger's team got a point. If the first player managed to hop to the other side successfully, their team got a point, and the barger was out. This game would carry on for hours, until only one person was left.

There was another whole tier of games, which came and went in cycles, such as making kites; making 'guidies'; bows and arrows (Bonenarras, in the vernacular); peeries; making paper aeroplanes; making wooden swords; spears; home-made yoyos; iron girds (hoops); jauries (marbles); home-made stink bombs, which were posted through letterboxes; pinhole cameras; swings; and slings (catapults).

One game which was played all year round was football (fitba'), which was played at every opportunity, and by every age group, but only by boys. The space between the lampposts and the nearest wall was the usual goalmouth. This meant that the pitch was diagonal to the street as the goalposts were on opposite pavements. The biggest problem was finding a ball, of any shape or size.

Consequently, the balls were made from anything, from a big tight ball of newspaper tied up with string, which inevitably disintegrated, to an empty soccer ball, which had long lost its inner bladder. This was stuffed tightly with newspaper, and laced with string, giving a reasonable sort of ball, which looked superficially like a real ball, but didn't perform like one. In between these, a wide range of bald tennis balls, solid rubber balls, hollow rubber balls of various diameters, were used. If no ball of any sort could be found, then a tin can would have to do instead. Kicking tin cans played havoc with our clogs, boots, or shoes, with the toecaps developing holes more quickly than if we were just kicking balls.

Street football was illegal, and frequently resulted in smashed windows, for those unfortunates who lived in ground floor apartments. We kept an eye out for the polis (Police) at all times, ready to pick up our ball and leg it to the nearest close mouth and back court, if we spotted the polis sneaking up on us, or if we heard the dreaded polis whistle. They were usually able to catch one or two kids, with the rest making a getaway into the nearest back, where we would clamber up to the roofs of washhouses and hide on the other side of the roof.

This usually did the trick, as the polis couldn't be bothered to climb up after us, knowing full well that we would dreep (no equivalent English translation) into the next back and be well away before they could get anywhere near us. On occasions, however, the polis would surround the whole tenement block before revealing their presence by blowing their whistles. We did our usual disappearing trick, only to be scooped up by towering polismen, as we scooted out of the closes into Crown Street.

They would go through the motions of booking us, as we tearfully gave our names and addresses, making sure that we were suitably terrified of being frogmarched to the Lawmoor Street polis office, before giving us each a heavy clip around the ear, and allowing us to run home as fast as our legs could carry us. The older street footballers, however, were taken to the polis office, where they were given a much harder time before being booted out.

The Glasgow Police Force was at that time run by Sir Percy Sillitoe. He had been recruited to stamp out the numerous gangs that had rampaged out of control prior to his appointment. The Gorbals gangs had been by far the worst of these. His first action was to remove from the force all policemen who were less than six feet tall and weighed less than fourteen stone.

New recruits were not selected by their IQ, but by their physical robustness and ability to handle themselves in a fight. Patrolling the streets in pairs, instead of singly, and keeping in touch with the nearest office by means of telephones in red painted policeboxes, (which were placed regularly, at strategic intervals,) the gangs were quickly subdued. Sillitoe also introduced the flat peaked cap for the force, scrapping the old-fashioned conical helmet. He also designed and introduced the black and white chequered band on the new caps, known at first as the "Sillitoe Tartan".

The cap and chequered band has since been copied by practically all police forces in Britain, and in many parts of the world. A polis box was the ground base for each shift of patrolling polismen on their beat. The boxes were constructed from precast concrete sections, bolted together and painted bright red. This was the original 'Tardis' of 'Dr Who' fame. On the outside there was a spring-loaded flap, meant to allow any member of the public to pull open the flap, exposing a large grille, and communicate directly with the nearest polis office, in an emergency only. This flap became the target of "Ah dare ye" games for the street kids.

Those who accepted the dare would open the flap, wait to hear someone replying, then yell "Yer Maw's a hoor" or some other insult, such as "Yer grannie's knickers ur full o' mince" into the grille, before releasing the flap to close with a loud bang, running back to join their pals, proud of their bravery. Other darees would follow, without stopping to think that the recipient of the shouted abuse would be taking some action. For the instigator of the game, who would have been the first to shout into the grille, the trick was to wait until he could see a pair of polismen rounding the distant corner, in hot pursuit from Lawmoor Street, then dare his chosen victim, usually a right wally, to take a turn.

The poor unfortunate, emboldened by watching the others perform, would run to the box, whilst we ran for our lives through the nearest close-mouth and away. He would just be shouting "Ah like mince an' totties" or something equally innocuous into the grille, as the polis arrived at the trot, and nabbed him red handed. The terrified and howling victim was led away, suspended in mid-air between two towering polismen. We would wait until the howling had faded away before emerging from our boltholes to carry on with some other street game.

We were quite confident that the unfortunate wally would not be able to give the polis our correct names and addresses, as he was highly unlikely to know them anyway. The usual polis modus operandi, in the case of very young offenders, was to extract a name and address if possible, and, after enough time at the polis office to put the fear of death into the kid, to take him home to face further retribution from the outraged parents, who would be mortified to be visited by the polis, and would belt his erse red raw, as soon as the door was shut.

Bobby and I were forced to undergo the terrifying experience of being locked up in a polis cell at Lawmoor Street only once, but it was a salutary lesson to us.

It happened like this. We lived practically on the corner of Kidston Street and Crown Street, which at that time was a major thoroughfare. Going up Crown Street in the direction of Govanhill, on the left was a high brick wall marking one of the perimeters of Dixon's Blazes, punctuated by a solid wooden gate. The wall continued up past Gushetfaulds, known locally as 'The Gushet', until nearly the top of the hill. Just before the railway bridge a shabby and neglected lane, bordered by high barbed wire, led to the left.

Down this unappealing lane was nothing for the first hundred yards, then a dilapidated kipper factory, where haddock were gutted and split before being placed on long narrow wooden racks to cure over a thickly smoking smouldering fire. The factory had no walls, only a corrugated iron roof, allowing the smoke to escape easily. Judging by the smell, they must have been burning damp unwashed second-hand underpants imported from Bengal. To the right of the factory was a railway signal box, nestling into the bank bordering the multitude of railway lines and sidings.

Beyond the kipper factory, a high brick wall surrounded a group of sombre buildings. This was the depot of a local Home Guard detachment and was in a dilapidated condition. I am not sure if the complex had been deliberately built to provide a training area for house-to-house combat, been bombed, or was just the result of enthusiastic and expert vandalism.

Whatever the reason, it was severely broken. A tall square brick chimney (lum, in the vernacular) rose from the roof of the largest and least damaged building. Somehow the older kids from our street had found out that the Home Guard was very rarely in residence but there was plenty of stuff of interest stored within the building.

The old-fashioned chimney had steel rungs up the outside all the way to the top. The local gang had climbed up to the chimney top and discovered that inside the chimney another set of rungs led down to the large fireplace inside. The only problem was that they couldn't climb down it as the there was insufficient room inside the chimney. Late one afternoon Bobby and I were approached by a playmate, Alfie Duffy, who said that his big brother Matt wanted us to go with his gang to the old barracks. We were overawed by this request, as Matt Duffy was an eleven-year-old with a big reputation as a tough guy, and was a recognised hard man, even at that age.

Unwilling to get beaten up if we didn't tag along, we sauntered up the road to the old barracks. Everybody climbed up onto the roof of the main building. "Youse go up furst, an' then clim' doon inside the lum, an' see whit ye kin see," said Matt to Alfie, Bobby and me. We were scared witless, but complied, scaling the iron rungs to the top, and after swivelling round we climbed down to the large open fireplace. When we were accustomed to the gloom, we looked around very nervously, all three of us, as Alfie was daring, but not a hard nut like his brother. "Whit kin ye see?" yelled Matt, from the outside.

We looked around. The large hall was a bit of a shambles, with piles of stuff everywhere, with some dim light coming in through the windows on the far side. We poked around with little success, until we came to the closed door of a side room. We pushed open the door. The room was full of wooden boxes painted khaki, with rope handles. Some of the lids were loose, so we lifted one up, and were surprised to see that it was filled to the top with rifle bullets. Most boxes were the same, but some contained much shorter bullets, silver in colour, which we could guess were pistol bullets.

It was like being in Aladdin's cave. We ran back to the fireplace, and shouted up: "Youse shid see this, there's millions o' bullets an' a boax o' haungrenades." "Wait a minit, ah'll get somethin' tae let doon tae yese, so we kin take some hame," shouted Matt. It seemed hours to us, before a coalbag tied to a freshly cut clothesline, dropped down into the fireplace with a thud, amid a cloud of ashes and coal dust. “Jist full it up, an we’ll pull it up,” yelled Matt down the lum.

Dragging a box of each kind of ammunition and the box of hand grenades to the fireplace, we loaded the coal bag with the contents. “Okay,“ we shouted up the lum, “ye kin pull it noo”. The boys on the roof took the strain, and slowly the bag disappeared up the lum, stopping at regular intervals, as the bag encountered each rung. As soon as we could see light at the top of the lum we scampered back up the rungs and climbed back down the outside of the lum to the roof and jumped on to the wall and on to the ground.

Everybody reached into the bag and filled their pockets and transferred their belts to the outside of their jerseys, cinching these as tightly as possible, and filled their jerseys with the loot. We filled our pockets with as much as they would hold and left it like that. Matt hid the remaining loot under a pile of bricks. Instead of heading off home, Matt led us to the middle of the Gushet railway overbridge. “Ah’ jist want tae drap some o’ thae haungrenades oantae the next train comin’ oot o’ Dixon’s Blazes,” he said. Horrified, but rendered immobile, we all hung over the parapet, waiting for the next goods train full of pig iron ingots to emerge from Dixon’s onto the main line.

It wasn’t too long before one appeared and chugged under the bridge. There was no mystery to us in arming a hand grenade and throwing it, we had seen it done plenty of times on the movies. Matt pulled the pin of the first one and dropped it accurately into the middle of a goods wagon, then quickly did the same with a second grenade. We waited, our nerves all on edge waiting for the explosions. The train rattled on, but nothing happened. “Must hiv been duds,” said Matt in obvious disappointment. As the wagons continued to roll below, Matt pulled pins from successive grenades, and dropped them, until all were gone. "Fuckin' useless haungrenades they were! They must hiv belanged tae the Salvation Army, no' the real army," he complained.

Running homewards, we were thankful for the duds, and to be clear of Matt Duffy and his gang of bampots. Once home we carefully hid our bullets under the bed. "In the name o' the wee man, where the hell hiv youse two been", yelled Mammy when she saw us properly, when the gas mantle was lit, "Ye're like a couple o' wee coalmen, so ye ur, where the hell hiv ye been tae git sae manky". "Dunno, Mammy we wur jist playin' roon at the stables". "It must hiv been the coalman's stables, ye wur playin' in, whit ur we gaun tae dae wi' ye, ah'll hiv tae get yer claes aff ye an' intae the sink if yere gonnae hiv any claes to get tae the school in the moarnin".

She grabbed us in turn and stripped us naked. "If yere cauld it's yer ain faut', an' ah've nae sympathy fur ye. She threw our soot encrusted clothes into the sink and put the kettle on to boil. "Dinnae think ah'm bilin' the kettle fur youse, its fur washin' yer claes, youse two are in for a cauld bath". We shivered as we stood up in the tub, in front of the fire, as Mammy scrubbed us with a scrubbing brush and the usual block of red carbolic soap, tipping potful's of freezing water over our heads.

Mammy washed our filthy clothes in the sink, wringing them out with her hands, and propped them up on chairs in front of the fire to dry, banking up the fire to keep it going overnight whilst we shivered in bed. We kept our bullets a secret for a few days, crawling under the bed to play with them. About three or four days later, Mammy announced that she was going round to Auntie Bella's for an hour or two and she would trust us to keep the door locked and look after wee Alec. "Nae bother, Mammy", we said, and off she went. As soon as she had gone we locked the door and put the heavy iron key back on the mantelpiece. We got our bullets from under the bed, and arranged them on the kitchen table in rows, pretending that they were toy soldiers. We were so engrossed in our imaginary game that we didn't hear Mammy's key sliding into the door lock and the door opening. Her scream jolted us back into the real world. "Whit the hell huv ye goat there, where did ye get a' thae bullets?"

Afraid of retribution from Matt Duffy's gang, we refused to tell her. We had never seen Mammy in such a rage, which scared us witless. "If ye wullnae tell me where ye goat thim fae, ah'll take ye tae sumbuddy who wull soon find oot." With that she scooped the bullets into an empty message bag. She took wee Alex next door to the Maloney's to be looked after, then grabbed us both by our arms in a vice like grip and frogmarched us all the way to Lawmoor Street police station.

When we realised she was deadly serious, and where we were going, we wailed and tried to wriggle free, but to no avail. Mammy marched us up to the front desk and emptied her message bag out on the desk, in front of the duty officer. "Ah've jist found ma' two wee boys with a' thae bullets, an' ah wid like ye tae fun oot where they goat thim fae." The polisman fetched his sergeant, who quickly summed up the situation and took Mammy aside out of our hearing, where they had a fairly long conversation.

When they came back to the front desk, the sergeant said, "Ah'm gonnae hiv tae loack you two up in the jile, fur stealing a' thae bullets," and with that the sergeant marched us into a nearby cell, complete with bars, where we howled hysterically. Mammy left us without a backward glance. "Honest mister we didnae mean it, we'll never dae it again, honest we wullnae". Nobody paid any attention. Some hours passed before Mammy came back, we could see that she had been crying as much as us. "Ah' think they've learned a lesson", said the kindly sergeant, "An' wull be more careful who they mix wi', in future". Mammy marched us home. It was long past our bedtime, and we tumbled into bed exhausted and still crying.

We felt deeply ashamed of letting Mammy down, more than anything else and it was many days before we could relax in her company. It turned out that the polis had caught up with Matt Duffy and his gang the day after the theft, when they had lit a large bonfire and were chucking handfuls of bullets into it, and then leaping about to dodge the bullets which were whizzing all around. Inevitably, a bullet struck someone and felled them. During the ensuing uproar and commotion, the polis arrived, followed by an ambulance. The polis were already dealing with the gang, as they were already well known to the polis. The lesson was well learned, as far as we were concerned. It was very difficult for law-abiding parents to bring up a family in these slum surroundings.

Chapter 8

The summer holidays were over, and it was time to go back to school. Bobby was starting school in the penny buff. He was very lucky, as his teachers were two pretty young women, one blonde, the other brunette, just out of teacher's college, and assigned to carry out their probationary year together in the same classroom, as there were no spare experienced teachers to break them in gently. I was very jealous when I found out, for my first year at school had been a nightmare, with Mrs Campbell constantly whacking away at my head at every opportunity and causing me to suffer constant headaches.

We entered our classroom in trepidation, and sat quietly, waiting to see who would be our new teacher. The headmistress entered the room, accompanied by a diminutive old lady, who was no more than four and a half feet tall. "Children, this is Mrs Woods, she will be your teacher for the present. I expect that you will be on your best behaviour for her and do excellent work."

She then left the room. Mrs Wood sprightly stepped up to the teacher's tall desk, taking her tools of trade out of her bag. We were pleased to see that there were no pointers, clubs, missiles, or other recognisable weapons in sight. "My name is MRS Woods, she said with emphasis, in a surprisingly strong voice for such a small woman, you will always call me MRS Woods, not Miss. I am aware that you had a lot of problems last year, but I want you to forget all that, and put it behind you. I can assure you that, if you work hard, we will all have lots of fun in learning lots of exciting things."

Mrs Woods, we gradually learned, had travelled widely during her life, having taught in Canada, Australia, Argentina, and of course Scotland. She had been retired for many years, prior to volunteering to rejoin the teaching profession in a time of great need. She should have been awarded a Victoria Cross and double bar for accepting a job in the Gorbals. Mrs Woods was true to her word, as she was very competent as a teacher, helping us to make up the lost ground suffered under the sadistic regime of Mrs Campbell.

Classes would be interspersed with interesting stories, culled from her worldwide travels. I listened spellbound as she rambled on about events in exotic places, and as she described the various cities, and the people who lived there. How did we get such a bum deal, living in the Gorbals? I wondered, it's nae wonder that oor faimily disnae really believe, in a' that Goad, an' the Virgin Mary, an' bliddy Jesus Christ noansense. If a' that wis true they widnae allow places like the Gorbals tae exist.

The school year rolled on with Mrs Woods taking us much further than anybody else could have achieved. This allowed time for diversions. She was always bringing in exotic articles that she and her engineer husband had accumulated over many years of travel. A favourite was a range of small stereoscopic viewers, with a circular disc. Peering through these, and rotating the disc, would reveal coloured pictures of British Columbia, the Canadian Rocky

Mountains, Sydney, and its harbour, Adelaide, and Tasmania. We also found out that her Christian name was Adelaide, named after the Australian city. I got on very well with Mrs Woods, as I really loved learning, and excelled in every subject, except arithmetic, which I found boring.

Towards the end of the school year, Mrs Woods decided to put on a full-blown play, to be performed in the school drill hall. The title of the play was "The Tardy Scholar" and was set in ancient China. I was fortunate, or unfortunate, to be chosen to play the lead role of the Tardy Scholar. The play was set to music, with all roles being singing roles. Mrs Wood lived in Mount Florida, in what must have been a large house, as she had the wardrobe to outfit everyone in the play in full period costume. We rehearsed for weeks, during which time I really began to enjoy playing the lead role, as I was on stage for most of the play. Our upbringing being what it was, I never mentioned to Mammy, or anyone else, including my brothers, that I was performing in the play. I enjoyed the dressing up, as even we could appreciate that we were wearing truly authentic garb.

Eventually the great day arrived, when we robed up behind the curtain, in the drill hall. Everything was going fine as we excitedly prepared for the curtain to rise, with a group of musicians arranged by Mrs Wood warming up. I felt just fine until I was silly enough to sneak a peek through a small gap where the curtains didn't quite meet. I froze, consumed with instant terror, as I saw that the audience, for the first few rows, consisted of what looked like posh people, who must be very important. I had assumed that only schoolchildren would be watching me performing. We retired into a side room behind the curtain, leaving the elaborate scenery to be revealed to the audience, as the curtains parted.

The musicians started playing, which was my cue to come on singing "The Tardy Scholar is my name, missing classes is my game." I froze with terror, rooted to the spot, in my full regalia. "Go on, QUICKLY!" said Mrs Woods, beginning to panic. "I can't, I can't," I replied frantically, keenly aware that I was creating a disaster for poor Mrs Woods. The curtains were hurriedly closed whilst Mrs Woods tried to calm me down. By this time, I was in total panic, and would not budge. There were no understudies, so reluctantly, poor Mrs Woods had to announce to the packed drill hall that due to sudden illness, the play had to postponed until further notice.

I was so ashamed of myself that I didn't know where to look, what to do, or where to go. I was stunned, and disconsolate. I can't remember anything else except that the play was performed the next week, with Mrs Woods herself playing my part. My relationship with Mrs Woods was, to say the least, cool, from that point onwards. I knew that it was all my fault, but I had no idea how I could make amends. This unhappy experience affected me for many years as I would always steer well clear of anything that would bring me to the forefront of any activity whatsoever.

As kids, we didn't automatically get pocket money, as my mother had to carefully keep every penny a prisoner, until she had to spend it. We would have to do allocated jobs, which we were expected to take care of, from about the age of four onwards, in order to get the odd thruppence or so, to buy sweeties or a comic. As we grew older we discovered ways to earn extra money. Knocking on neighbours' doors we asked if they had any old furniture, or wooden boxes, that we could have.

People were reasonably generous in this regard, as it got rid of surplus rubbish. We carted our donated wooden objects down to our back court and piled it up. Getting the only item in our tool collection, a hatchet, from our coal bunker, we would proceed to chop everything up, reducing the bits to a fairly uniform size. After tying the pieces of wood into regular size bundles, using rough string that we cadged from the lady in the next-door fruit shop, we then went from door to door, selling the bundles of kindling wood for thruppence a bundle. Kindling wood was always easy to sell, even though we were selling the kindling to the same people who had donated the wood in the first place.

Another potential source of money was the common midden. In the vernacular, a midden was called a midgey. Sifting through the rubbish, with bare hands, was known as 'midgey raking'. During the war everything was recycled and had a definite value. Our main targets when midgey raking were bottles of every description, rags, and any discarded item seen to be of value. Each type of bottle or jar, when washed and dried, was worth something. Using an old sack or pillowslip, we would go from midgey to midgey, raking through the ashes and rubbish, until the sack was as full as we could carry home. Mammy allowed us to empty our sack into the sink, so we could wash our collection.

These were then sorted into groups and sizes, before we took each group to the appropriate shop to be sold. Medicine bottles were sold to the chemist shop for a penny each; large jam jars (Jeely Jaurs in the vernacular) fetched tuppence and small jars a penny at the grocers, with sauce bottles also fetching a penny. Beer bottles had to be returned to the pub that had sold them, as they were stamped with the pub's name. The real prize was a soda water siphon bottle, especially if complete with cap and nozzle, which fetched between two and three shillings, depending on the condition and the shop buying. Rags were sorted carefully before being bundled up and taken to the rag store of our choice; woollens were worth about six times more than other rags.

The pinnacle of midgey raking involved taking our sack on the tramcar (Caur in the vernacular) which was cheap, as the Corporation had a penny fare, called a 'pennyhauf', which allowed kids to travel as far as they liked on any bus or caur for only a penny. We would travel to a neighbourhood which we regarded as being upmarket, inhabited by 'toffs'. Climbing over garden walls, we would sift through their dustbins, not just for bottles, jars and rags, but also for discarded toys and other treasures.

These were called "luckies", as we thought that we were very lucky if we came across anything of value at all. We were often chased away from our hunting grounds by irate householders, but that only forced us to range further in our quest for luckies. This was mainly how we made our pocket money, and how we got our toys, which were always faulty in some regard, but frequently fixable. If not fixable, we still treasured them anyway, and let our imagination take over, so that they worked just fine as far as we were concerned.

Other sources of income were running errands (messages), for people who were too old, or too lazy, to stir themselves. Someone would call down from an upstairs window, "cuid ye run a wee message fur me, son?" With our innate understanding of the tenement layout system, we could match an outside window to a house easily. Arriving at the appropriate door and knocking (chapping), the door would be opened by the old lady, or the idle housewife. A shopping list (message line) would be thrust into our hands, with the requisite sum of money, the appropriate ration books, and a message bag. If we were lucky the required messages involved only one or two shops. Running such messages could take hours, depending on the length of queues at each shop.

Queues were situation normal during wartime, and there was no guarantee that you would get what you wanted when you reached the head of the queue. This was especially true for kids obviously running messages for somebody else. The shopkeeper had no compunction in telling us that they were sold out, even when we knew that they were lying. They would prefer to act as gracious providers to young housewives that they could chat up as they served them. We were only street urchins who didn't rate a second thought, who could be ignored with no risk of any retribution. Eventually we would return with the laden message bag and knock on the door.

Now came crunch time, as we were entirely at the mercy of the woman as to how much we would get for our trouble. For running such messages, we hoped to get sixpence, but some old ladies were still living in Victorian times, and expected you to grovel in appreciation, when they handed you a penny and a jam sandwich wrapped in newspaper. Most gave sixpence, but the lazy housewife would frequently give ninepence, or even a whole shilling, which meant that we were rich, and could splash out on goodies to eat. We would keep our eyes on her window in future. We would certainly run her messages at the slightest opportunity.

Another source of funds was the regular propensity for the occasional woman to somehow lock herself out of her house. The unfortunate would present herself at her closemouth and try to attract attention to her plight. Seeing her and guessing her predicament, we would vie with each other to get the job of getting her into her home. The going rate was definitely sixpence and settled prior to the required burglary. If her window was close to one of the many vertical cast-iron down pipes which adorned the walls of tenement buildings, then the successful bidder was in luck. Shinning up the down pipe, to the first or second storey window was okay, but the third storey required better nerves than I had.

My brother Bobby could, and would, do this, as it was worth at least a shilling, maybe even two shillings or half a crown. After shinning up the pipe, which we were very adept at as a lot of our street games involved shinning up pipes, the rescuer would reach out with the nearest hand, and open the sash window as these were seldom locked. If it opened easily, then he would deftly transfer his weight to the windowsill and parapet, and clamber through the window to open the door to the grateful woman. If the window was locked or jammed, then plan B was followed, that of kicking in the door, breaking the lock. You might think that such a task would be beyond the capacity of a small boy, but if so you would be wrong.

From a young age I could kick in most doors, often at the first kick. The secret is that you have total faith in your kicking foot to withstand the shock, as the rest of your body follows through, in maximising the impact. I would hurl myself at the lock area of the door with the unshakeable conviction that the door would give way, which usually happened. The only problem with kicked in doors was that the lock was sometimes broken, requiring repair by the local blacksmith. Usually only the minor part in the door jamb was affected, requiring minor carpentry, which we could undertake if required.

By 1945 it was becoming clear that the war in Europe was nearing an end, and would soon be over, with Germany in ruins, and the Americans and Allied forces tightening the noose on Japan.

Everybody was becoming very cheery, and just waiting for the return home of their menfolk. On May 9th, hostilities in Europe ceased, except for a few diehard SS units in Eastern Europe which refused to give in, preferring to fight to the death.

When VE (Victory in Europe) Day was officially announced on the wireless, everybody stopped whatever they were doing and took to the streets, laughing, dancing, and crying, all at the same time. Street parties were quickly organised. For the teenagers it was a great chance to put their prior demolition experience and considerable vandalism skills to good use. They attacked the heavy wooden beams which protected each close with pointed steel railings, which were easily prised from the few remaining railing fences which had survived the Government's earlier drive for scrap metal. The beams were dragged out of the closes, and piled up in the middle of most streets, but especially high in our street. Further fuel was added to the bonfire material, by people dragging out old items of furniture, to add to the already huge and fast-growing pile of bonfire fuel. In years to come, old items of furniture like these would become potentially valuable antiques, but to the tenement dwellers they were regarded as being only old-fashioned rubbish. We all visited Granny Cunningham at Parkhead on the day of the big street parties.

As we passed each side street on the way home from Parkhead to Glasgow Cross, and from the Cross to Kidston Street, we saw giant bonfires, with revellers leaping around, and loud music coming from wide open windows, with everybody tuned into the same wireless programme. Getting off the tramcar and turning into Kidston Street, we were greeted by the sight of Fire Brigade trucks, a myriad of fire hoses snaking everywhere, and a crew of firemen training huge jets of water on the blazing bonfire, which was still issuing large columns of flames and huge showers of sparks, much higher than the tall tenement buildings.

Prevented by the ARP from going any further, we could not get home, so had to join the throng of yelling protesters gathered at the corner of Crown Street, who were incensed at being denied the freedom to burn the whole district down, which would certainly have happened if some sensible citizen had not called out the Fire Brigade.

Realising that it would be hours before the firemen eventually subdued the oversized bonfire, Mammy led us round to Caledonia Street to Auntie Bella's house. As we were climbing the six flights of stairs, we heard a commotion coming from Bella's house. "Ye're no' comin' hame tae ma hoose reekin' o' bliddy beer an' whusky, ye stupit wee bugger," rang out the dulcet tones of Auntie Bella. "Ye kin jist gae back to yer drunken pals it thi pub, fur ye're no' steyin' here."

Mammy took a look through the open door, before dragging us in behind her. On a chair sat poor wee Uncle Alec Dorans. "Bit Bella hen, ah only hid a couple o' pints an' some wee haufs, its VE night efter a'." At that time Uncle Alec, the whole four feet six of him, was working as a coalman. He must have been a right tough little bugger to cart the hundredweight (approximately 50kg) bags of coal on his narrow little shoulders, up and down flights of tenement stairs all day long, but he managed it somehow.

Auntie Bella, like all of her sisters except Auntie Jean, was implacably opposed to drinking alcohol, in any quantity, putting a total damper on their husband's potential social life. This didn't mean that they abstained completely, but it meant that they could go home and cop an ongoing tirade of abuse, or they could stay away from home until they were sober, then cop an even greater tirade of abuse for drinking and not coming home.

"Bella," said Mammy, "Alec's only hid a few wee drinks, an' it is VE day efter a', he's no' drunk or anythin' like tha', hoo aboot gie'n him a wee chance, eh?" "Ah'll gie him a few wee drinks, ah'll gie him a few wee drinks oan thi ither side o' his ugly wee mug," retorted Bella, still in full indignant flight. Uncle Alec looked up at Mammy, having found an unexpected and sympathetic ally. "Ye unnerstaun, Jessie, a man's goat tae hiv a wee drap noo an' again, fur the sake o' his sanity, if naethin' else." It was an awkward situation. "Aw' right," said Bella, "ah'll no' throw him doon thi sterrs, bit he's no' sleepin' in mah bed, he kin doss doon in the loabby, an' ah hope that he catches his death o' yoomony, so ah dae."

Uncle Alec smiled at Mammy, revealing a totally toothless, gummy mouth. "Ye're a real guid sister, so ye ur Jessie, ah weesh thit the rest o' yer sisters wur like ye." said Alec, not realising that he was inviting another broadside from Auntie Bella. "She disnae hiv tae live wi' the likes o' yoo. If she did, she wid be haudin' oan tae yer ankles, an' me yer hauns, while we flung ye right doon the sterrs," yelled Bella, "Ye're gettin' aff lightly, if ye hid ony sense at a' ye would shut yer stupit gub an' keep quiet, ye stupit wee bauchle."

Uncle Alec got the message at last and sat back in his chair to doze off in minutes. "Oor street's barricaded aff Bella, kin the weans an' me wait here tae the bonfire his been put oot, it shouldnae be that long bit Ah' didnae want tae jist staun' ther' wi' a' thae drunk folk," said Mammy, unthinkingly. "Dinnae yoo mention drunk folk tae me, ah've hid enough o' drunk folk fur wan night thank ye very much," said Auntie Bella in an irritated tone, "Ah dinnae want tae hear the word drink ever mentioned again."

We sat quietly not saying a word, but well aware that poor wee Uncle Alec would have been sleeping rough in some close or wynd, if we had not unexpectedly arrived at the critical moment. Apart from their unwavering opposition to drink, my Aunties were basically good natured and kind. If it hadn't been for the close family support which they supplied at all times to their "Wee Yin" and her family, we would have been very hard pressed to survive. We sat up until the early hours of the morning playing with our cotton reels and rubber bands, as Mammy periodically nipped round to Kidston Street to check if it was safe to return home. At about 3am, Mammy came back with the good news that the Fire Brigade had eventually doused the blaze.

Auntie Bella carried Alec and Mammy carried Bobby, whilst I tagged alongside. We collapsed into bed, fully dressed, and were dead to the world before Mammy could undress us. As far as the bonfire was concerned, when all the ashes and charred wood was removed by the Corporation, it could be seen that the street itself had been on fire also. The asphalt surface under the bonfire was deeply charred in a large circle. It was some weeks before the Corporation men arrived with a large tarboiler, which was coal fired, and with "Trinidad Lake Asphalt ", in big white letters painted on the outside.

A team of labourers dug away the charred asphalt, shovelling the debris onto a truck, leaving a large shallow pit. Meanwhile a team of asphalt layers had assembled, with each member wearing prominent leather knee and elbow pads, carrying two huge wooden trowels, one in each hand. The tar was transferred from the tar boiler in massive iron buckets with a swivel handle and a spout. The tar was poured into the shallow pit by the labourers, whilst the men with the trowels spread the asphalt out using both trowels and achieving a superfine surface. It must have been a backbreaking job, but when they finished, it was hard to see where the hole had been.

Chapter 9

My father had joined up in the Highland Light Infantry(HLI), based at the Maryhill Barracks, in 1934, as this was better than being on the 'Brew'. He was demobilised in 1937 and took a job as a bus conductor with the Glasgow Corporation. It was then that he met my mother, who was then Jessie Cunningham. After a brief courtship, they got married on New Years Eve 1937 at Martha Street Registry Office, with the only guests being the two witnesses, Shug Campbell, my father's friend, and Nellie Kerr, the best friend of my mother. The wedding feast consisted of four fish suppers wrapped in newspaper, consumed on the Auchenshuggle tramcar on the way home from town. For refreshments, they shared a large bottle of Barr's Irn Bru, drinking straight from the bottle. There was no honeymoon, with the newly marrieds moving into the sole bedroom of Granny McLachlan's apartment in Mc Duff Street, and Granny setting her bed up in the sitting room. The next morning my father set off, at 0530 to attend work as usual, as if it was just another day. Also, importantly, he had not requested time off work in advance, as he only proposed to mother on the morning of the wedding, and when she accepted, decided to do it without delay, that afternoon. Besides that, they needed the money. My mother informed her mother, and via her mother, her sisters, when she got back from the Registry Office, that she was now a married woman.

In mid-1939 when Hitler was making loud warlike noises, my father had been recalled back into the army. Trained soldiers like him were needed to act as instructors for the many thousands of volunteers and conscripts who were now being urgently drafted into the army. He was initially stationed at Fort George in the Highlands, where many of the new recruits were being trained. Daddy wasn't very tall, but he had grown up in an extremely tough world and could look after himself just fine.

An event which typified his nature took place in a barrack room at Fort George. He was a corporal at the time but had fallen foul of a very big English drill sergeant. He was sitting on the end of his bed polishing his best boots, a nightly task, when the arrogant sergeant appeared, and immediately started to needle Daddy, loudly boasting of his prowess in the boxing ring and in unarmed combat, saying what he would like to do to the short-arsed Scotchmen, who made up the majority of the HLI contingent, and Daddy in particular.

Daddy was very quick tempered, and would take no crap from anyone, which is no doubt why he had attracted the attention of the burly sergeant in the first place. Daddy quickly lost his temper. "Ah think that yir jist a fuckin' big blawhard, ah'll bet ye couldnae even beat the wee fella' hidin' under ma' bed", said Daddy. "Who's hiding under your bed?" shouted the sergeant, squatting down to have a look. As soon as his head was within easy range, Daddy leapt to his feet, and smashed the hobnailed heel of the boot that he had been polishing into the sergeant's forehead with all the force that he could muster, opening a wide gash from which blood spurted like a fountain as the sergeant collapsed, out cold. "Let's see hoo guid ye ur at fightin' noo, ye big ugly parcel o' English shite," yelled Daddy, as he gave the inert body a volley of hard kicks to the ribs and head with his hobnailed boots for good measure, before he was pulled away.

Daddy was quickly placed under close arrest and marched off to the guardroom. He was charged the next morning and sentenced to demotion to private, accompanied by three months in the military prison, also located at Ft George.

This pattern of promotion and demotion was repeated many times during his years in the army. He was a sergeant, corporal, and private, then corporal, then sergeant, with steady regularity. My mother must have been fed up trying to guess how to address his mail, as they corresponded weekly. When he was released from Fort George he was posted to the Dorset Regiment which was stationed at the Butlin's holiday camp on the Isle of Wight, where the battalion was being worked up for active service. All the training went for naught.

One night every officer was attending a boozy party in the officer's mess. A lone German bomber had become lost on a bombing raid on London. Returning to its base in France, it passed over the Isle of Wight. The pilot decided to drop his load of bombs, releasing them directly over the Butlin's camp. The officers mess took a direct hit, killing every single officer. The battalion was of no use without officers, so was disbanded, with the men being posted to a myriad of different regiments.

Daddy was transferred to a Royal Artillery regiment, and proceeded by troopship to the Middle East, where the regiment became part of the Eighth Army, fighting in the many campaigns which culminated in Rommel's Afrika Corps being driven from North Africa. He also served in Greece and was evacuated back to the desert during this time. Sicily and Italy were next, with the regiment being eventually happily stationed in Graz in Austria, when the war ended.

You might have noticed that I have never mentioned either of my grandfathers. There is a very good reason for this, which is that I know absolutely nothing about either of them. My paternal grandfather's name was Allan Gilfillan McLachlan, as was my father's, and as is mine. He was a paviour by trade, meaning that he laid heavy granite cobblestones all day for a living, and had hands as hard and unyielding as the stone he worked with. I only know that about his hands, as my father recounted one day, how Daddy and his brother used to hide under the bed when his father came home, to avoid getting skelped round the ear by his iron hard fists just for being there. I believe that Wee Granny's total deafness was caused by powerful blows to the ears.

Of my maternal grandfather, I know nothing at all about him, except that his name appears to have been Thomas Cunningham, and that he died before my mother was born. Not once did I hear a single word spoken about him by his large family, at any time.

Another member of the family was my father's maternal grandmother, Mary Fleming, who lay as if in state, on a bed by the window in Granny's room. We were terrified of her but were always forced to go in and pay our respects to her when we visited. She lay perfectly still with her eyes wide open, unblinking, and looked just like a corpse, which is why we were so frightened. Her hair was as white as snow, her skin too was pallid and white, and her eyes were the palest shade of blue imaginable, altogether an alarming vision for anyone, never mind young children.

With white sheets as a background, she looked like a contrived scene from a horror movie. Occasionally, she would say in a weak voice, "Ah kin hear the bell's o' Saint Mary's." When this happened without warning, we would be even more frightened than before, and scoot out of the room as quickly as we could run. She had been in this catatonic state since she suffered a stroke at the age of 65. She was 95 when she died.

Now that the war was over, we impatiently awaited the return home of Daddy, now stationed in Graz, Austria. Eventually in mid-1945 Mammy gave us the good news that Daddy was in transit from Austria to England, and that he would be home early on the following Thursday. We were very excited, with the exception of Alec, who had reached the age of three, without any contact with men. Even when the coalman came into the lobby to dump the coal in the bunker, Alec would scurry under the bed to hide, and not emerge until the coalman was long gone.

At last, the great day arrived, I doubt that any of us had slept during the Wednesday night. By 7am, we were all up and dressed, ready for the arrival of Daddy. Alec had already hidden under the bed and refused to budge. We were also apprehensive, as we hadn't seen Daddy for years, only remembering what he looked like from the framed photographs on the sideboard. I went down to the communal toilet on the stairhead. I was still in the toilet, when I heard the sound of heavy tackety boots entering the close and ascending the stairs.

I peered through the large keyhole, saw the back of a soldier, dressed in a heavy greatcoat, and humping a big pack, small pack, a kitbag over one shoulder, and a rifle over the other, clumping up the stairs to our single end door. Mammy flung open the door excitedly and tried to get her hands through the webbing and kit, to give him a big hug, which for our family was unheard of.

I followed him through the door, as he dropped his pile of kit and struggled out of all the webbing. Eventually he managed to get his greatcoat and battledress jacket off, and collapsed into our only armchair, which Granny Cunningham had got for us at an auction sale just the week before. "My, ye've a' shot up" he said, with tears of sheer happiness showing in his eyes. "An' you, Sheena, ye're still a right wee smasher." Sheena was Daddy's name of endearment for Mammy, claiming that it was the Gaelic equivalent of Jessie. Where he got this from I have no idea.

"Where's wee Alec?" asked Daddy, as he swept his gaze around the little room. "He's hidin' alow the bed, an' wullnae come oot fur naebody", I said. Daddy had never seen Alec before, except in the photographs that Mammy had included in her many letters. "Ah'm sure that he'll come oot fur me", said he with confidence, "Ah'll jist lift the valence, an' gie him a wee look at me first".

He lifted the valence and looked under the bed. Alec was curled up in a tight ball in the far corner, and refused to uncurl himself, never mind emerging from his favourite hidey hole. "Okay," said Daddy, "we'll jist gie him a wee bit o' time tae get used tae me afore ah try again". He turned to me and Bobby, "Ye'se kin stey aff school the day if ye'se want tae, it's a long time since yer Daddy's been hame". "Ah'd rather go to school as the teacher's goat somethin' special tae show us aboot big ships", I said. "Me tae," said Bobby.

We had, even though we were only six and seven years old, decided the night before that Mammy and Daddy should get some time to themselves, without us hanging around, and we knew that Alec would not emerge from under the bed until he was forced out by the need to go to the toilet. "Awright, aff ye go tae the school, but afore ye go, ah've goat something fur ye'se in ma pack." He unbuckled his small pack and rummaged around in the contents. "Here ye ur, hiv ye iver seen real aipples, perrs, an' bananas". He held out three pieces of miniature wrinkled fruit, one pear, one apple, and one banana.

We had never seen real fruit before, and thanked Daddy before we stuck our precious fruit in our schoolbags and ran around the corner to school. I was so excited about the fruit that I couldn't wait to show the teacher. She held the fruit up for the class to see. There were a lot of "ooh's and ah's" from the classroom, as they also had never seen real fruit before. I ate the fruit during morning playtime, relishing every bite, whilst the other kids looked on drooling at the mouth.

Daddy was only home on leave for two weeks before returning to Woolwich in London, which was the regimental headquarters of the Royal Regiment of Artillery. A month later he returned home, this time without the uniform, wearing his pinstriped 'demob' suit, supplied by the Army, carrying a compressed cardboard suitcase in one hand, and with his kitbag over his shoulder.

This time he was home for good. "Whit's in yer kitbag, Allan?" asked Mammy. "Ach, it's a' mah uniform an' stuff, fur ah'm still oan the Army Reserve fur years yet, and ah might need it a' again if anither war breaks oot." Daddy opened the neck of the kitbag, thrust his arm in and raked around by feel, extracting a webbed belt and two pairs of tackety boots and some pairs of socks. Putting those under the bed, he retied the neck of the kitbag, tossed it over his shoulder, and saying that he would be out for little while, slipped out of the door.

Within an hour he returned, minus the kitbag. "Whaur's yer kitbag?" asked Mammy. "Ah managed tae get ten shullin's fur it a' at Paddy's Market at the Saltmarket, nae bother," replied Daddy "Mah goad Allan, whit's gonnae happen tae ye if ye get called up again, ye'll get the jile so ye wull." "Fuck 'em, there's nae wey that they'll get me back intae the Army, the jile's faur safer oneywey, an' Barlinnie's miles better thin maist o' the places that ah had tae put up wae abroad. The only decent place wis Austria, an' they wurnae even oan oor side," replied Daddy with feeling.

Chapter 10

For the hundreds of thousands of returning servicemen, civilian jobs were difficult to find. We needed the money, as the Army allowance had ceased, so Daddy had little choice but to return to his old job as a corporation bus conductor, based at Larkfield bus depot in Govanhill, which was not too far away. Now that he was at home, we couldn't all fit in one bed. Daddy made a sort of sliding bed that was pushed under the recess bed during the day, and pulled out at night to accommodate us three, whilst he and Mammy had the curtained off recess bed to themselves, after they clambered over our bed to get in.

The living space problem was solved when the family living in the 'room and kitchen' next door moved to a new house in the Pollok housing estate, built on a part of the vast country estate of the Maxwell family. As soon as Mammy found out that they were moving, she shot round to McFie, the factor, and applied for the potential vacancy. Our family had a good tenancy and rent paying record and had been on the waiting list for a larger apartment for years. We were overjoyed when Mr McFie told

Mammy that we would get the house when the tenants next door moved out.

Moving was no trouble, as we had few belongings anyway, and shifted next door, in less than an hour with everybody helping, as soon as the door key was obtained from the factor's office,. As we moved out, a young couple, the Leydens, moved into the single end. We now had a bedroom as well as a kitchen. Both rooms had a bed recess, and a fireplace. Mammy got the local blacksmith to make an iron framed sprung bed to fit in the room recess for us.

The other innovation was the installation of electricity, to power a single light bulb, in the centre of each ceiling. We thought that we were real toffs, with a bedroom, and an electric light. On the first night, the light was eagerly switched on. Compared to the soft light from the gas mantle that we were used to, the electric light was harsh and dazzling to our eyes.

For the first few weeks, Bobby and I took our comics next door to the Maloneys each night after supper to read, sitting beside old Mr Maloney as he puffed on his pipe. Also Daddy constructed a small wooden table with a shelf underneath, and a metal top to sit the single gas ring on, instead of the floor. Not that long after we settled into the room and kitchen, Mammy told us that we would be having a wee brother or sister, very soon. As usual I hadn't noticed that she was pregnant, so the news was a big surprise.

One night she went into labour, with Auntie Annie from upstairs in attendance. We could hear Mammy's moans of pain through the wall separating the bed recesses, keeping us awake for most of the night. Daddy went off to work early in the morning, as childbirth did not appear on the Corporation's acceptable list of excuses for not turning up for duty. About seven o' clock, the midwife arrived, having been fetched by Grace Patterson, our teenage cousin. Shortly afterwards, Mammy's loud moans ceased, to be replaced by the shrill noise of a newborn baby crying. A little later Auntie Annie came into our room, carrying a tiny bundle wrapped up in a baby blanket. "Hiv a wee look at yir new wee sister, is she no' beautiful?"

We looked into the bundle. All we could see was a tiny red face, sucking one of its miniature fists. "Ah'll jist gie wee Grace back tae yir Mammy, then get you two fed an' ready for school." "Oor Grace'll watch wee Alec fur a few days untae yir Mammy is back oan hir feet." I was about an hour late for school and very hesitant as I knocked on the classroom door. "Come in," said the teacher, as I peeked around the door. "What's your excuse for being so late, McLachlan?" "Ah've got a new wee sister, she wis jist boarn this moarnin." "That's lovely, now you can concentrate on your lessons," said the teacher, who had replaced the aged Mrs Woods a few weeks before. She taught us for years afterwards, but I can't remember her name or what she looked like.

Shortly after Grace was born, I had to attend the local doctor's surgery, as I was continually suffering from severe headaches. The nurse took my particulars. "Is your face always that white?" she asked. "Aye, ah think so," I replied. She made some notes on her pad. "I think that you need some good fresh country air and building up", she said, handing me a bottle of some kind of iron tonic. A few days later a man knocked on our door whilst I was at school. After introducing himself as a child welfare officer, he told Mammy that our doctor had written to the department recommending that I needed some time in the country to build me up and improve my health generally. He then called at the school to quiz my teacher on how I was doing at school, and how she viewed my general health and learning ability.

In June 1946, I was asked to go to the headmaster's office, where I waited outside in trepidation, wondering what I had done to deserve the strap from the 'Heidie'. I was called inside and told to relax. The headmaster handed me an official looking letter. "McLachlan, tell your parents that you have been selected to attend the Residential School at Ardossan for a few months, to get some good fresh air and sunlight. Full instructions are in the letter for the train and bus times, and travel vouchers for you and one accompanying adult. There is also a full list of what you have to take with you." "Please sir, what's an adult?" I asked, feeling very nervous about the whole thing already. "Your mother or father are adults", said the headmaster as he ushered me out of his office door. I returned to the classroom with my head in turmoil. I was only seven years old, and apart from a week at Dumfries with Wee Granny, I had never been apart from my family.

When I got home from school I handed the letter to Mammy. "Ah think we'll leave this tae yer Daddy gets hame, he's much better at readin' these things than ah am." It was late in the evening when Daddy arrived home. He read through the contents of the letter, after Mammy handed it to him. "This is a' very well", he said, "bit who's gonny pey for a' this stuff that he's goat tae take tae this place in Ardrossan". "A' this stuff" consisted of a single change of clothing, a spare pair of sandshoes, a toothbrush, and two pairs of pyjamas. "It's a dampt disgrace that they expect weans tae hiv a' their orders, like pyjamas, they must think that we've goat nothin' better tae spend oor money oan."

As usual, Auntie Annie came to the rescue when Mammy told her about Daddy's predictable reaction. A couple of days later a little cardboard suitcase containing all the required items arrived on the kitchen table. I was very relieved, and so was Mammy, but Daddy just grunted and pretended that nothing had happened. In reality Daddy was a dyed in the wool communist, but never admitted this to anybody, particularly himself. "They" were always to blame for everything that Daddy disagreed with. We grew up thinking that "They" were some sort of entity which spent twenty-four hours a day conspiring against poor working-class folk. In reality "They" were a good excuse for not taking any responsibility for our own situation. He never ever cast a vote at elections, as he said that it only encouraged the bastards.

On the first Saturday morning of July, Mammy and I took the tramcar to the Saltmarket, and walked through the back streets to St Enoch railway station. Both of us were very apprehensive and nervous, as Mammy had no idea where Ardrossan was, or anything else about it. We found the right platform, where we saw a large woman with a banner on a pole, reading "Ardrossan Residential School Passengers". We joined a little group of children, each with mothers. There was not a man in sight. I was quite worried as the other kids were much older than I was.

The time came to board the train and we found that the seats were pre-booked, saving us the trouble of standing all the way, as the train was jam-packed with excited families travelling to Saltcoats, the 'Glasgow Riviera'. I had never been on a train before, and Mammy only twice, so we spent the time avidly watching the changing scenery, as the train chugged along at a fast clip.

When the train arrived at Saltcoats, the holidaying families disembarked with the maximum of fuss and bother, with yelling weans scattering in all directions and being chased by frantic parents The screeching weans waved their little wooden spades and buckets as if the seaside was right on the platform. From Saltcoats it was only a short time before we arrived at Ardrossan station. We disembarked, and followed the large lady, still waving her banner, to the pavement outside the station.

A single decker red bus was waiting with the engine running. The lady motioned the group to board the bus and followed us aboard. The bus drove along a narrow road which followed the general line of the shore. I would have been enthralled if I wasn't so nervous, as I had never seen the sea before, and it was much bigger than I could ever have imagined. The bus turned into a gravel driveway and stopped at the impressive front porch of a huge house, a veritable castle, with a large circular stone tower to one side. The large lady led the way through the open door, and into a large wood-panelled room which completely overawed me. Another lady appeared, and introduced herself as Mrs Ritchie, the headmistress. She beckoned the mothers to follow her, as she left us behind to look around nervously, and to size each other up.

When Mammy reappeared with the other mothers, she was obviously on the brink of tears, handing me the little suitcase, and abruptly left the room to rejoin the bus, along with the other mothers, who were equally upset. The Headmistress returned with another three ladies in tow. "I want you to meet your teachers and allocate you to your dormitories." She split us up into age groups, which was relatively easy, except for me. I was by far the youngest in the group, causing the Headmistress to tut tut to herself. "We've never had a seven-year-old before, ten years old is supposed to be the lower limit." The rest of the kids were led away, by the teachers, leaving me with the Headmistress, still tut tutting to herself. "Allan, how would you like to sleep up in the tower, in the small three bed dorm, the other two boys are ten, but they are the nearest to you in age."

I followed her up a spiral staircase, until we reached a circular room at the top, equipped with three beds. "You can have this bed, just leave your wee case here," she said, pointing to a bed on a higher level than the others. "I hope that you're not a bed wetter, Allan, as it is the one thing that I cannot abide." "Naw miss, Ah never wet the bed," I said with my fingers crossed behind my back.

I followed her down the stairs, feeling like bursting into tears, but biting my lip as she led me to my classroom. The classroom was brilliantly light and airy, with a panoramic view of the Firth of Clyde, with the island of Arran clearly visible with its steep mountain scarps. Immediately in front was the long harbour breakwater, stretching out for what seemed like miles to me, with wave surges breaking over it, sending sheets of white spray high into the air.

Our contingent was only a small portion of the pupils, as I quickly found out. The school had a floating population which changed as pupils reached the end of their stay and returned home. In the classroom were kids of all ages up to the age of fourteen, being taught individually according to their needs. At home in the Gorbals, there was a rigid vertical separation of kids according to age groups of about two years. Here ten-year-olds, who wouldn't even speak to me at home, were the closest in age. Most of my classmates ranged from twelve to fourteen years old, some of whom would be out in the workforce within the next year.

There were kids from different parts of Glasgow, most of which I had never heard of. Blackhill, Bishopbriggs, Airdrie, Calton, Shettleston, Partick, Newbank, Bridgeton, to name a few. To an outsider listening to us conversing, it would have seemed that we were all speaking the same guttural dialect. To us, however, there were many different accents, and intonations, subtle but plain to us. None of us had ever before spoken to a kid from a different district and spent many happy hours discussing the differences in word usage, nuances, and accents. The teachers spoke in a soft Ayrshire accent, which was also foreign to me.

I was intensely homesick and suffered from this affliction for the whole three months of my stay, which was a great pity, for in many ways it was a fantastic experience, allowing me to take part in many activities that would have otherwise been denied me. I can't remember much about the first day, except from being led up to bed in the tower, being shown how to brush my teeth properly in the tiny bathroom/toilet in the garret above, and the strange feeling of getting dressed up to go to bed in my new pyjamas.

The morning started at 7am, when the kindly housemother gently shook us awake, and waited to ensure that we got out of bed, washed, cleaned our teeth, and got dressed. A new experience for me was putting on a cold shirt in the morning, as at home we slept in our shirts. The three of us were lucky, living in our own little dormitory. The bigger boys lived in much larger dorms, sharing a single common bathroom, complete with actual baths.

As soon as we were dressed, we followed the delicious aroma of marmalade, toast, and burnt porridge, downstairs to the dining room, and filled up to our heart's content. Many years have passed, but I can still recall the particular combination of smells which heralded breakfast. Schoolwork started at eight o'clock sharp in the classroom with the brilliant views, which didn't help my concentration, as I couldn't help looking out of the windows and letting my overactive imagination run riot, as I thought of pirate ships, deep sea divers, giant fish, and all the other things that I associated with the sea.

Interrupted by lunch, school continued until 2.30 pm, when we rushed outside to play in the extensive woodlands behind the house. The house was a big one and must have belonged to one of Glasgow's rich trading families before being converted into a residential school. Magnificent topiary work covered most of the front garden. High stone and brick walls followed the boundaries, enclosing about twenty acres of woodland and some fields. In true Scottish fashion, the front façade of the house was constructed of the local pink sandstone, facing the waterside road, but the sides and rear were executed in plain red brick for the sake of economy.

The grove of trees closest to the classrooms had been turned into a cross between a kids' jungle gym and a commando assault course, with the emphasis on assault course. Heavy ropes were suspended in pairs between trees, which allowed walking on the bottom rope whilst holding on to the top one. I was much shorter than the twelve- to fourteen-year-olds for whom the rope bridges had been designed, so had to settle for swinging across, hand over hand, on the bottom rope. The trees were accessed by many ropes hanging to the ground, and nets hanging from substantial branches.

On my first full day, I was bailed up by the oldest boarders, who wanted to know how old I was, and where I came from. I expected to be picked on and bullied by these giants, but this was far from the case, as I was adopted into their group as a sort of mascot. I was given the name 'The Kid', which they all called me, and was extremely well treated by all the boarders during my three month stay.

The grounds seemed to go on for ever, in my eyes, which were accustomed to much more restricted horizons. There were trees, bamboo groves, ponds, a stream, and a swampy area. No place could be more perfectly suited to playing soldiers, cowboys and Indians, Tarzan, pirates, Flash Gordon, and cops and robbers. We carved pistols, rifles, and tommy guns, from suitable fallen branches, with a kitchen knife 'borrowed' from the cook and hidden for ongoing use under a small footbridge.

Freed from the slum environment, everybody grew in self-esteem and stature, without the constant hunger and mixing with the numerous petty criminals in training, which prevailed in the Gorbals and other slum areas, on an everyday basis. I don't remember exactly what the weather was like, but I think that it was pretty good for most of my stay. If it rained, there was a long timber hut with many windows for playing in, with plenty of room for everyone.

I was constantly homesick, not for my home, but for my family, which spoiled what was otherwise an idyllic existence. On those afternoons when the weather was warm, the teachers took us down to the waterside. There wasn't much of a beach, just patches of sand between rocky pools, but the rocky pools were the most interesting. The water was shin-numbingly freezing, but we took off our shoes and socks and waded in regardless. After my legs went totally numb and the pain faded, I would wade for hours looking for interesting shells and crabs. I remember the first trip to the rockpools and was thrilled to see that the rocks were encrusted with countless whelks. Remembering how delicious these were when bought from the street hawkers, I filled my bucket, and my pockets, sorry that I didn't have a pin to prise them from their shells, being surprised that nobody else was doing the same, as they were telling me that I was wasting my time.

Arriving back at school, I went to the back door of the kitchen and begged for a pin, then sitting down to have a real treat, started to get to work with the pin. I was surprised when the whelks spat out a small jet of water and clamped their little covers tightly shut. I was snuffling with sheer frustration, when one of the kitchen staff noticed what I was trying to do. "Ye'll niver get them oot tae they've been biled an' cooked right through, son," she said. "Kin ye bile thim fur me then," I asked. "Sorry son, it wid be mair thin ma joab's worth, the cook wid go mad if she thocht that her good pots wur bein' used tae bile up whulks fur wan o' the school bairns." I tearfully took my haul of whelks to the swampy part of the property and tipped them into a small pool. The bigger boys laughed when I returned with my empty pail and pockets. "We telt ye thit ye wur wastin' yer time, ye silly wee bugger, bit ye hud tae fun' oot the hard wey." I could see the funny side of it and burst out laughing with them. "A'll no be daein' that again, whit a waste o' time that wis."

Every Saturday was a visiting day, when parents or other relatives could arrive, and take the pupil out for the day or remain within the school grounds, as these were just like an interesting park. Each Saturday, I ran with all the others to the front gate at 1130 sharp, hoping that Daddy or Mammy would be on the local bus that met the Glasgow train. Six long weeks passed without as much as a letter, and no sign of a visitor. I had long since stopped hoping that someone would be on the bus.

On one Saturday morning I was playing with some of the boys up in the trees when I heard the bus drawing up at the gate and eventually pulling away. From high in the trees, we had a good view of the driveway. As the group of visitors walked up to the front door, I saw that Mammy was amongst them; I ran to meet her but drew up short as I suddenly felt shy and awkward, not knowing what to say to her after all the previous Saturday morning disappointments.

"Hoo ur ye Allan, ye look good wi' a' that colour in yer face, everybody wull be right jealous when they see ye", said Mammy in a happy voice. I grabbed her arm, but still didn't know what to say. "How did ye no' come before, Mammy? Ah've been waiting at the gate every Setterday moarnin' since Ah've been here, an' naebuddy's came yet." I whispered to her; in case I was overheard by one of the other boys. "A'm right sorry son, bit it's been hard tae get doon here, wi' yer Daddy oan shiftwork a' thi time. He hud tae swap wi' sumbuddy the day tae work the nightshift so he cuid watch the ither weans, while ah came doon here oan the train tae see ye," whispered Mammy. "Besides, it's no' chape getting' oan the train an' bus a' the wey doon here tae see ye." I clung to her arm and looked at her properly for the first time. I had never seen Mammy wearing lipstick or any sort of makeup before. She looked quite glamorous, even in her well-worn best coat.

Mammy needed to go to the toilet, before anything else. "Yir big sister's a right smasher, ah bet that she hisnae ony trouble gettin' lifted at the dancin'," said one of the older boys who were hanging around, as most of the other visitors had also headed straight for the toilets. "That's no' ma big sister, that's ma Mammy," I said. The boys laughed, "Aye an' ah'm Adolf Hitler," said one. "An' ah'm Charlie Chan, so ah am" said another. When all the mothers returned from the toilet, I could see why they were sceptical. The other mothers looked more like my older aunties than my Mammy did. "Whit dae ye want tae dae, Allan?" asked Mammy, as we walked towards the front gate. "Ah kin show ye aroon' the school, an' a' the places where we play Mammy, an' then we cuid walk along the seashore a' the wey tae Saltcoats, an' look at the shoaps."

Mammy agreed, and we started our tour of the school grounds. I was very excited and proud of the facilities and told Mammy about all the games we were able to play in these superb surroundings. "It's a wonder thit the loat o' ye hivnae broke yir necks, never mind yer legs or airms," Mammy said. We then inspected my dormitory. "Luxury, pure luxury, that's whit it is, you weans don't know hoo lucky ye'se ur tae live in a place like this, ah've nivir seen the like's o' it." When we came to the classroom and library, she said "Ah bet ye spend the maist o' yer time starin' oot the windae, an' no' oan yer schoolwork, Ah canny credit the view ye've goat, it's miles better than the hoaliday postcairds in the shoap at the station."

After inspecting the rest of the school, especially the large kitchen, which was so well equipped that Mammy's eyes were wide open with wonder, we set out along the waterfront towards Saltcoats. I removed my shoes and socks, and waded from pool to pool whilst Mammy removed her high heeled shoes and walked along the narrow strip of sand that masqueraded as a beach at low tide. "C'moan Mammy, it's brilliant paddlin' in the watter, ye'll like it, an' its good fur yer coarns, an' a'," I yelled. Mammy bent down and put a hand into a pool. "Ye must think that Ah came up the Clyde oan wan o' Fyffe's banana boats, if ye think ah'm gonny pit ma feet in tha' freezin' watter," she retorted with a shiver of her shoulders, "Ah'll jist stick tae the saun' thanks very much."

We continued towards Saltcoats, and its tacky rows of shops. I had an underhand reason for steering Mammy to the shops, as I ached to have a proper gun of some sort, instead of the crude wooden guns which I had whittled from fallen branches. Arriving in Saltcoats, we went from shop to shop without buying anything, which for our family was situation normal. Eventually we entered Woolworths and wandered along the aisles of merchandise. Eventually we came to a counter where toy metal revolvers were heaped up. "Mammy, kin ah hiv wan o' thae cowboy guns? Ah'll pey ye back when Ah get hame, honest Ah wull, Ah'll get enough jeely jaurs in nae time at a', please Mammy please!" Mammy looked stricken, "Ah've nae money tae buy cowboy guns even if Ah wanted tae, Ah've only goat enough money tae get me hame an' that's a' Ah've goat, period." I was bereft but knew that Mammy would have bought me a gun if she could.

We walked back to the school, this time by the road which followed the foreshore, and arrived back to find that it was already three pm. The rest of the visitors were milling around at the front gate, saying their goodbyes to their boys in typically stolid Glaswegian fashion, no hugs, kisses, or any of that sissy stuff for us. As the bus drew up at the school gate Mammy said, "Cheerio son, ah kin see thit ye're daein' jist fine, yer Daddy wull try tae get doon tae see ye the next time an' take ye fur a swim." With that she boarded the bus and took her seat, waving at me until the bus disappeared around a bend on its way to the railway station. I bit my lip until I had walked round behind the play shed, then sobbed my heart out where nobody could see me.

Having exhausted my store of tears, I rejoined my big pals, who were swinging from the trees on the ropes. "His yer big sister gone hame, Kid?" they called, in good humour, "we asked oor mammies, if she wis yer Mammy or yer big sister, an' they a' said she looked too young tae be anybody's Mammy, never mind yours." "She is so mah Mammy, an' Ah hiv two wee brithers, an' a wee sister an' a'," I responded, but this fell on deaf ears and was met by a chorus of derisory hoots from high in the trees.

In the grounds were several high stands of black and white banded bamboo. A favourite game, especially for me, was for the big lads to pick up the smaller boys by their hands and feet, and swing them backwards and forwards, until the momentum built up, then let go at the same time, propelling the small boy sideways into the thick bamboo, at high speed, bending the bamboo backwards, and on the recoil shooting the small boy back at the throwers. It sounds a bit painful, but it wasn't in the least. I could always go on until the bigger boys ran out of puff. "C'moan youse guys, dae it again," I would shout after each turn, until they gave up through exhaustion.

Every Saturday morning, I waited hopefully at the gate for the arrival of the bus bringing the visitors from the train. Trying hard to look nonchalant, I watched the visitors out of the corner of my eye as I pretended to be an uninterested bystander. Weeks passed slowly, but the promised visit from Daddy never eventuated.

Each week kids departed, and others arrived, until I was the longest serving boarder. My much older mentors were gone, and I was not too impressed with their successors. One Thursday afternoon after school I was summoned to the Headmistress's office, where I waited outside in trepidation, wondering what I had done to deserve her personal attention.

The Head emerged from her office and beckoned me to follow her inside. "Allan, you will be going home on Saturday morning, which I suppose you'll be glad to hear. I've written to your parents, to advise them to come and collect you, but your father has replied that he has to work, and your mother has the rest of the family to look after." I was totally at a loss, not knowing how would I get home on the train without an adult. "I've arranged for Mrs MacVicar to go with you on the train, as she has some family business to attend to in Glasgow over the weekend, and your father has promised that your mother will meet you at St Enoch Station," said the kindly Headmistress. "Thank you very much, Miss," I said as she motioned me from her office. I was on one hand saddened that I had to be escorted by a stranger instead of one or other of my parents; on the other, I was ecstatic to be going home at long last. I had been at the Ardrossan school for more than three months, which seemed like a lifetime to a seven-year-old.

I was up at the crack of dawn on the Saturday morning, getting dressed, and packing my little cardboard suitcase with all the treasures that I had accumulated in the months of beachcombing. There was too much to fit all in, so I had to make a trip down to the kitchen middens with the less valuable items carried in my stretched-out jersey front. Even so, the little case weighed a ton, as the majority of the contents consisted of exotic, in my eyes anyway, seashells.

After breakfast I was collected by Mrs MacVicar who worked in the school office and boarded the bus with her after waving goodbye to the kindly kitchen staff who had gathered outside the kitchen door. Mrs MacVicar chatted away in her soft Ayrshire accent during the bus ride and on the train, whilst I sat silently, my mind jammed up with conflicting feelings.

At last, the train arrived at St Enoch station. I felt strange as Mrs MacVicar took my hand and led me down the platform, and out into the station precinct. Beside the far wall I spotted Mammy with the pram, and Bobby and Alec standing alongside her. "Can ye see yer Maw?" asked Mrs MacVicar, "Aye, Ah kin see hur ower at the faur wa'." I led my guardian angel over to where Mammy stood. Mammy thanked Mrs MacVicar for her trouble before she scooted off, as she had a lot to do before the shops shut. I felt very awkward and out of place, not quite knowing what to say. "Ah've goat some brammers o' seashells fur everybody in mah case," was the best I could manage.

It was a hot day for Glasgow as we walked out through the ranks of soap box orators who crowded around the station precinct, yelling at the tops of their voices about every subject from radical Christianity to communism, with the communist attracting the biggest crowd by far. We had a long way to walk, with nobody saying very much, feeling uncomfortable in the clammy heat in our year-round attire of thick woollen jerseys. Eventually we reached the corner of Crown Street and Caledonia Road, where our home territory began. Everything looked strange, not how I remembered it, and this unsettled feeling was reinforced when we turned into Kidston Street itself. Looking around, everything and everybody looked very tawdry and dirty, especially in the unaccustomed heat.

The tenement wives had opened their windows wide and, with cushions protecting their forearms, were leaning out of their windows loudly conversing with their neighbours. Compared with the school at Ardrossan, it was like a scene from hell. We bumped the pram up the stairs and waited whilst Mammy unlocked our door. Everyone filed inside, including the pram, with me bringing up the rear. I stopped dead in my tracks, suddenly feeling very ill. The kitchen looked too small to accommodate a medium sized dog, never mind a family, and the décor was sickening.

As I looked around in horror, the kitchen seemed to rotate, until it was about 45 degrees from plumb. "Ur ye gled tae be hame, son?" asked Mammy, expecting me to eagerly agree. I said nothing, as I didn't have an adequate vocabulary to express the feelings of overwhelming oppression that were consuming me. Sitting at the small kitchen table, I dumbly opened my little suitcase, and pushed it towards my brothers who fell on the seashells as if they were gold plated.

I was in a peculiar daze, staring out of the kitchen window at the view of the galvanised iron roof of the washhouse, and the grime encrusted walls of the next-door church and other tenements. At no time in my young life had I felt so despondent, not even when we returned from our camping holiday at Luss, where we only had a bell tent and the fresh air and lochside to compare with Gorbals life.

Now I had what at some time had been a wealthy family's mansion to act as a comparison, and there was just no contest at all. "Oan ye go Allan, get yersel ootside wi' Boabby an' Alec an' play, that'll soon settle ye doon, fur ye've bin oan a train fur 'oors, an' it's gave ye a sair heid, "said Mammy "Jist take aff thit heavy jersey afore ye go fur it's hoat outside." I took off my jersey, which had survived for three months of hard country playing without it being all ripped and with holes in the elbows, as would have happened within days playing in our streets and backs, or at the outside, a week or two. Going down the stairs, and out into the street with my tanned arms legs and face, I was surprised at the deathly white complexions of my old pals, and the amount of grime sticking to their hands, faces, legs and clothes.

We mucked around as I didn't feel like joining in and getting as manky as the rest. Eventually Mammy called us in for supper in the usual way, by shouting out of the window. "It's your favourite Allan, mince'n totties," she said proudly as we filed through the door.

Sitting down at the table, I looked at the plate of watery mince, surrounding a couple of small boiled potatoes, and realised why we ate our meals with a spoon, rather than using a knife and fork, for the main ingredient was mince flavoured hot water, as Mammy had to eke everything out to make meals go round the whole family.

When Daddy came in from work, hanging his bus conductor's leather bag, hat, and jacket, on a hook behind the front door, he looked at me, saying, "Ye'll be missing a' yer orders noo thit yer hame, an' hiv tae live wi' yer faimily again," before adding "Ye're lookin' a' fit an' healthy the noo, let's see hoo long that lasts. Ah suppose yer too much ae a toff noo tae sleep in yer shurt tail, in the same bed as yer brithers."

"How did ye no' come tae see me Daddy, ah wis expectin' ye fur weeks?" I asked, "Dae ye think thit money grows oan trees?", he responded. "Ah hiv tae work every 'oor that god sends us tae keep youse lot in hoose an' hame, an oneywey it wid only upset ye if ah hid come tae see ye."

It seemed that Daddy didn't understand how much I had been looking forward to him visiting me at Ardrossan and showing him around, just as I had done with Mammy. It would take a long time, like never, before I accepted that living in poverty was our lot in life.

Chapter 11

Living in slum conditions meant living with constant puddles in the back courts, which seldom if ever dried out. These were our pretend seas, rivers, and beaches. Mixed with muck, they were unhealthy enough, but were additionally contaminated by sewage seeps and burst pipes which released bulk sewage, at least until a plumber arrived to repair the damage. It was an everyday sight to see kids, including my brothers and me, playing pretend boats with pieces of wood in a large filthy puddle where turds were also floating around.

We had no conception of the connection between these conditions and the many sicknesses which were endemic in the area. Cuts, grazes and puncture wounds were an everyday occurrence. These didn't heal cleanly, but invariably turned septic, and swelled with yellow and green pus. It was so normal to have septic sores that they were largely ignored. There is a name for such festering sores in Broad Scots, 'Beeling', that has no equivalent in English. Large boils on arms, legs, and elsewhere, were also suffered, and regarded as being another natural blight which had to be endured.

When I had boils, particularly on the back of my neck where my jersey collar rubbed and aggravated the boils, I tried to bear the constant pain, in case my father noticed, or Mammy brought this to his attention. Daddy had a certain method of dealing with boils, which was clinically effective, but excruciatingly agonizing in application. First, Daddy had to catch us, as we knew what was coming, and we would attempt anything to avoid the inevitable. After cornering and grabbing the boil sufferer, he would sit down and lock his legs around ours and hold both of our wrists with one hand behind our back, leaving his right hand free to smack our behinds as we wriggled and struggled to free ourselves.

He had already placed a milk bottle upside down in a pan of boiling water to reach as high a temperature as possible. He then wrapped a towel around his free hand, grabbed the hot milk bottle from the pan, and as quickly as possible clapped the boiling hot neck of the milk bottle over the boil, holding it firmly in place as we shrieked and struggled. The bottle neck formed an efficient air seal against our neck. The scalding hot bottle was bad enough in terms of pain but was nothing compared to the agony suffered as the hot air trapped inside the bottle cooled, creating a partial vacuum, which caused the boil to be sucked out of the neck complete with long yellow root, leaving a large bloody crater behind. "Ah don't know whit a' the fuss wis aboot, anybuddy hearin' ye wid think ye wur gettin' murdered," said Daddy. "Noo whaur else dae ye hiv boils?" he asked, as if we would tell him. Once he was on a roll, he would conduct a boil hunt, making us undress for a boil inspection. He invariably found some which had yet to develop to the suppurating and angry stage. "A'll jist get rid o' these wee yins afore they git ony wurse," he would say, as we dived under the bed to escape, even although we knew that any resistance was futile.

Hauling us one at a time from below the bed, he would repeat the procedure until we were pronounced boil-free. We then had to stand in the cast-iron sink while he would rinse out the craters, using a large red rubber bulb with a short pipe attached, filled from a bowl containing a mixture of bicarbonate of soda and water. Once the craters were rinsed out to his satisfaction, he would apply some black tarry ointment to the empty craters, warning us to keep the ointment off our sheets and pillows when we went to bed, as if this was even remotely possible. Although his skills in boil treatment were rudimentary, and extremely painful, no boil dared to grow in the same site again, so effective was his treatment.

The weather was so consistently inclement that we wore the same basic clothes all year round, with minimal changes for summer or winter. For young boys clothing consisted of a grey shirt, short trousers of thick material, fully lined, and held up with braces ('galluses'), which fastened to the buttons sewn on the outside of our trousers in the appropriate position, a woollen jersey with a collar, long socks which were always rolled down around our ankles (only sissies wore long socks to below the knee), and hobnailed boots or shoes ('tackety boots').

At the height of summer, during the school holidays, the tackety boots might be exchanged for cheap sandshoes ('saunies' in the vernacular), and in the winter for rubber Wellington boots ('wellies') with the addition of a navy blue trenchcoat, if a hand me down one was available.

In severe winter weather, which was not uncommon, we played outside in basically the same clothing that we wore in warmer weather, except for woollen mittens which quickly became saturated and therefore useless as hand warmers. The top edges of our wellies rubbed against our bare legs, leaving the skin red raw, which we mistakenly called scurvy. In really cold weather, if we were engaged in vigorous play, the bottom edge of our shorts would accumulate a fringe of icicles which also rubbed our legs raw, only higher up.

Of all the seasons I preferred the winter, the more severe the better, because of the snowfalls and the thickness of ice which developed. I could tell from my bed if snow had fallen during the night, or was still falling, without having to get up and look out of the window, as the snow acted as a sound baffle, deadening all the usual background noise made by buses, tramcars and horse drawn larries.

Even the clattering noise made by workers hurrying off to work along the granite flagged pavements in heavy tackety boots or clogs, was muffled. The rare sound of quietness was just pure magic. First thing in the morning, a snowfall transformed the slums into a different place, with all horizontal surfaces clothed in gentle pristine whiteness. This state lasted only for a short time, as the combination of traffic and pedestrians, with the pervasive black fallout from scores of industrial chimneys, all too soon turned the snow into blackened slush and muck.

If it wasn't a school day, Mammy would give us tuppence each for our fare, and we would cut across the Gorbals to Victoria Road, to board a tramcar for Queens Park, where clean white snow ('snaw') could be guaranteed to lie until it thawed or more snow fell. Always we travelled in strength, gathering up pals on our way, so when we got to Queens Park there were enough kids to play at building igloos, castles, aeroplanes, trains, with each game inevitably ending up in a snowball fight, and rolling in the snow, stuffing handfuls of snow down the necks of each other's jerseys, or up the trouser legs.

Normally, without the cover of snow, the grassed areas of all public parks were liberally dotted with metal plaques, bearing the hated words 'Keep off the Grass' in raised lettering. Each park attendant, 'Parkies' to us, carried a long pole to enforce his authority, and must have been recruited according to his implacable hatred of small boys from the poorer districts, who only went to a park to play on the grass, as this was the only grass available.

If a Parkie spotted us before we spotted him, he would immediately rush into attack, wielding his pole like a demented fencer, landing blows right and left as we scattered and ran away. If the Parkie realised that he had been spotted at a distance, he would often sidle off to find reinforcements. Having found some other Parkies, he would try to block off all escape routes, by placing Parkies behind the many bushes available.

Rather than falling into the trap by scattering, and being caught by our ambushers, we would form a tightly packed flying wedge, and run like hell, taking a route that we knew well, ignoring the 'keep off the grass' signs and the gravel walkways, heading straight for the high iron railings surrounding the park perimeter. Reaching the railings, we would be up and over with ease, into the nearest street, calling back to the enraged Parkies, "Ye couldnae catch a cauld if ye were loast in a snawstoarm ye useless bastarts, we'll get oor big brithers tae come back, an shove yer poles up yer stupit arses," and the inevitable "Yer drawers ur full o' mince," as we ran away before they could call the polis.

When it snowed, however, the Parkies retreated to their snug bothy, with a roaring coal fire sending grey smoke up the lum and curling up into the air. Short of a bomb falling directly down the lum, nothing would budge them. This allowed us to use the park as it should be used, going anywhere we pleased, and being able to really enjoy the outdoors without being attacked on sight by some evil-minded curmudgeon in uniform.

One Saturday, we had a very heavy snowfall with snow drifts, and with permission from our mothers, and dragging a collection of hurriedly constructed sleds, we made our way on foot to Queens Park, as the tramcars were not running. It was a long drag for us uphill all the way.

Arriving eventually at Queens Park, we slogged towards the nearest hill to put our sleds to the test. On the way we had to pass by the Parkies bothy, with its lum belching smoke, so we motioned to each other to keep completely quiet. The bothy was tucked into the side of a small steep knoll and was now buried in drifted snow to the eaves at the rear, and sides. To get into the bothy, the Parkies had shovelled the deep snow from the only doorway, but only enough to get in and no more. I signalled to my pals to stop and to keep quiet. I thought that it would be a good idea to very quietly pile snow against the door which looked like it opened outwards. It didn't take long to pile large armfuls of snow against the door until we could reach no higher.

Encouraged by the lack of any response from inside we continued to reinforce the snowbank, until we were sure that the hated Parkies would never be able to open the door. We plodded on towing our sleds, thinking that it was a great pity that we would not be around when they tried to open the door. When we were safely out of earshot we stopped to let our suppressed laughter explode, rolling around in the snow, as we giggled about the joke that we had pulled. Looking down on the bothy, from higher up the hill, I could see that it would be easy to walk straight on to the roof and reach the lum. I couldn't help myself and told the others to keep dead quiet as I went back down the slope.

Nearing the roof of the bothy, I lay flat on my stomach, and 'swam' the rest of the way on top of the deep snow until I was up against the lum. I slowly stood up and easily made a large snowball, which was a bit bigger than the chimney pot. Reaching up I placed the snowball on top of the pot, and pressed it into place, cutting off the flow of smoke, and turning around made my way back up the hill as fast as I was able to in the snowdrifts.

I didn't get very far before I could hear a muffled drumming on the bothy door as the Parkies were getting well smoked. Rather than hang around, as I was now frightened that I might have gone too far, we took off as fast as we could to the top of the hill, where we had intended to do our sledging from. By the time that we reached the top and looked back, three Parkies were outside the bothy coughing their lungs up and wondering what had happened.

They didn't look up at us at all, but one climbed up to the lum to see what the blockage was. By this time the snowball had melted without trace, and the smoke was pouring from the lum with no trouble. The Parkies went back inside the bothy but put a big lump of timber between the door and the door jamb, to prevent another snowslide from the roof blocking the doorway, obviously surmising that this was what had happened. Relieved that I was not going to be charged with suffocation of the Parkies, however much despised, we carried on sledding without a single Parkie interfering.

Our sleds were made from the backs of chairs, sheets of plywood bent up slightly at the front, with a piece of rope to hold on to and try to steer with, and bits of old broken prams cobbled together to resemble a sled. Reluctant to leave, we stayed on until it was getting quite dark. During the course of the day many others had joined us on the hill, but by the time we reluctantly decided to go home everyone else had drifted off. It was now getting so cold that my short trousers had frozen stiff around the bottom edges and a row of sharp little icicles were suspended from the cloth. By the time I noticed them it was impossible to scrape them off. Walking was now very painful, and I was a long way from home. I sledged down the hill for the last time on my old chairback.

At the bottom of the hill was a dark object, hard to distinguish in the gathering gloom. Plodding over to it with my ice-abraded legs, I was amazed to see that it was a properly designed and built sled, with two runners turned up at the ends, a proper steering system controlled by ropes, and seating for two. Looking around, not a soul was in sight except Bobby and me. Dumping our homemade wreck of a sled, I sat on one of the seats and steered whilst Bobby pulled when necessary, but the route home was downhill for the most part, so both of us could ride.

Eventually arriving at our close, we grabbed an end of the sled each, and wrestled our new acquisition up the stairs. I thumped on the door to be let in and Mammy opened the door. "Where the holy hell hiv youse two been a' this time? Ye've been oot fae early this moarnin' in the freezin' snaw," she yelled. "Ah've been worried sick aboot yese fur ah didnae know where yese wur, ah wis jist gettin' ready tae go and get the polis, ah wis that worried. Yere pals goat hame 'oors ago, an' they didnae know how ye wurnae hame."

Suddenly, she stopped dead. "Whit's that ye've goat?" "It's a real sledge Mammy, Bobby an' me foun' it at the boattom o' the hill efter everybody else hid gone hame, honest Mammy, it disnae belang tae anybody, honest it disnae."

Mammy wasn't listening as she gave the sled a close inspection. "Ye cannae tell me thit somebody jist left this sledge lyin' aboot, it must hiv cost somebody a fortune. Yere no' bringin' that intae this hoose." Mammy reached behind the door for her coat and shrugged into it. "Ah'll jist ask Mrs Leyden tae watch Alec an' wee Grace, while we take this roon' tae the polis oaffice." Mrs Leyden was perfectly willing to look after the two younger ones, whilst Mammy dragged us round to Lawmoor Street police station.

We were now quite scared, as we remembered our last forced march to the same police station. We knew we were innocent of any intentional wrongdoing, but were scared stiff of the police, regardless of anything else. Arriving at the police station, Mammy went in front, whilst we bumped the sledge up the steps and through the swinging glass doors. Mammy went up to the counter where a bored looking constable was scribbling away.

"Ah'd like tae report a missing sledge that mah two wee boys hiv foun'", said Mammy in a firm voice. "Hoo kin it be a missing sledge missus, if it's already been foun'?" asked the constable, knitting his brow in concentration as he turned over to a fresh sheet in his foolscap pad. "Ye know whit ah mean, the weans brought it hame efter finding it at the big hill in Queens Park, an' there wis naebody else aboot, except themselves," replied Mammy.

The constable looked over the edge of the desk at us, "How did ye no' jist leave it where it wis, in case somebody came back fur it?" "Mah legs wur rubbed red raw an ah couldnae walk hame, mister, honest ah couldnae," I said, pulling up the leg of my shorts to display the raw red abraded and bleeding skin.

"Ah'll believe ye although thousands widnae, ah'll jist take doon a few wee particulars before ye go hame, tae keep the record straight like, ye can jist fill this form in." "Ah'm no' that good wi' forms, but Allan here wull full it in nae bother," said Mammy, passing on the form to me. I filled in the form to the constable's satisfaction eventually. "Ye kin go hame noo," he said, "If a' folk wur like you missus McLachlan, oor joab as polismen wid be a helluva sight easier, but jist make sure that yer weans leave things where they foun' them an' leave a' the trouble tae somebody else tae fill a' the forms in, an' a' tha' nonsense."

Mammy took us each by the hand, as we set off home. "Let tha' be a lesson tae yese, ah'm right annoyed wi' yese, causin' a' this bother, ah' hiv a good mind tae tell yir Daddy, when he comes hame fae his work the night." "Don't dae that Mammy, we're sorry an' wullnae dae anythin' like tha' again, we didnae think that we wur dae'n any hairm tae anybody," we howled, for getting a belting from Daddy was always agonising. As soon as we arrived home Mammy thanked Mrs Leyden for her help, and put us to bed, after she had rubbed some ointment into my glowing red raw thighs. We got no supper although we were starving but dared not complain in case Daddy heard about our brief ownership of a real sledge.

Another game opportunity, brought on by Jack Frost, was the making of slides, in the street or on the pavement. Wellington boots were absolutely useless for sliding, so we wore our tackety boots. The first requirement was an icy surface, which would lend itself to being extended. To make the slide required a degree of skill and experience.

Starting off at some considerable distance from our chosen icy patch, we would run at full tilt at the target, and when reached, we would turn sideways, legs splayed rigidly, arms outstretched, and slide as far as we were able, getting out of the way fast to avoid being knocked over by the next slider. Depending on the weather conditions, preferably freezing, the slide of slick ice would improve in slipperiness, and length, as each slider took his or her turn, eventually reaching equilibrium, as the length equalled the energy level of the best sliders.

Once the slide was established, a long queue of sliders formed, to await a turn. The instigators of the slide exercised the right to inspect the soles of the footwear of potential sliders, as rubber soles would quickly destroy the slick surface, and ruin the slide. The best footwear was definitely tacketty boots, as these acted like ice skates. Girls didn't wear such boots so had to make do with plain leather soles, which meant that even the tomboys were rendered uncompetitive in length of slide achieved, unless they went home and changed into a pair of their brothers' tackety boots.

If anyone tried to slide wearing rubber soles, they would tend to fall over as soon as they hit the slide proper with the momentum of the long runup. Such culprits were barred from the game, and were booed by the kids waiting in line, until they sidled off, often blushing in embarrassment. Slides in the street were subjected to interruption by traffic, and could easily be ruined by rubber tyres, or a large Clydesdale horse letting out a small steaming waterfall over our laboriously constructed slide.

To avoid this problem, a slide could be set up on the pavement, which avoided vehicular traffic, but made pedestrian traffic a slippery proposition, not to mention the gaggle of kids, bunched up, waiting for their turn, and blocking the footpath. The main problem was with the 'wee wimmen', as we called the middle aged and elderly women who, whatever the weather, were invariably dressed in a thick tweed coat buttoned up to the neck, with a woollen muffler wrapped tightly round their neck, and topped off by a headscarf. They always carried a large message bag in each hand, regardless of the purpose of their outing.

When one of the wee wimmen approached, we would yell out "Hey missus, the pavement is a' slidey, ye better walk in the street." The wee wumman would nearly always tuck her chin even more deeply into her muffler, and continue to walk towards the slippery slide, saying "A'm no gettin' aff the pavement for the likes o' youse wee buggers, ye kin jist get oot o' mah wey, afore ah get the polis tae ye." There was nothing else we could do, as we recognised determination when we saw it, but open ranks to let the wee wumman through.

As the wee wumman got to the beginning of the slide, considerate kids would grab her elbows from both sides to steady her when she lost her footing. This usually provoked a furious reaction as the wee wumman shook off the helping hands, "Dinnae touch me ye wee buggers, ah kin manage by masel', ah wis walkin' oan this pavement afore yir mothers wur even boarn, an' ah'm no' stoappin' noo." She would just get her tirade out, before her feet shot out from under her, and she landed on her back with a thud.

Regardless of her screams and yells, we would try to get her to her feet as soon as possible. I don't know what the wee wimmen wore under their coats but it must have been heavy gauge sheet lead, as it always took at least six kids to get them to their feet and support them until they were clear of the slide. "Ah've goat a broken back, an' a broken bum tae go whi' it, jist you'se wait tae ah get tae the polis, ah'll get ye a' the jile so ah wull, ye'll no be making slides fur poor folk tae fa' doon an' hurt themsel's oan the pavement," yelled the wee wumman in obvious pain. Feeling ashamed of ourselves, and being terrified of the police, we would then render the pavement slide unslippery, by pouring buckets of water over it until all the ice had melted. In really cold conditions this method of ruining a slide didn't work, so we had to resort to scraping the ice off, using small shovels borrowed from the coal bunker.

One aspect of icy weather which always upset me was the danger to the carthorses of slipping on icy streets and main roads. The majority of main roads were surfaced with granite cobblestones, or setts. On inclines, the road surfaces on which the cartwheels would run on consisted of long strips of granite, forming a much more even surface than the cobblestones, which paved the rest of the road, and between the parallel granite strips. At the bottom of every incline was a large, galvanized bin containing sand. The carter would stop at the bin to fill the bucket which swung from a hook underneath the cart.

Having filled his bucket, the carter, if he was alone, would walk up the hill, with his horse drawn larrie hopefully following behind, scattering sand between the strips to prevent the horse from slipping, as it struggled to maintain traction on the uphill slope. In severe icy conditions horses could easily slip and fall between the shafts, still harnessed, struggling wildly to get back on their feet. This was usually unsuccessful, as the harness prevented the poor horse from being able to stand up again.

The carter would try to unbuckle the harness whilst the crazed horse thrashed around in panic, foaming at the mouth, and surrounded by anxious onlookers. If he was unable to undo the harness the carter would cut the leather straps and try again to get the horse on to its feet. Often, by this time the horse was frequently too exhausted by its struggles and would just lie on its side with its eyes rolling in terror, with chest heaving, as it struggled for breath. I don't know how the message was passed on to the owner of the horse, but somehow it was.

Within a reasonably short time a man would arrive with another type of cart and placing a pistol to the side of the poor horse's head, would shoot it dead. At this the women and children in the watching crowd would burst into tears, the women sobbing softly, and dabbing at their eyes with hankies, while the children wailed loudly, as the dead horse was dragged onto the horse murderer's cart with the aid of a hand operated windlass, and some ropes. "It's awright hen dinnae ye greet", a woman would comfort her wailing daughter, "the hoarse is no' really deid, it's only gaun tae the hoarses' hoaspital, oan the hoarse ambliance, an' it'll be back pullin' it's cairt afore the week's oot, jist you wait an' see." Unfortunately, during spells of icy weather, which wasn't that uncommon, the 'hoarses' hoaspital' got lots of patients, keeping the 'hoarse ambliance' very busy.

Chapter 12

It was about this time, I think, that Gaumont Cinemas, a countrywide chain, started their "Saturday Morning Film Club". Our local Gaumont cinema was the Cinerama in Govanhill, near Eglinton Toll. Since Daddy had barred us from attending the Crownie, we hadn't been to the pictures at all, and were desperate to find a cinema that he would let us go to. As the Cinerama was as upmarket as the Crownie was downmarket, Daddy allowed Bobby and me to queue up to join and get our club badge. It was made plain by the little booklet, issued with the badge, that a high standard of dress was required when attending the club.

The following Saturday was the opening session of the club, starting at 10am sharp. Half past nine, on the Saturday morning saw us dressed as if for Sunday school, standing halfway down a long queue, which reached nearly as far as the Good Samaritan Hospital, with our club badges proudly pinned to our jacket lapels. As the queue started to shuffle forwards at ten o' clock, we were consumed with excitement, wondering what we were about to be entertained by.

At last, we reached the box office, and passed over our sixpences in exchange for two tickets, and headed for the stalls, where we would be close to the action, but without our street pals, who would cause a 'rammy' anywhere at the slightest excuse. The lights dimmed, and to our amazement a huge Wurlitzer organ appeared slowly from an unseen pit directly in front of the screen, playing loudly as it rose. A smarmy looking character, with heavily Brylcreemed hair plastered to his skull, large horn-rimmed glasses, and a smile that would have put a skeleton to shame, was driving it. When the organ had risen to its full extent, the smarmy character switched it off with a theatrical flourish.

Taking advantage of a captive audience, which didn't know what to expect, he rambled on at length about the cost of such an organ, where it was made, and the unending range of noises it was capable of creating. To demonstrate its versatility, he made the sound of a steam locomotive pulling away from a station, a series of church bells, a cock crowing, an elephant trumpeting, a lion roaring, and a tramcar, followed by his obvious piece de resistance, a thunderstorm, complete with flashing lights for lightning.

He then asked the audience for requests. Everybody started calling out together, drowning each other out. Waving his arms like a demented traffic cop, he eventually restored order. "Just one request at a time, boys and girls, just hold up your hand but don't say anything until I point to you directly." A forest of hands shot up. He pointed to his first choice, confident that he couldn't be beaten by a bunch of young kids. "Kin ye make a noise like a German erryplane crashin' intae Dixon's Blazes?" was the first request.

The organ driver was English, which was his first big mistake. "I'm afraid that I don't know anything about Dixon's Blazes, or what it is," he said into his microphone. "Ye must be a right daftie, 'cos it's jist doon Cathcart Road, an ye must hiv passed it oan yer wey tae here," shouted the requestor, to a roar of laughter from most of the audience. "Please be serious, club members," said Brylcreem Bill. " We can have a lot of fun if you ask for serious requests." He pointed to another straining arm. "Kin ye make a noise like a firemigade?" He frowned, beginning to realise that he was going to be struggling with his first Glasgow audience. "What's a firemigade?" he asked. "Ye know, thae big rid lorries wi' ladders oan toap, an' full o' firemigademen, an' big bells ringin'," replied his second tormentor. Brycreem Bill was none the wiser, shaking his head. "I'm afraid we have time for only one more request, as we have to keep to the programme, so last one please." "Kin ye make a noise like a big parcel o' shite hittin' the grun', efter bein' flung oot o' a three storey windae?" someone at the very front shouted at the top of his voice before Bill got a chance to point to anybody.

The Saturday Film Club was not going to be as sedate as the promoters had hoped. Brylcreem Bill sat down, playing the organ, with his head bowed down over the controls, as the whole assembly disappeared back into the floor, to be snuffed out as the lid slid into place. The lights above the stage brightened as a bald man wearing a tuxedo strode out and grasped the microphone, as if he would have fallen down if it hadn't been there. "Welcome to the Saturday Morning Film Club, I'm sure that we are going to have lots of fun every Saturday morning from now on. As far as the programme is concerned, we will kick off with some talented club members, who will thrill you with some dance numbers on this very stage." He paused as the audience groaned loudly in unison. "Then we have two films that I am quite sure that you will enjoy," pausing again as the audience cheered and clapped, "and so on with the show, starting with Edna Smellie, as she shows off her considerable ballet skills."

Edna came out of left stage in her tutu and ballet slippers, as the audience muttered and shuffled their feet noisily, to the strains of the Sugar Plum Fairy, and did her stuff quite competently, bowing deeply to the club members as she exited the stage. Baldy came back on stage, clapping his hands, as if he was trying to beat the world hand clapping record, completely drowning out the few who were clapping in the stalls. "Faaaantastic! Edna, how are we going to cap that performance? Buuut the next act might manage it, I give you Archibald and Maryjane O'Driscoll, who have won many competitions in Irish dancing."

With that Baldy scooted off stage as Archie and his sister pranced on, with someone out of sight playing on a penny whistle, both dressed in somebody's idea of Irish national costume, staring rigidly ahead as if hypnotised, and dancing like a couple of puppets on strings which were only connected to their legs, as nothing else moved at all. They were very good at stamping their feet loudly, which was greatly applauded by the audience, reasoning that anyone who could stamp like that must be worth a wee clap, if nothing else.

When the foot stampers had finished, Baldy came back on stage. "By your applause I'm sure that you really enjoyed the last act." "Ah hope that wis the bliddy last act!" someone bellowed from down the front to Baldy's obvious discomfort. "Now for the first film, which is all about young people living on a cattle station in the Australian outback, and how they help everybody, and have exciting adventures. I know that you will just love it." With that the stage lights dimmed and the film started. I had never heard of the outback of Australia, but when the film finished that was where I wanted to live. To be able to ride horses all day and go anywhere I pleased, as long as it was to rescue stranded travellers who had wandered off the track and fallen down a gorge into a billabong, that was the life for me. Faaaantastic! I thought, where do I sign up?

The next film was just as good, about poor children in Mexico, who didn't have a school to go to, spending the mornings helping their mothers prepare foodstuffs, or anything else that might be saleable to sell in the town marketplace. In the afternoons, they were allowed to board luxury cruise liners, and dive from the superstructure for coins that the passengers threw from the promenade deck. It must be brilliant to have no school to go to and get to do high dives from luxury liners every day, I thought, tossing up between the outback and a Mexican childhood.

When the second film ended the show was over, and all emergency exits were thrown open, letting blinding daylight into the normally darkened auditorium as the audience streamed out the nearest exits. To cover our bets, Bobby and I rode our horses home by running at the crouch, left hand holding the reins firmly in front, and right-hand slapping at our right buttocks, urging our steeds onwards and faster. It is amazing how much faster we got home this way, than if we just ran.

"How wis the Cinema Club?" asked Mammy, as we cantered into the lobby and tied our steeds to the coal bunker, just in case they strayed. "It wis smashin' Mammy, kin we go tae Australia, or Mexico?" we asked. "Nae bother, Ah'll jist check ma purse tae make sure thit ah hiv enough money fur everybuddies bus fares an' enough jeely pieces tae last us tae yer Daddy gets his furst pey." "We're no' kiddin' Mammy, an' ye cannae get tae Australia or Mexico oan a Corporation bus, their baith across the sea, and miles further than America, we'll hiv tae start savin' up fur the boat fares." "Boat fares, boat fares, if ah saved up fur the next ten years oot o' mah hoosekeepin' money, we widnae hiv the boat fare tae Gourock," said Mammy, with a wry grin on her face. "Ah'll tell ye whit, if ye help me aroon' the hoose this efternin', ah'll gie ye a shullin tae get the caur tae Rouken Glen, an' buy yersel's a big boattle o' Tizer or Irn Bru, an' ye kin take wee Alec wi' yese, tae gie me a wee break fur a chainge." "Okay Mammy but ye'll hiv tae gie us anithir sixpence, if we take Alec wi' us," I said, "or we'll no' be able tae buy the Tizer." "Ye cannae pull ma leg sae easy, wee weans under five dinnae pey onythin' oan the caurs, an' he wullnae drink that much o' yer Tizer," replied Mammy.

We scraped past our horses which were still tied up to the coal bunker and climbed up on to our bed. Pulling all the bedclothes and pillows into a big pile in the corner and stripping down to our underpants, we climbed on to the ship and started diving for money, landing headfirst on the mattress, and swimming really deep to pick up the money from the gleaming white seabed. "In the name o' the wee man, whit ur yese daein' noo, an' look at the right mess ye've made o' yer bed, yere supposed tae be helpin' me, no' hinderin' me," exclaimed Mammy in astonishment, as she came into our room.

"We're divin' fur money Mammy, fae the tap deck o' a luxury liner," I said. "In that case, ah'll hiv hauf o' a' the money ye get, ah cuid dae wae some new claes fur the warm weather that Glesca' might get wan day, if ah live that long," replied Mammy, "Yese kin jist stoap the deep sea divin', an remake the bed, afore ah haud ye underwatter an' droon' baith o' ye, besides yer Daddy wull be hame fae his work in aboot hauf an 'oor, an' wullnae like the deep sea divin' instead o' a well-made bed."

At the mention of Daddy coming home earlier than usual, we were galvanized out of our Mexican daydreams, throwing the pile of bedclothes onto the floor and getting dressed, before making the bed look as good as possible. "Ye kin go fur mah messages, that'll help me a loat," said Mammy, handing me her message lines, message bags, and the ration books. Bobby and I took a message bag each, untied our patient steeds from the coal bunker and led them down the stairs into the close, where we mounted and galloped off to start our queuing at Guthries the butchers in Cumberland Street. When we had finished getting the messages, we tied our horses to the lamppost nearest the closemouth, as Daddy wouldn't tolerate horses in the lobby.

On entering our kitchen, we laid the full message bags on the table. Daddy was sitting in his fireside chair, with his stockinged feet on the mantelpiece, smoking his customary Capstan Full Strength. "How was the Cinema Club? he asked. "It wis great Daddy, kin we go tae Australia or Mexico?" I asked. "If you think that ah spent a' thae years abroad in the army, tae get hame safe fur youse an' yer Mammy fur nothin', ye must be aff yer heids, we're gaun naewhere, an' yese can like it or lump it," Daddy growled. That was the finish of our exciting futures abroad.

The format of the Cinema Club changed each week as the club members showed their disapproval of the organ driver and the dancing acts, before letting us watch the films that we had really come to see. The final format came down to two adventure films, which always stimulated our imaginations, and some cartoons. We attended the Cinerama Film Club on Saturday mornings for many years.

Chapter 13

With the war over, the men of our extended family returned home to 'civvy street', to the usual dead-end jobs. Uncle Rab Cunningham, my mother's only brother, had served in the Royal Navy as a stoker on corvettes escorting convoys across the Atlantic. Uncle Rab was my favourite uncle. He had married Nellie Kerr just as the war started, and they now shared Granny Cunningham's house in Parkhead.

Rab and Nellie had two daughters, Betty, who was a couple of years younger than me, and Grace, who was just a few months old. For some reason, Uncle Rab and I had always got on like a house on fire, perhaps because he didn't have a son of his own, well not yet anyway, as he and Auntie Nelly were not as prolific in creating new family members as my parents were. The extended Cunningham household was always a happy place to visit, and although I have difficulty in remembering how or when, I knew that at some time it had been home to Mammy and me. Betty was a very pretty little girl, and we played happily together.

My first concrete memory of Uncle Rab was us both squatting on the bedroom floor, with a large round tin of Players Navy Shag tobacco between us. Uncle Rab had a pile of small, lidded tins, roughly the size of sardine tins, which he was filling with the finished cigarettes as he rolled them, using a little hand-held double roller machine which, with Rizla cigarette papers, was almost universally used to produce reasonably shaped home-rolled cigarettes. He gave me a spare roller and a packet of Rizlas to keep me occupied. By the time I managed to turn out one oddly shaped and soaking wet cigarette by overdoing the licking, he would have rolled at least twenty perfectly proportioned ones. He explained to me that on his ship there was not a lot of spare room for rolling cigarettes, and it was easier to roll his Royal Navy issue tobacco ration in advance and keep them in the little sealable tins.

My father's older brother, Uncle Alec McLachlan, had served throughout the War, mostly overseas, as a ground crewman in Spitfire squadrons, having married Auntie Annie McEwan in 1935 (not to be confused with my other Auntie Annie, whose married name was Patterson.) They had a daughter, who was universally known as 'oor Margaret' who, as an only child, was spoiled rotten in our family's opinion. What 'oor Margaret' wanted 'oor Margaret' got, in total contrast to our family. We invariably got sweet F/A, no matter how much pleading was done. Alec, Annie, and 'oor Margaret' lived as an appendage of Annie's family, the McEwans, which was firmly ruled by her mother.

Annie was seldom seen without 'Maw McEwan' in tow. Maw chose what everyone ate and drank, and how they dressed. Maw's extended family ate all their main meals at Maw McEwan's house no matter where they actually lived. The only time that Uncle Alec was able to separate himself from Annie and her Maw was when he visited us on Friday nights, when he and my father played cards, usually a game called Newmarket, noisily as they would have a couple of large bottles of beer (Screwtaps) to enjoy as they played.

The only problem with this, from my mother's point of view, was that they continually swore as they played. "If youse two don't stoap swearin' a' the time, ah'll hiv tae plug the weans' ears, tae stoap thim hearin' yese, thirs nae need for a' that terrible language, an' ye should know faur better at your ages." Daddy and Uncle Alec would try, but within a few minutes were at it again, to my mother's despair, as she rounded us up and put us to bed in the other room out of immediate hearing range of the bad language.

Uncle Rab Duncan, Auntie Jean's husband, spent the whole of the war years on some sort of home posting, as his health was too poor to be posted overseas on active duty. I think that he served as an orderly in the officers' mess at the Maryhill Barracks. Despite this he regularly turned up full of his own importance, dressed to the nines in full highland regalia as if he was a real soldier. Even as kids, we could see that he wasn't too bright. His fatal mistake which always gave me the giggles was to try to speak "proper", and sound important, even when conducting a trivial conversation. His attempts to speak proper fell straight into the "Could I have a pund of pototties please?" class. Phrases like "When I was travelling here on the tramcaur, I nearly felled down the sterrs when the tramcaur stoapped far too quick." "I was just walking up Maryhill Road, when a small wean runned out of a closemooth and pished all over my boots an spats. It is just a disgrace how some folk dinnae control their children," rolled continually from his lips. Auntie Jean never called him anything but Duncan. "Shut yer gub Duncan, ye're talkin' shite as usual," without looking up from whatever she was sewing or mending, was her normal response to his prattling. He never caught on to the fact that he was regarded as a harmless but irritating adjunct to Auntie Jean.

Another strange thing about Rab Duncan was his hair, which he wore in a weird style as if he existed in some type of time warp. His hair was cut in the conventional military short back and sides to the extreme, to well above his ears. But there any resemblance to the conventional haircut ceased. The rest of his hair went straight upwards like a cliff, much longer than was fashionable. As long as he was wearing any type of headgear such as a Glengarry bonnet he looked okay, but when that was removed the weird hair took centre stage. According to my mother, who told me when I was much older, Auntie Jean had left home without permission, and had married Rab Duncan when they were both only sixteen years of age, spending their wedding night on an old second hand mattress, in a rough Bridgeton single end, with not another possession or any income to their names.

Another uncle, who I have so far failed to mention, was Uncle Louie Patterson (nothing to do with the Pattersons of my mother's family). Louie had been adopted by Granny McLachlan, some years before she produced any family of her own. Louie was universally known as a 'flyman' and would do anything to earn a quid except work. He was a tall man with an ever-ready cheesy fake smile, heavily brilliantined hair, and was always working on some scheme or other to make money. He had been crafty enough to know how to avoid being called up for the armed forces.

My first memory was of Uncle Louie turning up at our house one day unannounced. "Ah wis jist doon the street Jessie an' I thoat that Ah wid jist drap in an' see how ye wur gauin' hen," he said, as he edged through the doorway and sat down uninvited at the kitchen table. I could see that Mammy was not too comfortable and didn't quite know what to say. "How's Annie an' the weans?" Mammy asked (referring to yet another Auntie, Annie Patterson). "Ach thir jist fine Jessie hen, jist fine," replied Uncle Louie, "an' hoo's Allan, is he still sodgerin' oan oot there in the desert?" "As fur as ah know, but ah'm jist waitin' fur his next letter so ah kin send him a birthday present that ah boat fur him," replied Mammy. Mammy had joined a sort of club that allowed members to get a sum of money in advance, to be repaid with cripplingly high interest over the next year or so. "Whit hiv ye goat him? asked Louie. "A wristlet watch," replied Mammy. "Kin ah see it?" asked Louie. Mammy hesitantly fetched her treasure from the wardrobe shelf and handed it over for inspection. "It's jist as well that ah came by," said Louie, "This particular sort of watch wull be ruined if it's no' worn a' the time, an' wull jist seize up dead solid." Louie wound up the watch and nodded sagely, "Jist as ah thoat, it's no' workin' right. Ah'll jist take it fur ye tae a wee pal o' mine who soarts watches an' cloaks' an' things like tha'."

Uncle Louie stuck the watch back in its box and put it in his pocket. "Ah'll drap it back intae ye when it's soarted Jessie hen." He was out of the door and away before Mammy could get a word in. When he had gone, Mammy looked at me in distress, "Ah bet ye thit we'll niver see that watch again, Ah don't know whit came ower me, Ah'll niver forgie' masel fur bein' sae stupit, as tae listen tae his patter, the rotten big bugger," she said before bursting into tears. She was right, for we didn't see Louie again for a long time, and never saw the watch again at all. Mammy never told Daddy about the watch, as she knew he would have immediately rushed over to Louie's place with his eyes bulging with rage and got himself arrested for severe assault and battery, or even worse, for murder.

Louie was a born conman. Not long before he died my father told me, when I was questioning him about his childhood, about the dog that he had once, an Airedale named Bonzo. One day he was playing outside his house in McDuff Street, when Louie, already an adult, appeared. "Whaur's yer dug Allan?" he asked. "In the hoose, sleepin', my father replied. "A big dug like tha' needs a loat o' exercise," said Louie." Ah'll take him fur a nice long walk if ye like, if ye jist show me where his lead is." My father got the lead from the kitchen, clipped it to Bonzo's collar and handed it to Louie, who set off in the direction of Shettleston Park.

It was some hours before Louie returned with the lead but no dog. "Whaur's Bonzo?" asked my father in distress. "Ye wudnae believe it, but ah hid jist goat him intae the park when we saw some rabbits. Ah thoat it wid be a good idea tae get the dug tae get a couple o' rabbits' fur oor supper, so ah slipped aff his lead an' he ran like hell efter the rabbits, ah waited fur ages but he never came back." My father burst into tears, as he loved Bonzo, and knew that he wouldn't be allowed to have another dog after losing this one.

Some days later my father heard something scratching at the door. Opening it he was overjoyed to see Bonzo standing there, with his little stumpy tail wagging at full tilt, and a doggy grin on his face. "Bonzo, ye're back, where hiv ye been a' this time ye stupit dug?" my father cried, as Bonzo jumped up and licked his face in obvious joy at being home. A few days later he was taking Bonzo for a walk along London Road when a boy stopped him. "That's oor dug ye've goat there, he's been missing for days noo." "Naw he's no', he's ma dug, an' his name's Bonzo," retorted my father, elbowing the boy out of his way and continuing on his way home. He had hardly had time to unclip Bonzo's lead when the door shook as somebody violently pounded on the outside. Father opened the door to find an irate man standing on the doorstep, with the same kid clinging to his leg. "That's him Daddy, that's the boy that stole oor dug," cried the boy. "That's oor dug ,an' ye kin jist haun' him ower this minute, or ah'll gie ye a bliddy good clip roon the ear fur yer bliddy thievin' cheek," said the man, with a fierce scowl. At this point Granny McLachlan, who being stone deaf, had heard nothing of the interchange so far, arrived at father's shoulder. "Whit the hell's goin' oan here?" she asked father. "This man says that Bonzo's his dug an' ah've tae haun him ower or he'll clip ma ear Maw." Wee Granny swung round to face the stranger. "The dug's oors an' his been since he wis a wee pup, so ah'll trouble ye tae take yer ugly mug aff oor doorstep or ah'll hiv the polis tae ye." "It's oor dug, ah boat him fae a big fella in the pub aboot five days ago, an' ah peyed fifteen shullin's fur him," said the aggrieved man, as my father relayed what the man was saying by shouting into Granny's best ear. The penny dropped for father and Granny, at the same time. Granny slammed the door shut in the man's face, opened the flap of the letter box, and shouted "Get the hell oot o' here before mah man comcs hame fae his work an' knoaks ten different colours o' shite oot o' ye, ye bliddy nuisance ye, an' don't bother tae come back tae mah door again."

The man and his son muttered together for a few minutes, as my father listened at the letterbox, then drifted away, deciding that to risk any more confrontation was a total waste of time. "That bliddy Louie Patterson, he selt yer poor wee dug doon at the pub the rascal, ah'll get yer faither tae gie him a right hammerin' so ah wull, whit wull he be up tae next? Ah'll gie him loasin' the dug chasin' rabbits, he's a boarn liar, it's nae wonder his Maw didnae want him, the bliddy eejit toerag," yelled Granny. It was many days before my father dared to take Bonzo for a walk, and never in the direction of London Road. When Louie did show up eventually, Granny chased him all around the house with a heavy iron poker, getting in a few good blows around his back and shoulders before he managed to get the door open without being smashed across the knuckles in the process, and made good his escape.

Years later I saw Uncle Louie in action for myself. We were visiting Granny Cunningham, and I was playing outside in the grassy backcourt. The backcourt adjoined a railway line, with substantial railings separating the lines from the back courts. On the margin of the railway property a level area had been cleared for the installation of a barrage balloon unit during the war and was now given over to a good crop of weeds. The local layabouts and inveterate gamblers used this level area for playing 'pitch and toss', which was a gambling game with serious money at stake. As we played, a tall man in suit and trilby hat came through the close, and edged along the tenement wall, until he was as close to the railings as possible without showing himself.

Somehow the man looked very familiar; with a start I realised that the man was my long unseen Uncle Louie. Just as I was going across to talk to him, he dashed towards the railings, climbed quickly over these, and ran down the embankment shouting "Police, Police, stey right where yese are," waving what was probably a Corporation Library card in his outstretched left hand. I was thunderstruck as I had no idea that Uncle Louie was a polisman and ran to the railings to watch the action. The gamblers immediately scattered in all directions before Uncle Louie got close, leaving the 'kitty', a decent pile of money, behind in their panic. Louie raced to the kitty, scooped up as many notes and silver coins as he could quickly stuff in his pockets, turned around, and running back the same way as he had come, clambered over the railings and jumped back into Granny's back court. "Uncle Louie, ah didnae know that ye wur a polisman," I said as he was rushing past.

He only slowed slightly, obviously not recognising me, and looking dismayed to have been himself recognised. "Don't ye tell anybody whit wey ah went," he puffed as he ran through Granny's close, and away down Glamis Road. "Aye, that wid be yer Uncle Louie tae a 'T', said Mammy when I rushed upstairs to Granny's house to tell her what had just happened. "Wan day he's gonny get caught at his tricks an' get himsel' murdered, so he wull, and nane tae soon fur mah taste, God forgie me, ah've never telt yer Daddy aboot him stealin' his watch, fur he would hiv swung fur him ah'm sure." That was my Uncle Louie. We were always glad that he was not really our uncle as he was a real liability. In spite of my mother's prediction, Uncle Louie went on to be married three times, with three different families, and lived to a venerable old age.

Uncle Alec Dorans, and Uncle Bill Robinson, I have covered briefly before, and will mention again later on.

Auntie Annie, my mother's older sister, was married to George Patterson, known in the family as 'Big Geordie'. I don't know what he did during the Second World War, as I don't remember him being in evidence whilst the Pattersons lived at 29 Kidston Street. I can only remember him appearing on the scene some time after Auntie Annie and her family moved into their new three-bedroom, kitchen and bathroom home in Deanston Drive in Shawlands in 1946. Uncle George had enlisted in The King's Own Scottish Borderers (KOSB) in the First World War when only aged fourteen. He had lied about his age. He was a relatively tall and well-built boy, and they accepted his word that he was eighteen. He survived the horrors of that terrible war to return home an older and weary man, instead of the boy who had so enthusiastically enlisted. During his time in the trenches, living alongside much older men, George had acquired a taste for beer and spirits, as part of his premature transition from boy to man.

For whatever reason, Auntie Annie had developed a type of split personality. To us, the wee McLachlans, she was a greatly beloved fairy godmother, keeping us just above the poverty line by a constant stream of hand me down clothing and discreet financial assistance when my mother was frequently at her wits' end. We thought that she was very rich, being able to distribute largesse to those in need, and also being the owner of a fur coat. It was some years later that I found out that throughout our younger years she had worked a twelve-hour nightshift seven days a week cleaning tramcars, in order to support not only her own family, but partly supporting those of her sisters, mainly ours.

The other side of her very strong character, which we never saw, but occasionally heard about second-hand, was her implacable hatred of any alcoholic beverage, of any type and any quantity. I can't be certain, but I think that Uncle George wasn't allowed to live at home unless he abstained completely. If he came home with even the slightest whiff of booze on his breath, he was immediately subjected to a torrid tirade of abuse and shown the door, with his personal belongings being thrown down the stairs after him.

Uncle George, in terms relative to the stunted population of the slums, was a magnificent specimen of a man, standing over six feet tall and broad of shoulder. His rugged face looked more like that of John Wayne, than did John Wayne's own face, and he had an unusually deep gravelly voice that John Wayne would have killed for. He was invariably kind, and always willing to spend time talking and joking with us when he was around and had the time available.

In later years, during one of his homestay spells, he would volunteer to take us swimming at the Pollokshaws swimming baths. I never heard him raise his voice or appear to be angry. In short, Big Geordie Patterson was a very nice uncle to us when he was around. We never quite understood how Auntie Annie could banish him from the family home, or how he survived between homecomings, but even Mammy knew better than to ask her older sister any such question.

George and Annie had five children: Jimmy, who was old enough to serve in the Royal Navy for the duration of the War, Young George, who had been invalided out of the Navy, and spent some considerable time in Hairmyres Hospital in East Kilbride, Grace, Nancy, and Bobby, who was about three years older than I was. Grace and Nancy were always very kind to us, taking us to the cinema, parks, the Glasgow (Glesca') Fair during July on Glesca' Green, which was always stomach tremblingly exciting, and the great Kelvin Hall Shows in December. All in all, we had a lot to thank the Patterson family for and were very lucky to have such relations acting as backstops for Mammy, the Wee Yin of the Cunningham family.

Uncle Alec McLachlan had a very good friend from his Royal Air Force days, George Jeffries, whom he had introduced to Auntie Mary at some time. George and Mary married in 1946, and settled in Poole, Dorset, where George worked as a motor mechanic. They were the only people in our large extended family of the time who actually owned their own home, a small bungalow. This achievement earned them celebrity status, as we thought that they must be incredibly rich to do so. This also meant that I had another Uncle George to add to the list. I had two Uncle Georges, two Uncle Rabs, two Uncle Alecs, one Uncle Bill, one Uncle Jimmy, and one Uncle Louie (which was one Uncle Louie too many). As can be seen, Glasgow families in the early part of the twentieth century were very conservative when it came to choosing names for their offspring.

How George Jeffries became friendly with Uncle Alec will always be a mystery to me, as George was a very quiet non-smoking, non-drinking, non-swearing, unassuming man, not quite in the same mould as Alec, or my father for that matter. When these two were together, my mother would get really angry, upset by the amount of swear words that they managed to inject into even the simplest sentence. If the word 'fucking' had been removed from their lexicon, they would have found it difficult to carry out a simple conversation, as they used this in all of its variety of inferences, to convey half of a dictionary of meanings.

Auntie Murn (Marion) was married to Jimmy Carty. I seem to remember that they lived much further south along London Road in a very nice Corporation house with many more rooms than we were used to seeing. They also had a big family, but somehow they seemed to move in a different orbit from our family, and consequently I never got to know any of the Cartys very well.

I also had Uncle Shug Campbell. He wasn't a real uncle, but a close friend of my father since their school days, and who had joined up in the HLI with my father in 1934, the first time around. I should explain that Shug is the most common Glaswegian pronunciation of the name Hugh. It is difficult to explain to non-Glaswegians why Hugh is pronounced as Shug, but to a native of the city it makes perfect sense. How else could you pronounce Hugh, just as 'bureau' is pronounced 'brew'. The only possible softer alternatives to Shug which were utilised were 'Shuggie', 'Shooie', or by those social climbers determined to be stuffy and formal, 'Shoe'.

Shug was the classic friend from hell as far as my mother was concerned. She didn't drink, smoke, or swear, but was not so implacably opposed to these habits as were her sisters Annie and Bella, adopting a live and let live attitude in general, which normally served her very well. Shug Campbell was another matter. Shug tended to show up unexpectedly. If Mammy had any warning she would have immediately locked and barred the door, hidden us gagged under the bed, and stood behind Daddy's chair with her hands over his eyes and mouth, until the menace had got fed up knocking and peering through the letterbox and gone off muttering.

To us Shug was okay once you got used to his badly battle-scarred face with a prominent broken nose, and his generally rough tough appearance. He wasn't a big man, but he looked like someone who should be steered well clear of in most circumstances (which would be best translated as always). As soon as Shug arrived in our house, he would reach into his pocket and generously fish out some loose change, giving us some each. Mammy would retreat as far away from him as was possible in the small room, as he beamed and spoke to Daddy. "Hoo ur ye gaun' Toaffy (my father had liked toffee so much as a young boy and youth that he attracted the widely known nickname Toaffy), could ye go a few wee pints the night?"

Mammy's face screwed up in distaste and disapproval. She knew from experience that Daddy was loath to turn down such an invitation from Shug, which meant that any money spent in the pub was money that was not available for her to buy essential items like food.

Daddy was generally more likely to save face and go to the pub with Shug and face the wrath of my normally meek and mild mother when he came home, rather than turn down the invitation. Daddy carefully avoided Mammy's baleful stare and picked up his jacket. "A couple o' wee pints wull dae nae herm, Jessie, ah hivnae been oot in weeks, ye know that" said Daddy as he followed Shug out of the door and closed it behind him. We seldom saw Mammy in anything other than an affable mood and were frightened to see her like this. "Jist wait, if he comes hame the worse for drink, an' wi' nae money left oot o' mah hoosekeepin', ah'll gie him a few wee pints, so ah wull, he'll be laughin' oan the ither side o' his face afore the night's oot, the stumour."

We were upset at Mammy being upset and didn't know what to say. I actually liked Uncle Shug, as he was just like a lot of characters in the cowboy pictures that I liked so much. I could imagine him driving the chuckwagon at top speed across the range like the eccentric Gabby Hayes or Andy Clyde, or the other professional sidekicks of Roy Rogers or Gene Autry ('Jee Nottry' to us) and was upset that Mammy disliked him so much. The only difference was that Shug would have spent all his time getting drunk in western saloons and fighting much bigger men, just as he seemed to do in real life.

There was no doubt that Shug was a habitual pub brawler. The trick was to get him to leave the bar before he reached the fighting stage, which didn't take that long. Otherwise, he would size up the crowd propping up the bar and take a purely technical dislike to another patron. Somehow he would manage to convince himself that the guy was doing or saying something detrimental to himself or his friends. At the first available opportunity, he would challenge his target to a fight outside. As the other man put his pint down on the bar, Shug would land a king hit to the face before his opponent knew what had hit him. If this well tried and proven tactic worked, dazing his opponent, Shug had already won, and would pound away with his fists until he was hauled off. If his first punch missed or was ineffective Shug would take off out of the pub door as fast as he could run, hoping that he could get clear of likely pursuers.

Of course, Shug was banned from every pub anywhere near his home territory, which is why he had to travel all the way from Parkhead to the Gorbals to get a drink. I heard all this from Shug himself one day when he was carefully explaining to me how to win a pub fight, when I would be old enough to go to pubs. "Jist you always mind, WeeToaffy, a man's only goat wan decent punch in him, an' that's how ye hiv tae always get the furst punch in, ur ye've hid it fur sure." As Uncle Shug often said, a man must have a wee pastime of some kind, to keep him happy, and out of mischief. It just happened that Uncle Shug's wee pastime was punching strangers in pubs. Despite this he had his own code of what was acceptable, and he would never use weapons as others were prone to do, as this was breaking the law and someone would end up badly injured, attracting the attention of the police, who didn't really worry too much about a few punches between drunks and some blood on the pub floor. This was far too common an occurrence for the police to waste any time on.

If the normal closing time brawl got out of hand, with large numbers of protagonists spilling out into the streets, the Gorbals police would arrive in force accompanied by a couple of Black

Marias. Waiting patiently behind the Crown Street wall of the Wynd Church, the police were far too experienced to try to break up the fight immediately. The sergeant in charge would carefully judge the point at which the fighters were now getting exhausted, before blowing his whistle to signal his waiting troops to rush in with batons cracking heads, fists smashing faces, and heavy hobnailed boots kicking shins, knees, arses, ribs, and groins.

The police knew very well from experience who the instigators and petty criminals were, ignoring the victims of the fight and dragging their targets to the waiting Black Marias, continuing to beat the holy shit out of them until they had been literally thrown into the back of the vehicles, one at a time, where another fresh crew of policemen would take over and continue the treatment until the vehicles reached Lawmoor Street and the cells. During such a fracas, the populace of the street would be hanging out of windows, loudly cheering on the police, as most of those being arrested were detested by the law-abiding tenants, being well known for violent behaviour, burglaries, and general antisocial habits.

Daddy wasn't really a drinker and would be sorry for himself for days afterwards if he transgressed. We would make sure that we were well in bed before he got home after drinking, as Mammy would rip into him as soon as he got through the door. Even worse, she would refuse to speak to him at all for days afterwards. "Don't even try tae apologise tae me, ye're jist a dampt eejit wastin' oor guid money oan drink, ye stumour, whit am ah gonny feed oor weans oan?" she would erupt, when she had had enough of silent fury. "Fresh air an' cauld watter is aboot a' ah kin afford tae feed the weans oan tae ye get peyed; ah suppose ah kin send thim ower tae Ellen Campbell's tae get fed, they must be rollin' in money by the wey they spen' it oan booze." "Jessie hen," Daddy would groan, "Ah didnae mean tae spen' that much, bit ah goat cerried away in company, fur ah hid tae staun' mah turn at the baur like a' buddy else."

Nothing would calm Mammy's fury. "Ye'll hiv tae dae a' the cookin' untae ye're able tae gi'e me some money tae buy stuff fur eatin' an' drinkin', we're lucky thit the weans get free school mulk, an' kin eat at the dinner school, otherwise they wid a' be starvin'. Ah suppose ye'll be eatin' oan tick at the Larkfield Garage canteen?" Daddy looked bereft and left the house after grabbing his bus conductor's uniform jacket. As soon as he had gone, Mammy gathered us in her arms. "Ahm sorry if ah've frightened yese, bit ah really loast mah rag wi' yer Daddy, ah jist don't know whit tae dae fur money tae he gets peyed oan Friday efternin', an' ah've goat nothin' left in the press." She then noticed that his leather coin bag and ticket machine were still hanging on the big hook on the back of the door. She groaned, "Ah bet that he'll get a' the wey tae Larkfield afore he notices, an'll loass a day's pey, as well as gettin' intae trouble." About three hours later Daddy returned, his arms full of brown paper parcels, and with a beaming smile on his face, despite his hangover. "Whit hiv ye goat in thae parcels?" asked Mammy, as he laid them down on the kitchen table. "An' ye left yer bag'n stuff ahint ye when ye went oot in a hurry, how did ye manage withoot them?" "Jessie hen, Ahm no' due tae start work untae hauf past three this efternin," replied Daddy. "Ah jist went tae the garage canteen wi' the wee bit o' money that ah hid left, an' played billiards fur money. Ah managed tae win enough tae get plenty o' butchermeat, an' some ither stuff fae Cochranes tae keep us gauin' tae Friday."

Mammy was so relieved that she burst in to tears. "It's no' that I'm forgein' ye, but Ah'm sae gled that the weans urnae gonny go hungry efter a', an' Ah hope that ye'll no' forget last night in a hurry, fur ye kin be a right eejit at times." "Don't you worry Jessie hen, ah'll no' be gaun' tae any pub again unless it's jist tae hiv a couple o' pints, an' nae mair than Ah kin afford at the time, withoot leavin' you an' the weans shoart o' stuff tae eat an' a' tha'," replied Daddy, looking ashamed of himself. "An' ye kin jist steer well clear o' that Shug Campbell an' a', Ah dinnae care whit yese did afore we goat merrit, but ye're responsible fur a faimily o' weans noo, an' canny afford tae go oot boozin' wi' the likes o' him when he feels like it," Mammy berated him.

Daddy unwrapped one of the brown paper parcels, and watched us go round-eyed at the sight of a whole Lorne sausage (a large square block of specially spiced sausage meat, that is sliced prior to being fried). "Jist you weans wait fur hauf an 'oor, an Ah'll hiv this cut up, fried, an' oan yer plates afore ye kin say Lorne sausage." I had never seen a whole Lorne sausage before, except on a counter in Guthries the butchers, and was salivating at the thought of hoeing into a couple of slices for lunch, preferably between slices of bread. It tasted even better than I remembered, particularly when washed down with a cup of Barrs Irn Bru from the large bottle that Daddy produced from his jacket pocket. When we had finished, we all went out to play without the normal feeling that we could easily eat another couple of meals immediately. Daddy waved to us when he set off for his shift to Larkfield Garage.

We were still playing in the street a couple of hours later when I saw Uncle Shug rounding the corner from Crown Street. "How's it gaun, Wee Toaffy?" said Shug when he spotted me, "Ah've jist goat tae drap a wee thing intae yer faither afore Ah furget it." "He's gone tae work, an' wull no' be hame tae late the night Uncle Shug, an ma Mammy's roon at mah Auntie Bella's," I lied, hoping that he wouldn't knock on our door and get Mammy wound up, as I knew that she would refuse to even speak to him through the letterbox, never mind letting him through the door. "Yer faither gave me thurty shullins tae haud ontae fur him at the pub last night, in case he goat cerried away efter a few pints an' spent a' his money, an' left yer Maw shoart o' hur hoosekeepin' money," groaned Uncle Shug, "an' noo Ah've missed baith ae them, efter gau'in well oot o' ma wey tae come here, afore yer Maw needed it fur her messages." "If ye gie it tae me Ah kin keep it tae ma Mammy gets hame, Uncle Shug. Ah'll no' loass it, Ah'll keep it in mah poacket, wi' ma haun' tight roon' it tae she gets hame fae Auntie Bella's hoose," I said, hoping to avoid Shug being spotted by Mammy, if she looked out of the window to check up on what we were doing. "Right, Wee Toaffy, Ah'll jist hiv tae trust ye tae no' loass it, an' make sure that yer Maw gets it afore she hauf kills yer Daddy fur spendin' a' his money ower the baur," Shug shrugged.

I took the two notes from Uncle Shug and held them in my pocket with my fist clenched as tight as tight. I had never held so much money in my whole life before. Waiting until Shug had disappeared round the corner into Crown Street I ran up the stairs as fast as I could and battered on our door. Mammy opened it just enough to see out, as I had been too excited to use the family code knock. "Whit's the maitter wi' you, huv ye messed yer troosers?" "Naw Mammy, Ah've goat a loat o' money fur ye fae Uncle Shug, that he wis haudin fur mah Daddy at the pub last night. Ah telt him thit ye wir roon' at Auntie Bella's, so that he widnae chap at the door an' get ye intae a bad temper again," I said, in trepidation that she would lose her temper with me instead of Uncle Shug. She looked down at my tightly clenched fist, where paper money protruded at each end, and took the two notes in wide eyed disbelief as my fist opened. "Mah Goad, an' Ah gave yer Daddy a right roastin' fur somethin' he didnae dae. An' Ah called that Shug Campbell fur everythin' under the sun, but he'll dae somethin' tae deserve it afore long oneywey, the rotten toerag, sae Ah dinnae feel sae bad aboot him. Ah'll tell ye whit Allan, don't say a word tae yer Daddy aboot the money, let him suffer, fur as faur as he knows he spent a' mah hoosekeepin' money when he wis knoacked silly wi' mair beer than he could haundle. Ah'll plank this money away fur some time when we really need it." Mammy put the money in her apron pocket and gave me a pat on the head.

I felt really good that Mammy now had an emergency fund to call on if things got tricky. I don't know if my father ever found out that he hadn't really spent my mother's housekeeping at the pub that night, if he did, I never heard anything about it.

Chapter 14

Another subject that I remember very well from when I was six or seven years old was our dependence on comics for reading matter. These were not the American comics, but the home-grown types, which were published in Dundee, of all places, by a chap named Dudley D. Watkins, hardly a common Scottish name. During the War and immediately afterwards paper was in short supply, meaning that our publications were more or less rationed, even if we had the money to buy them, which we didn't.

We started off reading the 'Dandy' and the 'Beano' as five-year-olds. To read about 'Korky' the cat, 'Eggo' the ostrich, 'Desperate Dan', 'Lord Snooty and his pals', and all the other characters inhabiting the pages, was a lot better than not reading at all, and contributed greatly to honing our reading skills. The Dandy and Beano led on to the other publications, the 'Rover', 'Hotspur', 'Adventure', and 'Wizard'. These were supposed to be weekly publications, with the Adventure and Wizard being on sale on Tuesdays, and Rover and Hotspur on Thursdays. During paper rationing each publication dropped back to being fortnightly only.

These publications were very good for improving reading capacity, as they contained no pictures at all, being text only. It was essential to get every issue as each 'ripping yarn' type story was in serial format. If a copy was missed, then it was difficult to keep abreast of the unfolding saga. I will always remember the issue where one of my heroes, "Strang the Terrible", ended up in a small cell, heavily chained into a cast-iron chair, with the walls and roof which were covered in sharp steel stakes slowly moving inwards to inevitably impale and crush him. I liked Strang and spent the following week worrying about how he was going to escape but could only come to the conclusion that this was the end of the road for Strang, as there was no possible way out of this trap. When the next issue came out, I turned the pages to the Strang story with my fingers trembling, and half expecting to find out that Strang was now heavily muscled high-quality mince. I read the opening paragraph, not daring to breathe. I let my breath out in pure relief. "Mighty Strang burst from his bonds, and fled from the ever-encroaching spikes," was the opening sentence. Why didn't I think of that, it was so simple, I had totally underestimated Strang's capacity to deal with any dangerous situation. After this I never worried about Strang again, no matter how much of a predicament he was in at the end of a chapter. I tried to earn enough money to buy these comics each Tuesday and Thursday but found it impossible to keep up.

Even when I had the money it was not often possible to buy the relevant comic, as most paper shops only supplied on permanent order, leaving no copies for casual sales. An exception to this was a small Dickensian shop just around the corner in Crown Street, owned and operated by an eccentric little old lady named Kate Dunning. It was said that Kate had been there longer than anybody could remember, and during all of this time had never been known to throw anything out. Looking at the shop with its ancient gas lighting glowing dimly, and the piles of papers and other rubbish stacked up at crazy angles, you could well believe it. Kate wore her hair up in a straggly bun over her heavily wrinkled face, and always seemed to be wearing the same Victorian clothes, with a long dress trailing on the floor. Despite all that, Kate was the leading stalwart of the local company of the Salvation Army based in Kidston Street and the highest-ranking member. Kate looked quite different when she was all dressed up in her full regalia, leading her brass band and some tambourine-clashing ladies, and giving her own tambourine serious laldy around the Gorbals streets at weekends. We found that Kate ordered copies of many publications without insisting that customers place advance orders.

Bobby and I started hanging around Kate Dunning's shop after we had eaten supper, our heads cocked at all angles as we tried to read the comics without picking them up, as we had no money to buy any. Many people were frightened of Kate, as they were basically uneducated and believed in witchcraft, ghosts and anything else that they could summon up to frighten themselves.

I personally had long since stopped being scared of Kate, and it was all due to my Granny Cunningham's habit of taking snuff. When Granny arrived at our house, she would invariably sit in the fireside chair, putting down all the small or not so small items that she had picked up mostly at auction sales, to add to our meagre possessions. I remember one day her coming round the Crown Street corner with a large and heavy brass fireside fender over one shoulder." Wid ye run up the sterrs an' tell yer Mammy tae open the door, as this fender's nae lightweight," she puffed. "Where in the name o' the wee man did ye get that Maw? It's a brilliant fit," said Mammy as she helped Granny to lower the fender into place around the hearth. "Ah goat it at an auction sale, fur only three shullins," replied Granny, "An Ah wis lucky enough tae get a good conductress who let me lie it doon oan the boattum flair o' the caur, as it wis too big tae fit under the sterrs." "It's a hard life, Allan," wheezed Granny, as she slumped gratefully into the fireside chair. "Wid ye be a good wee boy an' jist run roon' tae Kate Dunnin's an' get me a penny's worth o' Irish Mixture," which was her favourite snuff. When I returned with the little paper poke, Granny would tip a little pile of the snuff onto the back of her left hand, and sniff it up each nostril in turn, then sneeze loudly. "Ah!, that's better son, there's nothin' better thin a wee pinch o' snuff fur clearin' yer heid," Granny would say in a happy voice. I had been getting her snuff like this for years and was quite comfortable in the company of the old shop lady.

Kate had noticed us squinting at her stock of comics from all angles. "Dae ye want tae buy anythin', boys?" she asked as she turned up the gaslight from very dim to just gloomy. "We're jist lookin' Missus Dunnin'," I said in embarrassment. "Ye can look through them if ye like, an' jist let me know when ye find the ones ye want to buy. I know that you're Allan, but I don't know the name o' the ither wee boy." "His name's Bobby an' he's ma wee brother," I explained. "That's fine Allan an' Bobby, ye kin take yer time sortin' oot whit ye want tae buy," said Kate kindly. I felt terrible and blurted out "Ah'm sorry Missus Dunnin', but we hivnae goat any money tae buy anythin' at a'." She sat on her high stool behind the littered counter in silence and just looked at us. We sidled sideways toward the door, getting ready to break into a sprint if she shouted at us for wasting her time. "Come back here, you two, Ah want tae talk tae the baith o' ye." We slunk back into the dim and cluttered shop, fearing that she was going to give us hell. "If ye promise tae be good boys and sit quiet at the coonter, oot o' the wey o' customers, ye can read a' the comics ye like, as long as ye dinnae tear them, or get them a' runkled." I was stunned. "Ur ye sure Missus Dunnin', that we kin dae tha'?" "Ah said it, an' ah meant it, whit else wid ye like me tae say, besides, ah cuid dae wi' some company oan daurk nights," replied old Kate.

Old Kate was as good as her word, allowing Bobby and me to rush around to her little shop every night as soon as we finished our supper, and climbing on to the old-fashioned high stools, read voraciously through every comic that Kate had piled up ready for us. My father and mother were flabbergasted when we rushed home the first night and told them that we could read comics every night at Kate Dunnings, without paying as much as a penny. "Ye must think that Ah came up the Clyde oan a banana boat, tae believe that. Ah know thit she's a wee bit funny but she cannae be that daft, as tae let two wee boys read brand new comics every night fur nothin'," snorted my father. "Honest Daddy, she dis, an' she says that she likes oor company," I said in exasperation. We hunkered up on our high stools at Kate Dunning's in the early evenings for years, hardly ever saying a word to each other or to her, squinting to read in the sputtering gaslight, until Kate suddenly died one night during her sleep at home, with her shop then being closed and barred by her executor.

On the day of Kate's funeral Bobby and I trailed sadly behind the amazingly long funeral procession, led by her Salvation Army brass band and tambourine-carrying ladies, all the way from the Salvation Hall halfway down Kidston Street and down Caledonia Road to the gates of the Southern Necropolis. We then realised that old Kate musn't always have been the elderly eccentric lady that we knew, or the very large number of mourners would have no reason to pay their respects to another of the great characters in the life of the neighbourhood.

Since I was now seven years old, I was seen by my parents as being sufficiently responsible to take Bobby and Alec to visit both of our grandmothers on Sundays. All trams to the city northbound along Crown Street went past Glasgow Cross, so there was no chance of getting on the wrong tramcar. When I was first entrusted to travel I would ask the conductress to put us off at the Cross, but within a week or two I was confidently able to handle the disembarkation myself, making sure that we were on the platform as the tram reached our stop at the Saltmarket side of the Trongate. We then crossed the main road to the Glasgow Cross underground railway station, which then formed a triangular island in the middle of the busy thoroughfare.

Waiting for the number 9 Auchenshuggle tram was no trouble, as they ran frequently. Getting off at the correct stop was easy, because it was the stop for Belvedere Hospital and plenty of hospital visitors got off there. Wee Granny lived at the beginning of McDuff Street and would be hanging out of her scullery window in wait for us, so we always visited her first. After saying hello, and taking off our jackets or coats, and having slurped down the milky tea that she served in bowls, not cups, and eaten a jam sandwich, we hurried back out of the door, running across the backcourt and through the close on the far side.

In the next street was our target, a large playground known as the 'swingy park', with a full range of equipment. In addition to the normal swings, roundabouts, and small slides, there were two grand devices called 'swingy boats', and a very large slide, plus some outdoors gymnastic equipment, such as parallel bars, a vaulting horse, and round hoops hanging on chains. We were accepted by the local kids, as we were frequent users, and faced no risk of being beaten up or chased away, as most 'strangers' were.

My favourites were the swingy boats and the big slide. The swingy boats were suspended from heavy duty pipe framework, and each consisted of a huge solid baulk of timber about fifteen feet long, with steel bars like an inverted U spaced out at regular intervals for kids to hold on to as they straddled the timber, with their feet on the wooden running boards that ran down each side. At each end was a very substantial cast-iron saddle shaped like those on old fashioned motor bikes. Once the boat was fully loaded with kids, including two sitting on the saddle at each end, came the part that I liked best. Two kids, one of whom would be me, held onto the outer edge of the cast iron saddles, at each end. Working in unison by shouting to each other, we would push and pull, gradually overcoming the considerable inertia of the heavy apparatus. As the boat gained momentum, the ends rose up higher and higher, with the pushers hanging on for dear life to the saddles, being lifted up high into the air with each swing, and running, pushing as hard as we could, on the down stroke. Having to look after Alec, and to a lesser extent Bobby, meant that I had to spend some time pushing swings, catching them as they slid down the smaller chute, and keeping Alec from being brained by swings. Only through injury or hunger did we return to Granny's before lunchtime.

After lunch we walked up McDuff Street to Glamis Road to visit Granny Cunningham, Uncle Rab if he was at home, Auntie

Nellie, and Betty. Granny Cunningham was quite different from Wee Granny, being relatively tall for her time, and was very easy to like. At some time before we moved to Kidston Street, Mammy and I had lived with her, and I never felt more secure than in her house, with the heavy orange chenille curtains which were drawn at nighttime, giving a lovely warm feeling all round. The apartment had its own toilet and bath, and that epitome of luxury, running hot water, heated by a 'wetback' fitted to the rear of the fireplace.

The back court was well grassed, unlike our heavily puddled expanse of muck at home, so we were able to play outside without getting filthy. If Uncle Rab was at home he could always produce a ball of some kind, and sometimes joined us in a game of 'three and in'. If we weren't playing football we would play chases with Betty and her friends -- this was noisy as the girls squealed all the time, rising to a piercing shriek when we caught one of them.

At some time, Granny Cunningham had lost half of her right pinky finger and the whole of the two adjoining fingers, leaving only her right index finger and thumb intact. I would often ask her how she had lost them. She always joked about it, saying such things as "That's whit happens when ye pick yer nose too often." "Ah loast thim when Ah wis skelpin' the weans' bums too hard when they were wee." "Wan day the weather wis that cauld, that they fell oaf when Ah took ma haun oot o' mah poacket tae pey the caur fare." "Ah used tae bite ma fingernails that much that Ah didnae notice that Ah hid chowed ma fingers aff as well." She never told us what had really happened.

I asked my mother what had caused the amputations. "It happened long afore Ah wis boarn, an' she wid never tell me either, but Ah found oot fae ma Granny Reddoch that it happened when she was only thirteen, when she was workin' in a cannin' factory," said Mammy. "She had only been workin' therr fur a day or two, when her haun' goat caught in wan o' the machines, and wis draggin' her in, tae her fingers goat cut aff, lettin' her go." "At the hoaspital the doactor hid tae cut aff mair o' the bones, tae leave enough skin tae cover up the mess, when he sewed her haun' up. He made sich a guid joab o' it that she wis back at work in a foartnight, wi' a leather bag ower her right haun'." "Did they gie her a loat o' money tae make up fur her loast fingers?" I asked. "Naw, in thae days they goat away wi' blue murder, ma Maw thought that she wis lucky tae keep her joab."

At the stroke of half past three, Granny would call us inside and give us a jam sandwich each and give me a silver sixpence. "Jist divide that amongst yersels, when ye get hame, an aff ye go the noo before yer Mammy starts tae worry aboot yese." Shrugging into our jackets, we headed down towards the tram stop outside the Belvedere Hospital, catching a number 9 to Glasgow Cross, and changing to the Cathcart tram which took us southwest along Crown Street to our stop at the Wynd church. "Did yese huv a good day, an' Ah hope that ye bahaved yersels at baith yer Granny's, an' didnae gie me a showin' up?" asked Mammy as we entered our tiny home. "Naebody goat their heids banged oan the swings, an' we a' hid a right good time a' day Mammy," I replied.

I wonder if anyone today would let a seven-year-old take a five-year-old, and a three-year-old, halfway across a busy industrial city and back again on public transport. I doubt it very much, but then in 1945/6 nobody thought that it was anything out of the ordinary. We continued to visit relations on Sundays under our own steam until we were teenagers.

Some other aspects of slum tenement living would be looked on as anti-social today but were regarded as being normal then. We used any sharp piece of metal to chip away the horizontal mortar between bricks at specific areas on the high walls separating the back courts. This provided grips for our fingers and toecaps, enabling us to scale all the walls, and stand up or straddle the top when we reached it.

Four types of wall capping were prevalent: plain brick, glazed terracotta tiles inverted vee shape, the same in half round shape, and wall tops consisting of broken glass embedded in a mortar screed. The plain brick tops were easy to cope with when we were straddling or walking along them. The terracotta tiles were easy to straddle too, but the vee shape quickly gave wall climbers a sore bum. Walking along the tops of the tiles was not too easy, as the half round profile required that the climber walked carefully on the very top only, or else the feet would shoot off sideways, resulting in a painful fall. The inverted vee shape was even more difficult, with the climber having to walk as if he had seriously bandy legs. To walk along the vee shaped tiles required a lot of practice, good leg muscles, and a suicidal disregard of the consequences of slipping. The walls topped with broken glass were to be avoided, unless there was something very attractive on the other side.

These walls linked the various washhouses, midden enclosures, and air raid shelters still standing. Climbing on top of these structures, and jumping from one to another, was a sort of constant test of courage that continued year by year as we grew up. Each jump had a name and a rating of difficulty, ranging from 'The Wee Easy,' up to 'The Kingy'. It wasn't just the jumps and walls in our own backcourts which were rated; back courts for miles around, all the way from Rutherglen Road to Govanhill, and sometimes beyond, were included in the unwritten rating system. Some unfortunate residents had concrete roofs of outbuildings butting up to their windows, which meant that they were subjected to a lot of noisy kids yelling just outside as they ran to jump to another outbuilding or landed on their one. Kids can be cruel and thoughtless, particularly in a slum environment.

One lady in our back court, Mrs Dale, with the concrete roof of a midden just outside her window, had a very short fuse, and would fling her window up to yell at her unthinking tormentors to get off the roof, or she would call the police immediately. Poor Mrs Dale had called the police so many times that the police were reluctant to attend, because when they got to the backcourt, the kids would jump into another backcourt and be well away, before the police could follow. Knowing this, we reacted in a very cruel manner. The making and throwing of 'ashy bombs' was second nature to us -- all that was required was a single sheet of newspaper, with a few double handfuls of dirty white ashes from the nearest midden placed in the middle. The edges were folded into the middle and twisted tightly, allowing some degree of handling. Thrown at any target, the paper wrapping would burst on impact, showering the immediate area with a dense cloud of ash.

To torment poor Mrs Dale even further, a couple of the more malevolent kids would make some ashy bombs, and creep up the outbuilding roof until they were directly under her window. When they were in position, everybody would start yelling their lungs out. When Mrs Dale threw open her window, the pair under her windowsill stood up and threw their ashy bombs through the open window, to burst inside her house. I can only imagine the mess that was caused, as the fine ash dust penetrated into every nook and cranny.

In retrospect our behaviour was appalling, but at the time it seemed like fun, especially in the overall context of our grim environment, where the unacceptable was considered acceptable. If someone had thrown an ashy bomb through our own window, our family would have gone berserk with rage, but our sense of right and wrong was so distorted that we failed make the connection.

Another thing that we were inclined to indulge in without much thought for the consequences was the collection of wood, paper, cardboard, and any other flammable materials, to pile up against the inner corner of two walls and set fire to as a bonfire. Bonfires were so common that nobody regarded them as anything out of the ordinary. Once the bonfire had really taken hold and was roaring, sending showers of sparks and cinders high in the air, we chased around frantically looking for additional fuel to keep it going at that intensity. This propensity to light fires indiscriminately was deeply imbued within the slum mentality.

My own disaffection with fire lighting happened when our gang was playing one evening in Hutchesons stables at Gushetfaulds. Entering the stables by climbing over the high wall, we made our way to where scores of various types of horse larries were parked. This was well away from the gloomy brick stables where the many Clydesdale horses spent their miserable lives when not pulling larries. We spent hours jumping from cart to cart, pretending these were pirate ships, and fighting off boarders with wooden swords made from the many pieces of wood which were lying around.

As always, we ignored the passage of time, and continued to play until it was too dark to see each other. The older boys who led our gang decided that a bonfire built on top of a larrie deck would allow us to keep on playing pirates, and additionally would add to the authenticity of the game. A brief collection of the combustible material laying around produced more than enough for a decent bonfire. Once this was piled up on a larrie deck and lit, we soon had sufficient light to continue our game.

Additional wood was occasionally added to the bonfire to keep it going. Unfortunately, far more wood was added than required. By the time that we realised that the wooden deck of the larrie was also alight, the fire was too intense to get close enough to put it out. Running to the wall, we clambered over, and ran home as fast as our legs would carry us. I was frantic with worry about what had happened and ran into the room and hid under the recess bed as soon as Mammy opened the door. "Whit's wrang wi' you? Hiv ye seen a ghost or somethin'?" asked Mammy. 'Aye, ah've seen a monster runnin' oot the back close, it wis that terrible, that Ah wis too frightened tae move fur a long while", I replied, thankful that she had provided me with an excuse. "The trouble wi' you is thit ye've goat faur too much o' an imagination fur ye're ain good, God only knows whit ye'll be seein' next, Adolf Hitler oan roller skates, or somethin' jist as stupit", laughed Mammy, as she laid the table for supper.

I was invariably fast at eating anything that was put in front of me at mealtimes, but tonight my stomach was so tied up in knots with terror because of the stable fire that I felt more like throwing up than eating. Additionally, I had developed a terrible migraine. "Ah cannae eat anything Mammy. Ah've goat a sair stomach an' a sair heid. Ah need an Askit powder tae make mah sair heid go away", I moaned in serious distress. "Ye must be really sick tae be no' eatin' yir supper, an' yir face his gaun a' peely wally intae the bargain", said Mammy. "Ah'll gie ye jist hauf o' an Askit, that wull be plenty fur a wee boy, an' Ah'll pit ye straight intae yer bed," said Mammy with real concern. At that I heard the sound of a convoy of fire engines approaching fast up Crown Street, with their distinctive bells ringing, which were joined by another group of bells coming down Cathcart Road. "My God, there must be a really big fire tae hiv a' thae fire engines gaun tae it. Ah wonder whaur it is?" said Mammy. I raced over to the sink, throwing up on the way, and climbed up the sink cupboard to hang over the sink, retching my heart out.

The arrival of the Fire Brigade, at any time, always attracted a large number of spectators. In this case the fire had got a really serious hold, and it seemed that many larries had caught fire before someone called the Fire Brigade. The whole neighbourhood turned out to watch the spectacle. The intensity of the fire was such that all the firefighters could do was to prevent the fire spreading to neighbouring premises, including the actual horse stables themselves; fortunately, all the horses had already been evacuated to safety. The numerous larries parked in the large stable yard were reduced to ashes. I only found this out second hand, as I was in bed with churning guts and such a severe migraine that even a whole Askit powder did nothing to alleviate the pain.

For many months afterwards I was terrified that I or the others involved would be arrested and incarcerated in Barlinnie prison. I avoided playing with the ringleaders of the stable bonfire incident and ran home and hid under the bed at the sight of any policemen, the sound of a police whistle, or the bells of fire engines. It was a long time before my fears over the stable fire abated.

For some time after the War, the numerous air raid shelters that were hurriedly built on school playgrounds, back courts, and in the middle of streets, remained untended and unloved, used only by street gangs as somewhere to beat up someone unobserved, and providing a cosy home for multitudes of large rats. I had always thought that the design and construction of these buildings was flawed, with skimpy walls supporting a heavy concrete roof.

The first shelters demolished in our locality were the four built on our school playgrounds. No particular precautions were taken to keep spectators out of danger during demolition activities. One morning five or six men turned up at our school equipped with sledgehammers, shovels, a water barrel, a wide selection of pieces of rough-sawn timber and a large serious looking cylinder with flexible hoses attached. Without any fuss the workmen entered the shelter and, using some heavy timber dunnage, set up the cylinder halfway up horizontally, across an internal doorway. The flexible hoses were led outside and attached to a long-handled handpump located on top of the water barrel. Once preparations were completed to the gaffer's satisfaction, we keen spectators were told to move back a few yards.

The gaffer satisfied himself that no schoolkids were close enough to be flattened before signalling one of the men to start pumping. About ten pumping strokes were all that was required to displace the internal walls sufficiently. With a sudden bang followed by loud booming noise, and a sudden hurricane of dust which whooshed out in every direction, the whole structure collapsed, leaving only a flattened pile of bricks, capped by the concrete roof slab which remained in one piece. All spectators were fairly evenly coated in a layer of pulverised mortar dust. We all looked like a passable imitation of the 'Claymen' in the Flash Gordon movie serials. "That'll learn youse weans tae hing aboot in case ye miss somethin', when ye didnae hiv tae", grinned the gaffer, as he started his men off breaking up the massive concrete roof slab using sledgehammers. The whole process of demolition, to the sledgehammer stage, had taken less than half an hour.

Helping each other to get rid of at least some of the white dust by slapping at our clothing, and shaking our heads vigorously, we ran to the main school door, where we were intercepted and lined up by the school janitor to get four strokes of the strap from the assistant headmaster for being late for school, and an additional two for turning up at school looking like refugees from Bilslands bakery. Despite this I thought that watching the demolition men reducing the air raid shelter to a pile of rubble in next to no time was well worth it.

The four air raid shelters built on our playgrounds were soon demolished. All traces of them were removed within three days, with all work carried out manually, including loading of the trucks with the resultant rubble. I doubt that the average labourer nowadays could, or would, carry out such demanding physical work every workday, without all the machinery that now carries out all the previously backbreaking work with consummate efficiency. One thing is for certain, a fat or even slightly overweight workman was as rare as an SS trooper leading the prayers in a synagogue when I was a boy. Broad shoulders were common. Broad behinds and fat bellies were not.

Inspired by the ease with which the demolition men had removed the shelters from the school playgrounds, three of my friends and I prised some pointed railings from a fence to use as crowbars and set out to emulate them. Straight after school on the following day, we collected our steel spikes from the hiding place in the 'dunny'. The dunny was a dank and dark passageway which led from the back court, down underneath the tenement, and emerged in the first close around the corner. As a starting place we chose a derelict wash house, which abutted ours. Access was gained by removing one of the galvanised roof panels and dropping to the floor inside. The noise we had made removing the roof panel had obviously alerted the rats, as the tail enders of the rat community were squirming to escape under the locked door as we dropped down from the rafters. Pausing for some time to allow our eyes to get used to the dim light we looked around. Piles of rubbish and rubble covered the dirt floor. The unmistakable smell of decay and dampness hung heavily in the air.

Selecting a part of the far wall, we used the points of our improvised crowbars to gouge out the mortar, until there was a sufficient gap to allow our spikes to lever the first brick free. After we removed a few more bricks we could see that the wall was two courses thick. Aware that the adjoining building was only another abandoned wash house, we prised more bricks away, until we had created a hole through both walls, at shoulder height. From that point onwards, with our newly discovered skills, levering bricks from the rapidly enlarging hole was very easy. At that point we hid our spikes under the rubble, and climbed out through the missing roof panel, to jump to the ground, and scurry home in time for supper, just as Mammy was calling us in from our back court window.

"In the name of the wee man Allan, whit hiv ye been playing in? Yer claes ur a' covered in glaur, it's even a' through yer hair", shrieked Mammy as soon as she saw me. "Ah've been helping Mrs Moloney clean oot her fireplace, an' carryin' a' the ashes doon tae the midden", I said lamely, using the first plausible explanation that came into my head. The gloom inside the derelict wash house meant that I hadn't noticed the thick coating of mortar and brick dust which had accumulated on all my external surfaces during our first attempt on the world amateur demolition title.

"Ye kin jist take a' yer claes aff, an' staun in the sink while ah wash ye doon wi' cauld watter an' carbolic soap. A'll hiv tae wash yer claes, an' hing thim oan the fireguard a' night, tae be ready fur ye tae wear tae school in the moarnin'", said Mammy in an aggrieved tone. "God only knows whit kind o' glaur ye'll be trailin' through ma door next, ye must think Ah've goat a' day tae run efter stupit weans that should hae mair sense than tae come hame a stane heavier than they left the hoose, wi' a' the glaur that they must roll aboot in efter the school is oot".

I sheepishly stood shivering and naked in the sink, as Mammy poured potfuls of freezing water over my head, lathered me from top to toe using the ubiquitous carbolic soap, and with obvious relish rinsed me off with more potfuls of frigid water than were strictly necessary. Our towels were thin and scratchy, and felt like medium grade sandpaper against the skin. This high friction design feature helped tremendously when we were standing in front of the fire shivering, rubbing ourselves down as fast and as hard as we could manage. Whatever dirt remained on the skin was efficiently removed by abrasion.

Despite my mother's warning, after school the following day we climbed back into the wash house to continue our self-taught lesson on demolishing brick walls. By the time that I could hear my mother calling me in for supper, we had created a massive hole between the two wash houses. After jumping down into the back court, we dusted each other down as best we could. Feeling that I was still too filthy, I took off my jersey, and washed my face, hair, hands, legs, and boots, with water scooped from the least filthy puddle that I could find. I used my jersey as a towel, and put it back on inside out, before running up the stairs, and into the house.

I sat down at the table. As Mammy was dishing out supper, she started to sniff the air. She continued to follow her nose, until she was directly behind me. She paused, and loudly sniffed my hair, before reeling backwards at high speed. "Staun up an' get back fae ma table, afore we a' get mair diseases than the hale o' the Royal Infirmary has goat. Ye smell like ye hiv been rollin' aboot in fifty different kinds o' shite", she yelled. I blushed deeply under the layer of sludge coating my face and backed into the corner by the recess bed. Bobby and Alec were trying to hide the grins on their faces, as Mammy grabbed the broom at the bristle end, and prodded me firmly in the chest with the handle, continuing to yell at me. "Jist you stey whaur ye ur, an' get a' yer claes aff the same as last night, an' staun up in the sink".

I underwent the same treatment as the previous evening, the only difference being that she spent a much longer time scrubbing me down with carbolic soap, before the extended rinsing. I was so cold that my shivering was violent and my chattering teeth were clearly audible. I stood as close to the fire as I could manage without burning my behind. Using the broom handle, Mammy speared my discarded clothing, and dumped it into the sink, with the tap running at full bore, and stirred the clothing around for some time before she judged it safe to approach. She plugged the drain and allowed the water level to rise sufficiently, before placing a cast-iron pot on top of the clothing to ensure that it was kept submerged.

"Ye kin jist tell me hoo ye goat in that state, ye durty wee eedjit. Ah've never smelt oneythin' like it in ma hale life before, ye're lucky thit yer faither isnae hame fur he wid hiv taken the skin aff yer bum wi' his belt", hissed Mammy. Realising that I was in deep trouble, and had greatly upset my beloved mother, I racked my brains to find an excuse. "The dunny wis flooded fae a burst lavatory pipe, an' a big boy pushed me in when ah wisnae lookin' Mammy", I ventured with a degree of hesitation. "Ah dinnae believe a word ae tha', fur the dunny wis bone dry when ah wis hingin' oot the washin' this moarnin', so ye cannae tell me sich stupit rubbidge, an' hope thit ye'll get away wi' it ye stumour," replied Mammy.

I was terrified that she would be angry enough to tell Daddy. We didn't see much of him, because of the iniquitous practice of the Corporation Transport in rostering of 'split shifts'. This meant that staff might start at 0530am, work until the early morning peak period eased at 0830, wait in the garage canteen, work again from 1130 to1330, wait in the canteen, work from 1630 until 1830, wait in the canteen, and then work from 2200 until 2300. Despite the overall time spent on the job staff were only paid for the hours spent actually working, and not for the long hours spent waiting in the canteen. This meant that staff might attend work for seventeen hours but were only paid for eight hours ordinary time. The shift quoted may have been at the extreme of the 'split shift' spectrum, but invariably staff spent many more hours away from home than they were paid for. During the years that my father worked for the Corporation, he was either working or sleeping, with little time to spend with us, except on his rare days off.

I implored Mammy not to tell Daddy. "Ah'll tell ye whit, ye'll hiv tae come straight hame fae school every day, an' help me aboot the hoose, instead o' gettin' yersel' clatty, tae Ah'm ready tae trust ye tae no' get yer claes a' durty, fae rollin' aboot in glaur", she said. I would have agreed to anything to avoid being bent over my father's knee, and getting a severe thrashing as he applied his old army belt to my bare bottom, until it would have glowed red in the dark, if the light had been switched off.

For a few days I went straight home from school, despite being called a 'feartie' by my three fellow demolishers. Then they told me that they had found an air raid shelter, in a Camden Street back court, that offered much more scope for our freshly gained expertise than the old wash house.

Next day on the way to dinner school, I went with them to look at the shelter. Already they had succeeded in making sizable holes in the internal brick walls and were starting on one of the external walls. When school ended, I didn't go straight home as promised, but went with the other three to the shelter. We were busy engaged in enlarging the hole in the outside wall with our spikes, when my mother arrived on the scene livid with anger. after I had failed to arrive home straight after school, mother had left Bobby and Alec with old Mrs Moloney and started to search for me. By asking kids playing in the streets if they had seen me, she had soon tracked me down to the air raid shelter. "Ye stupit durty wee eedjit, if Ah hid known whit you an' yer bampot pals wur daein', Ah wid hiv died o' hert failure. Dae ye realise thit the shelter cuid fa' doon oan toap o' ye, wi' a' the holes yese hiv made in the wa's?" she screamed. "This time Ah'm gonnae tell yer Daddy what ye've been daein', an' Ah hope that he belts the holy shite oot o' ye, so ye'll never go anywhere near an air raid shelter again. A'm sae gled that Ah goat tae ye before the thing fell doon oan yese, an' kilt yese a'." My mother was so shaken that she was visibly trembling. She held my right wrist in a vice-like grip with her left hand and dragged me home using her right hand to repeatedly skelp any part of me that was within reach. I had a severe migraine by the time that my father got home.

My mother was true to her word and told Daddy what I had been getting up to after school. "Ye deserve a' thit yer gonnae get, ye stupit wee bampot," he growled as he caught me by the scruff of the neck. I got the worst belting possible, without being actually flayed, though it felt like it at the time. The weals on my bottom were so severe that I had to be kept home from school for some days as I was unable to sit down without experiencing agonising pain, despite the soothing cream that my mother was applying every couple of hours. The bruising was so bad that it looked like my behind had been painted over by an expert in black and blue camouflage, when I used the wardrobe mirror to see why I was suffering such pain.

I didn't worry again about being called a 'feartie' by my former fellow demolition pals and went straight home from school every day. About a week after my monumental thrashing, I took Bobby and Alec to visit my grannies in Parkhead on the Sunday. I was still too sore to sit down on any of the swings or swingy boats and had to content myself with being a pusher for my brothers.

When we arrived back home in the late afternoon, I was surprised to find Auntie Bella sitting beside Mammy at the table, with one arm around my mother's shoulder, comforting her as she wept with great heaving sobs. By her appearance, she had been crying for some time. "Whit's ma Mammy greetin' fur?" I asked Auntie Bella, with a fair degree of apprehension, dreading to find out the reason for my mother's deep distress. My question only served to increase the flow rate of my mother's tears. Auntie Bella removed her arm from around my mother's shoulders and took me by the hand to the outside landing. "Ah don't rightly know Allan, she hid promised tae come roon' tae see me aboot three o' cloack fur a wee cup o' tea, an' a bit o' a blether", whispered Auntie Bella. "When she came tae mah door she wis greetin' hur eyes oot aboot some accident that happened in a back coort in Camden Street. She saw a loat o' ambulances, an' fire brigade lorries, oan her wey tae oor hoose. It seems that some wee boys were makin' big holes in the wa's inside wan o' they auld air raid shelters, an' the hale loat fell doon oan tap o' them, an' they wur a' kilt." I was immediately struck dumb with horror and had to struggle to stop myself from joining my mother in her tears.

I was so thankful to have parents who cared what their offspring did, even if it meant using draconian punishment as a means to keep us from potential harm. After Auntie Bella left I sat by Mammy until she could weep no more. I felt that I understood why she was so upset.

Chapter 15

The Wynd Church, located next door to our close, hosted a wide range of organisations on a permanent basis:

Church Choir
Ladies Hymn Singing Group
Band of Hope
Boys Brigade
Lifeboys
Girls Brigade
Rosebuds

As far as I can remember, in the Gorbals, if nowhere else, the Boy Scouts, Cubs and Brownies were principally Catholic in their membership.

The members of the organisations listed under the Wynd Church were principally Protestant.

When I reached the age of eight, my father gave in to my pestering, and allowed Bobby and me to join the Lifeboys. The uniform consisted of a navy-blue jersey, with a little brass lifebouy badge pinned to the left breast, and a navy-blue sailors hat. The two women who ran the show dressed in navy blue, with a tricorn hat.

We were taught how to tie basic knots, and a wide range of team games. About two months after we joined the older lady addressed us from the lectern. She held up a foolscap size sheet of cardboard, with a plastic cover on one side, and explained what it was all about. "The Scottish Missionary Society is raising funds to help the poor starving children in Africa and would like us to help them. I will be giving you all a card each to take home with you. All you have to do is ask your parents, relatives, and neighbours, to contribute sixpence each, which you slip into these little slots in the plastic cover. When you have filled the card you will have forty sixpences, which is one pound. I know that you all will raise a pound each, with little trouble".

My heart sank, as I accepted a card. I was wondering how I was going to cadge forty sixpences from family and neighbours, particularly as Bobby also had a card to fill. At the first opportunity, I tackled Mammy. "Kin ah hiv sixpence"? "Whit dae ye want sixpence fur this time"? she asked as she opened her purse. "It'll hiv to be yer pocket money in advance, fur daen a' thae joabs oan the list". "It's fur a' thae starvin' weans in Africa. Ah've goat tae get forty sixpences fur the Lifeboys'. Mammy responded by snapping her purse shut like a rat trap. "Ah need a' mah sixpences fur the starvin' weans in this hoose, ye can try yer Daddy if ye like, but Ah don't fancy yer chances".

I waited until my father came home, had eaten, and was sitting in his chair by the fire, reading the evening paper and puffing contentedly on a cigarette. "Daddy, kin ah hiv sixpence fur the missionaries tae send tae starvin' weans in Africa?" I might as well have shoved a live grenade down the front of his shirt and buttoned up his collar. Daddy went rigid, and his eyes bulged. "Fuck the starvin' weans in Africa. If they're onything like the wee thievin' bastarts I came across in North Africa durin' the war, ah wid faur rather shoot them than feed them. The rotten wee buggers wid steal the teeth oot o' yer heid while ye were eatin' yer dinner, then come back fur yer eyes afore ye even noticed that yer teeth were missin'."

I next tried Mrs Mathieson. She ran the fruit shop downstairs and was a native of Aberdeen. "Ah hiv tae sell a hale bag o' totties, tae make sixpence, an' Ahm damned if ah'll gie it away tae people thit Ah don't even know. If they were runnin' a fruit shoap in Africa, Ah doot that they wid send me as much as a green snotter," was her considered response. I next tried Peggy Sidey, who lived in the ground floor house. "Mrs Sidey, wid ye like tae gie sixpence tae the Lifeboys tae help the starvin' weans in Africa?" "Naw, Ah widnae", was her terse response, as she slammed her door.

I next tried Auntie Bella. She was quite happy to give me sixpence, which I slipped into a slot in the card, which I produced from under my jersey. I had learned from the string of refusals that it was fatal to mention what the sixpence was for. "Whit's the big caird fur?" she asked. I tried to ignore her question as I sidled out the door, but she grabbed the sleeve of my jersey. She took the card and read the spiel printed at the top of the card. "If ah hid any idea that ye wur collectin' money fur thae greedy missionaries, ah widnae huv gied ye a farthin', never mind sixpence. Ah bet ye that they spend a' the money oan themsels, afore any o' it gets near a starvin' wean". "Ah'll jist take the sixpence aff the next sixpence thit ah wis gonnae gie ye, so noo yer sixpence short o' the sixpence that ye didnae know that ye were gettin, afore ah found oot what the sixpence that ah hiv jist gien ye wis fur." I sort of understood her logic, but not entirely.

I tried various neighbours and local shopkeepers, but I found that the rest of the Lifeboys had already snared all the sixpences from the minority of people who were happy to donate. I tried in a desultory fashion to get more sixpences before the dreaded day arrived when the donation cards were to be handed in. In desperation, I inserted my own sixpence pocket money, making the other sixpence look less lonely.

Bobby had managed to get seven sixpences in his card. On the night of the handing in I tried to convince myself that somebody might have got no sixpences at all. The leader stood up at the lectern announcing that she was going to get each Lifeboy to come to the lectern in alphabetical order, to hand over their cards. She would announce each total as she received the card. First up was Kenneth Archibald, who couldn't get his card to her fast enough, with his spectacles misting over in excitement. "Archibald, a full card", she announced.

I felt sick and tried to figure out a way to get the hell out of there without embarrassment but knew that the door was always locked to keep hooligans out. The leader was glowing with pride as she worked through the list of names towards mine. So far the poorest result had been thirty-two sixpences. When my name was called out my face was sweating, and my legs were trembling. I reached the lectern but felt that I was floating up to the ceiling. The leader took my card and looked at it in disbelief. "McLachlan, two sixpences", she murmured. "Is that all you could collect?" "Aye Miss, ah had tae put baith in masel, 'cos naebuddy ah knew wid gie me anythin'."

Bobby was afforded the same treatment. I sat on the bench seething with anger. As far as I was concerned they could shove their Lifeboys up their smug arses, sideways. At the first opportunity, I shot outside and went home. Mammy looked at my glowing face. "Whit's the maitter wi' you?" she asked. "Ah'm no gaun' back tae the stupit Lifeboys, everybody else had full cairds o' sixpences, an' ah had only two," I said through clenched teeth. "Aw ah kin say tae that is that some folk must hiv mair money than sense, tae gie good money tae ither folk, so that they kin travel aboot the wurld, wi' a' thir orders", said Mammy. "Ah'll trust missionaries the day they come tae oor door dishin' oot money instead o' askin' fur it".

When my father arrived home my mother told him what had happened. Predictably my father unpinned our badges from our Lifeboy jerseys, and threw them into the blazing fire, closely followed by the two sailor's hats. "The jerseys wull dae ye fur school, ur ah wid burn them as well", he grunted. "But Daddy, we're supposed tae haund thae uniforms back in", I cried. "Ah just took a wee shoart cut, if the buggers want them they kin poke aboot in the ashes, afore ye take them doon tae the midden", growled Daddy, and that was the end of the Lifeboys for us.

My father used the fire a lot to achieve order and tidiness. We had learned to our cost to make sure that any small toy or comic, or anything else, was tidied away before he came home. He never said anything, just picked up anything that wasn't in its proper place and chucked it straight into the fire. Our cries of distress were always ignored.

I remember the time well when he took his mouthful of broken and rotting teeth to the dental clinic, after days of agonizing toothache. The dentist decided that the only course of action was to put him under general anaesthetic, extract the lot, and send him home with a set of false teeth. I know it sounds far-fetched, but this was standard practice then. The gums were supposed to mould themselves to the teeth rather than the other way around. He arrived home just after we got home from school, with an expression that suggested that he had a mouthful of marbles that would escape if he as much as unclenched his jaws. My mother suggested that he should only have soup for the first week or so, to allow time for his gums to heal, and his false teeth to bed in properly. Speaking with difficulty out of the corner of his mouth, just like the Hollywood gangsters in the pictures, he said that he would rather have the meal of ribs and cabbage that had been prepared for supper.

The meal was duly served, and we glimpsed his new gleaming white teeth as he gingerly attempted to chew his food. After about five minutes, he stood up, walked over to the fireplace, removed his new teeth, and threw them into the fire. The fire flared up as the teeth were rapidly consumed. My mother was horrified. "Ye shouldnae have done that Allan, ye cannae dae withoot teeth, an' the dentist wullnae gie ye anither set." "Tae hell wi' the false teeth, ah couldnae enjoy eatin' wae thae things stuck in ma mooth," rejoined Daddy. He rinsed his mouth out under the cold tap and sat back down to his meal. Despite being in obvious pain, he managed to eat everything on his plate. He never went back to have a set of teeth fitted and carried on for the rest of his long life chewing as well as anybody equipped with a full set of teeth. His jaws never collapsed, giving no clue that he was toothless.

The winter of 1946/47 was bitterly cold, with heavy snowfalls, and unusually icy conditions prevailing for months at a time. My beloved Granny Cunningham was taken ill, too ill to allow visits by her numerous grandchildren. The severe weather produced a serious shortage of coal, with prices soaring higher than anybody could remember. Even if households were willing to pay the inflated prices, the coal merchants were forced to ration single bags of coal to loyal customers only.

The only alternative fuel supply was to buy by-product coke from the large gasworks at Eglinton Toll, but even this was subject to rationing, and it was too heavy to transport easily. We procured an old pram from somewhere. I was put in charge of stripping it down to the bare chassis and wheels. Our galvanized bathtub was then tied on top of the chassis and secured by lacing short lengths of clothesline through the end handles and lashing it down. My mother had to look after the younger kids, who were put into bed to try to keep warm, so it fell to me to have to trudge through the snow and freezing slush to the gasworks, trailing the wheeled bathtub behind me on a length of rope.

I was wearing an old navy blue trenchcoat which was several sizes too large, over my shorts and jersey, and a woollen balaclava, to protect me from the elements. Unfortunately, as usual, my shoes leaked badly because of holes in the soles. Within a few yards, ice cold water seeped in, soaking my socks and feet.

Squelching my way to the distant gasworks, with increasingly numb feet, the falling snow turned to soaking sleet, compounding my misery as it easily penetrated my clothing and balaclava. By the time I reached the gasworks I was soaked to the skin and couldn't even feel my feet or hands. As I reached the gasworks I saw that a long queue had already formed at the office. I waited in line in the driving sleet for what seemed to be an eternity.

My mother had given me a ten-shilling note, to ensure that I could afford to fill the bathtub. I couldn't even feel the note as I scrabbled around in my pocket and handed it to the man who was serving behind the counter. He looked down at my bathtub, using experience to guess how much coke it would hold. "That'll be six shullins son", he said as he handed me a paper slip and my change. Fumbling as I tried to put the change into my coat pocket, my numbed hand refused to cooperate, allowing the coins to fall into the deep slush. I was forced to kneel down in the deep mucky slush to try to find the spilt coins, helped by the kind man who was next in line.

He then helped me to get my right hand into my pocket. I shook my hand to drop the coins in safely. By this time the flimsy paper receipt had got so wet that it had disintegrated. The clerk had to give me a replacement, which held up proceedings, causing loud muttering from the queue behind me.

I then followed the rutted trail around the corner of the building. I was dismayed to find another long queue waiting to collect their coke, which was being shovelled from a large pile by a lone labourer into whatever container was presented. By the time I reached the head of the line, handed over my disintegrating ticket, and had got my bathtub filled to the brim, I was so cold that my teeth were chattering like castanets. I set off home, now with the heavy load to tow behind me. The sleet had now reverted to a full-on snowstorm, which was rapidly piling up on top of the slush.

The new snow looked much prettier, but my feet were still plodding through the freezing mushy wetness underneath, and the rapidly deepening snow was acting as a brake on the wheels. The effort of dragging the fully laden bathtub helped to keep my circulation going at a slightly higher temperature, but by the time I reached our closemouth I was so cold and exhausted that I had to sit on the coke for some minutes to recover. Somehow I found enough remaining energy to climb the stairs and pound on our door.

"Allan, Ah'm sae gled you're hame," said my mother, "Ah wis that worried aboot ye that ah was just thinking to leave the weans wi' Mrs Moloney an' come lookin' fur ye. Ah'll just put the kettle oan tae heat up while we get the pram up the sterrs." Getting this upstairs was more difficult than it looked, defeating all our pulling and pushing. Only by unloading the tub and using a shovel and bucket to transfer half of the coke to the coal bunker, were we able to wrestle the lightened pram up the stairs and into our lobby.

My mother used some of the newly arrived coke to bank up the ailing fire. I stood as close to the fire as possible, shivering violently, teeth chattering, and with my numb hands held as close to the flames as I could stand. My mother had to unload the remaining coke into the bunker, untie the tub, and give it a quick rinse, before pouring the boiling water into the tub and putting the refilled kettle back on the gas ring. "Oh, ye're soaked right tae the skin," murmured mother in distress as she unpeeled my layers of sodden clothing and put them into the sink. When the bathwater was ready, I crouched down into it, as my mother poured potfuls over my head and shoulders, to warm me as quickly as possible. "Ah hope that ye don't get yoomonia. Ah've never felt anybody sae cauld," said Mammy. "As soon as ye're warm an' dry, Ah'll make ye a big mug o' Bovril, an' hap ye up in some blankets in front o' the fire for a while."

I didn't contract pneumonia, as my mother kept me in a warm bed with two Irn-Bru bottles filled with hot water at my feet, until she was sure that I was in no danger. Luckily for me, Earnoch our coalman was able to keep us supplied with sufficient coal to keep our fires going for the remainder of that cruel winter, thus saving me from ever having to go to the gasworks again.

One Saturday morning in November 1947, Bobby, Alec and I were playing around the kitchen table. Mammy was busy at the other side, slicing bread for sandwiches. Someone rattled the doorknocker, using the family code. I opened the door to find Auntie Annie dabbing at her eyes with a hanky and looking very pale. Pushing past me without a word, she went straight over to my mother. Putting both arms around my mother's shoulders, she sobbed something into her ear. The effect on my mother was instantaneous. "Naw, no mah Maw!! No mah Maaaawww!!, she wailed in a keening voice that frightened the tripe out of the three of us.

She collapsed over the table, with loud sobs that racked her body. Auntie Annie came over to us, as we watched Mammy with a great deal of apprehension, dabbing at her eyes with her sodden hanky. "Dae you weans want tae come hame wi' me untae yer Mammy feels better?" she asked. "Whit's up, whit's ma Mammy greetin' fur?" I asked. "Yer granny's deid Allan, an' ye know how close yer Mammy was tae her, so it's nae wonder that she's taken it sae badly," sniffled Auntie Annie into her hanky. For me the news was an unexpected bolt from the blue. I had been vaguely aware that Granny Cunningham was ill, but to me she was such a strong determined and loving character, that I assumed that she would carry on forever, to be there for all of us when needed. As the terrible news sank in, tears jetted from my eyes, and I found it difficult to breathe. This was my first contact with death, and I was totally bereft. Ignoring everybody, I crawled under the recess bed, where I remained until well past bedtime, sobbing my little heart out.

The following day I still burst into tears every time I thought of Granny. My mother had got over her immediate grief and tried hard to console me, but it made no difference. Our Cunningham relations prepared for the funeral. Granny had left instructions that she wanted to be buried in the Reddoch family plot in the Southern Necropolis. This graveyard actually bordered the end of our street, although the main entrance was well down Caledonia Road.

I seem to remember that the funeral was held on a Wednesday. The funeral service was held in one of our local churches, but I can't remember which one. I don't think that we younger family members were allowed to attend. The weather on the preceding days had been horrendous, with the heaviest snowfalls and coldest weather recorded in living memory. No vehicular traffic was able to operate, so the roads and streets were buried in deep virgin snow. What I do remember very clearly was being hoisted up on someone's broad shoulders, to follow the poor men who were carrying Granny's coffin on their shoulders.

The only way to get the coffin to the cemetery was to carry it all the way. It was difficult to recognise most of the men attending, as everyone wore the gloves, overcoats, bonnets, and mufflers up as far as the nose, leaving only the eyes exposed. The snow was still falling thickly as the procession proceeded. Men took it in turns to go out in front of the lengthy procession, and break a track for the coffin bearers, who took turns carrying, and those following behind. The snow was as much as three feet deep for most of the way, making progress painfully slow.

Under normal conditions, we could have walked the whole length of Kidston Street, round into Caledonia Road, and been in the cemetery in less than fifteen minutes. Granny's funeral procession took about three hours to reach the graveside. The open grave had been dug the day before, but the poor gravediggers had to get down into the grave at the last minute to clear out the deep snow that had accumulated overnight and was still falling. The internment ceremony was carried out as speedily as possible, in order to reduce the threat of exposure and potential frostbite to the mourners, not to mention the poor freezing gravediggers who were waiting to fill the grave back in.

Getting home was almost as difficult, following the track made on the way to the cemetery, which was already being obliterated by the falling snow. We were lucky, as we lived in Kidston Street where the procession had set out from. Most of the mourners had to make their way home on foot to distant parts, as no tramcars or buses were able to operate in such deep snow.

Granny was buried, no question about that, but the saga was not yet over. One spring Sunday after the snows had finally melted, my mother's sisters held a get-together at our house. After lunch, everyone including me walked to the cemetery to visit the grave and pay our respects. The weather was still cold and bleak, so we walked briskly to keep warm.

Entering the graveyard through the elaborate gate house arch, our group headed over to the far right-hand corner where we had watched the coffin being interred. Her headstone had been ordered and paid for. Everyone agreed exactly on the precise spot where she had been buried, but no headstone or an additional inscription on any of the elaborate family memorials could be found. Although we knew otherwise, it appeared that Granny had vanished.

Mammy and her sisters were upset and were conferring over the matter of the missing grave site when Auntie Jean became suddenly agitated. "Ah feel that somebody horrible is right behind us, an' lookin' ower mah shooder", she said in a quavering voice. I had never known anything to frighten Auntie Jean, except for the snake's incident at Luss, and nor had her sisters. Without further discussion, they all sprinted towards the gate, leaving me to catch up as best I could. Outside the gate, and safely back in busy Caledonia Road, they stopped to get their breath back.

Gathering in a huddle, they all agreed that that they felt the same cold creepy feeling at the same time as Auntie Jean did. As was common at that time, they really believed in the supernatural and were ruled by superstition. As far as I can remember, the matter of the missing headstone was never followed up properly, or the precise location of the grave established. Despite the fact that we lived very close to the cemetery, my mother was so unnerved by the imagined ghostly presence that she never again went near the place.

A facet of Granny Cunningham's character that I have omitted to mention was that she had been much respected and widely known for her skill in reading teacups, for which she charged sixpence a time. Sessions were arranged regularly by her daughters, including Mammy, to allow neighbours to have their fortunes told.

On these occasions Granny would sit at our kitchen table looking extremely serious as women queued from our door down into the street, each clutching the teacup from which they had last drunk. Mammy would take the opportunity to do her shopping, taking all of us with her, in order to provide some privacy for the customers.

Despite this, I remember being allowed to watch Granny at work during one session. She was very serious, as she skilfully swirled each cup to get the best possible pattern of tea leaves, before draining the tea dregs into a jug. I was hugely impressed with my clever Granny, as she made her prognosis, using information easily gleaned from the chatter of the garrulous clients, to customise each prediction in a manner that made them excited and grateful.

The proof of Granny's gift or skill was the fact that her clients always came back for more. Granny wasn't in any way a charlatan, as she really believed that she had this special gift. The money was also very useful, as she invariably gave it to those of her daughters who were most in need.

Chapter 16

Auntie Annie had quietly moved from the room and kitchen above us in Kidston Street to what seemed to us to be a palatial three bedroomed, sitting room, bathroom, and separate kitchen home in Deanston Drive in Shawlands. She was then able to have my older cousin George discharged from Hairmyres hospital in East Kilbride, where he had been for some years after being invalided out of the Royal Navy on medical grounds. He was now living at home, but bedridden. I had often heard the name of George mentioned in conversations but had never met him.

My mother had to take us along, when she visited her sisters, as there was no other option available. During my first visit to Auntie Annie's house after George had come home, I was taken into his bedroom to be introduced. I immediately took a strong liking to him. He had been ill for some considerable time and was painfully thin. During his lengthy sojourn in hospital, he had accumulated a large number of books, jigsaw puzzles and other games. I was speechless when I saw a large Meccano set in a pristine box by his bed.

George and I hit it off straight away, despite the disparity in ages. I sat on his bed chattering away as we played cards and the many other games which were stacked up beside his bed. To me his bedroom was the ultimate Aladdin's cave. When the time came for leaving, he said that I could visit any time I liked as he had really enjoyed my company, as much as I had his. After this, more often than not I ran home to dump my schoolbag. I washed quickly under the cold tap (the only tap), and quickly made my way to the nearest stop where I could board a tramcar to Shawlands. My mother didn't mind as long as I returned home by 8pm.

Arriving at the Pattersons, I was sure of a warm welcome from George. Sitting on his bed and using a table that spanned his bedframe, we played various games for hours on end. At about 5.30 Auntie Annie would bring in a tasty meal for both of us. George didn't have much of an appetite and would push his plate away after having a few desultory mouthfuls. Auntie Annie would remonstrate with him, but to no avail, as he would just not eat any more. Always ready to eat everything and anything put in front of me, I invariably finished off his leftovers. Making bridges and cranes with the large Meccano set was our favourite activity.

I can't remember how long my special friendship with George went on, but it was many months if not years. One day my mother informed me when I came home from school, and was getting ready to go to Shawlands, that George was presently too ill for me to visit, but I could go to see him when he was feeling better. Weeks passed without news. I missed George greatly, as I had grown much fonder of him than anyone else I knew, excepting my own immediate family.

I don't think that my mother ever really understood how close George and I had become. This became plain when I was helping my mother to carry a heavy bag of vegetables and potatoes up to our house from Mathieson's fruit shop downstairs. As I was loading the stuff from the shop counter into our largest message bag, Mammy said quite casually, "Oh! Allan, Ah forgoat tae tell ye that young George Patterson died yesterday." I felt as if the whole building had collapsed on my head. Everything became a grey blur, and I dropped the message bag to the floor, with the contents spilling out. I ran from the shop and up the stairs, opened our door with my key, and crawled under the recess bed. I had sobbed my heart out when Granny died, but this was much more devastating. My world had been turned upside down without warning, and all I could do was cry as I had never cried before.

When Mammy came into the room she located me under the bed by the noise of my crying. Bending down and lifting up the valence curtain, she asked me what the matter was. Choking on my tears, I tried to speak but couldn't. "Ur ye greetin' aboot your cousin George?" she asked. "Ye must have known that he wis dyin'; everybody else did." I found the whole thing mystifying: how was I expected to know that George was dying?

To me death was something that only happened to very old people, or by sudden accident. The thought of my beloved cousin George dying had never crossed my mind. How could God allow such an inherently good and blameless person to die? I immediately lost my already tenuous faith in God and religion. My hurt and sorrow lasted for a lot longer than anyone realised. His games and Meccano set were passed down to his younger brother Bobby, who was about four years older than me. I was certain that he never even opened the boxes, as he never showed the slightest interest in them when his brother was alive.

I knew better than to ever expect my parents to buy such a luxury item as a Meccano set. During the time that I built many things with George's set, I had noted that the system was relatively simple, and could be duplicated easily by anyone with a proper workshop and access to suitable materials.

A workshop and materials were well beyond our resources. Drawing on my imagination, I started to collect the discarded sticks from the ice lollies that had just been introduced to the market. These were approximately the same size as the main Meccano pieces. I made a simple template out of tin with the same dimensions as the lolly sticks, with holes punched at each end. Each night I sat beside the fire, with that day's collection of lolly sticks.

As we had no drill, I heated a piece of wire of the desired dimension in the fire, using pliers to handle it. When heated sufficiently I held the tin template against the lolly stick and burned a hole through the stick by pushing the red-hot wire through the template hole. It was smoky and smelly, but it worked. When I had sufficient sticks bored to fill a large shoebox, I built a crane by using matchsticks to join the sticks by means of the holes. It wasn't as good as the real thing but it was much better than nothing. When my Aunties saw this and other models built from the same simple materials the next time the sisters' hen session was held in our house, they were very impressed. "Whaur does he get his imagination fae?" Auntie Jean asked Mammy. "If Ah gave any o' mah bliddy tribe a shoeboax full o' lolly sticks an' matchsticks, the only thing they wid build wid be a nice wee bonfire, an' likely burn mah hoose doon intae the bargain."

On some Saturday afternoons, Bobby and I were allowed to dress in the more presentable of our clothes and take the tram to Glasgow

Cross. This was our starting point for an afternoon of city centre window shopping, with no money to spend. We referred to this as 'Goin' Doon the Toon'. First stop was visiting the two pet shops at the Saltmarket, one on each side of Crown Street. After spending some time with our faces pressed against the shop windows, looking at the goldfish, canaries, budgies, kittens, day old chicks, and puppies, we set off down Argyle Street towards our main target, the Argyle Arcade.

The arcade was mostly tenanted by high class jewellery shops, selling expensive merchandise which was of no interest to us. Even if the ladies serving behind the counters had been dressed in nothing but samples of rare pearl necklaces and stiletto heeled shoes, performing erotic dances on top of the thick glass display counters, whilst throwing handfuls of five-pound notes in customers' faces as they entered, we would never have known. To us these expensive shops might as well have been located on Mars, for all the impact they had on our lives.

Entering from the Argyle Street end the arcade had a right-angle bend to the left halfway down. Our mecca, 'The Clyde Model Dockyard', was located right on the bend. It boasted large well-lit windows, displaying a dazzling range of brass and copper steam engines of all sizes mounted on highly polished wooden plinths. in addition, model warships, aeroplanes, tanks, artillery pieces, toy forts, beautifully painted lead soldiers, and model steam trains, were placed to best effect.

We spent ages staring with wide open eyes at the comprehensive range of models on display This was many years before affordable plastic models were introduced to the market. Everything here was constructed from genuine wood, metal, fabric, or glass. An amazing range of miniature metal parts, wood and fabrics was stocked. Numerous splendid hardback books on every aspect of model making were tastefully arranged on shelves.

My imagination ran riot as I pressed my face against the windows. Being penniless had its advantages, as there was no real impediment to dreaming about owning any or all of the items on display. We were not alone in this. Many other kids joined us in crowding around the windows, constantly jostling to get the best views. It was obvious that they too had no money. Kids didn't enter this shop unaccompanied; only expensively dressed adults did, sometimes with snooty looking children in tow, after pushing through the throng of penniless potential model enthusiasts milling outside.

Having looked and dreamed our fill, we exited the arcade, and sped across the street to Lewis's department store, which was at that time rightly recognised as being world class. To prevent unaccompanied children from entering the store, and possibly shoplifting, two large men were stationed at either side of the main entrance. For us to gain entry by just walking in was totally impossible, as one of the doormen would just grab us roughly by the scruff of the neck and deposit us outside on the pavement, to be told in unminced words that it would be very unwise to try again.

Having learnt this the hard way, we used our wits to get in. Being reasonably dressed, it was no great problem to split up and stay on the pavement well out of sight of the doormen and watch the ingoing customers carefully. As a suitable couple approached the door, one of us would walk beside them, as closely as possible, but lagging slightly behind, in order that they didn't know that they had just adopted a strange child.

As we passed through the door, we held a hand out towards one of the couple, as if reaching for a parent's hand, and talking loudly to ourselves as if conversing with the couple, and kept on walking, until we were safely out of sight of the doormen. We used this method of gaining entry to Lewis's for years, without once being stopped and ejected.

Once inside, our meeting place was the stair landing outside the entrance to the third floor. The third floor was magic to us, as it contained not only the Pets department, but the Toy department. The Pets department should have been better titled 'The Lewis's Zoo' due to the large and unusual range of animals sold there. It contained all the common sorts of pets sold in a regular pet shop, but there any comparison ended. Bear cubs, tiger cubs, lion cubs, snakes, baby alligators, chimpanzees, all sorts of monkeys, a multitude of parrots of different species, donkeys, and Shetland pony foals, were all displayed for sale. Who bought such expensive and potentially troublesome animals I never knew, but some people obviously did, as there was a high turnover of these exotic pets from week to week.

Spending an hour or two going from cage to cage was all too easy, for the time passed amazingly quickly. The toy department was next and last on our mental list of things to drool over. Staffed by young people yet to be bruised by life, and who obviously enjoyed demonstrating the latest toys and gadgets to hit the shelves, it was just great. Going from counter to counter with wide eyes, we kept ourselves up to date with the latest offerings from the international world of toys. I was always most interested in the sorts of toys that I could copy and build at home, using commonly available materials.

At chucking out time a loud bell rang to warn customers to leave the building and allow staff to lock up until the following Monday morning. Sunday trading was not even remotely on the radar screen in those days. Things have changed dramatically, so much in fact, that nobody living in the late forties and fifties would have believed just how far the scales would slowly be tilted in favour of commercial interests and practices.

If we had spent our penny for the tram fare on something very trivial, as we usually did, then it was a long walk home, turning right at the Trongate, and walking the whole length of Crown Street. On our walk home we would excitedly chatter about all the things that had most impressed us 'doon the toon'.

To make anything at home was very difficult, as there were few tools, and nowhere to work. The only place where I could safely make a mess with woodchips, shavings and sawdust was inside the coal bunker. I would lift the top of the bunker, climb inside, and crouch down on top of the coal. This was okay for quick rough work, but useless for any attempt to make a reasonable model, or anything of use around the house. Working at a crouch inside the bunker inevitably meant that I emerged aching with cramp and looking like one of the cast of 'The Black and White Minstrel Show'.

My salvation arrived when I was told by our teacher that evening classes in various hobbies were commencing shortly at our school, Camden Street. Despite being much younger than the organisers intended or foresaw, I was allowed to enrol in the woodwork class. The classes were held on Tuesday and Thursday evenings from six to eight pm. This was perfect for me, as I was now nine years old, and considered myself to be practically grown up. The first night was a revelation. The instructor/supervisor was a retired cabinetmaker and was very good at explaining things in a very patient manner.

The first hour was taken up with explaining which tools were which and what they were intended to be used for.

A lot of this was already known by my much older classmates, who ranged from about fourteen to forty years of age, but not by me. He also explained how to look after each tool, how to keep edges sharp, the necessity of returning items such as saws to the correct storage rack in order that they could be shared by everyone when needed. To find out the level of understanding and competence of his pupils, he gave everyone two pieces of dressed wood, identical in length and dimensions, along with a single sheet drawing and typed instructions outlining how to make a simple rebated cross. This seemed reasonably straightforward to me, but I had never used proper tools before. Going from bench to bench, he got everyone under way, leaving me to last. He explained how to use the necessary tools, and in which order.

Under his close guidance, I managed to finish my cross satisfactorily before the class finished for the evening. Looking around, I noted that some pupils had made a right old hash of it, ending up with two pieces of chisel-scarred kindling wood. I raced home to show everybody my rebated cross. "That's fantastic Allan, Ah'll put mah order in noo fur a new chist o' drawers an' wardrobe right away, so ye kin finish them aff afore the night school finishes," exclaimed Mammy, with a beaming face. This made me feel quite accomplished, as I put the cross on the mantlepiece for Daddy to see when he came home after his shift.

On the evening of the next class, the instructor listed possible projects on the blackboard, ranging from small cupboards, fretwork pipe racks, to some models. I made my mind up instantly, as I noted that second to last on the list was a model of a deep-sea trawler.

The instructor got everyone started on their chosen project, before attending to me last again. To help me get underway quickly, he cut the rough shape of the hull from a large piece of timber using a bowsaw.

I spent the next three or four classes shaping the hull correctly, with some help when needed. At last, the instructor declared his satisfaction with the finished and well sanded hull. "Ye should be right prood o' that, young Allan. Ah've worked wi' a loat o' so called tradesmen who couldnae dae as weel as that, if they wur chained tae their bench tae they goat it right," he said in satisfaction. "Noo ye kin make a start on the superstructure an' the fittin's." I was so proud of myself that I couldn't wait for the next class, to get ripped into the fancywork.

On the next class night, I was at the classroom door before anybody else. While I was waiting a scruffy looking boy about fourteen years old arrived, with the elbows out of his dirty jersey turned up, and who I hadn't seen before. "Is this the widwurk class?" he asked somebody further back in the queue. "Aye son, it is that", was the reply. The instructor duly arrived and opened up. The stranger spent some time talking to him at the lectern, before they walked over to my bench.

"Ah'm jist gonnae pit this new boy at the ither side o' yer bench, he tells me thit he's done a wee bit o' jinery work before, an' should be nae bother tae ye Allan, his name is Wullie." I wasn't that impressed with having to share my bench, but there was no other choice. The instructor returned with a handful of tools for Wullie. I took some of the superstructure parts to the bench down to the front of the room where the glue pots were simmering. It took some time to do the glueing and clamping to the instructor's satisfaction.

When I returned to my bench I noticed that some of my razor-sharp chisels were missing. Looking over to Wullie I could see that he'd taken them. "Hey, you, how are ye usin' mah chisels, an' no yer ain'", I called out. "Mine are a' bliddy blunt," he replied.

Even as I watched he was hammering one of my sharp chisels into the gap between two pieces of wood that he had roughly nailed together. I raced around the bench and grabbed my chisels, wrestling the one he was using out of his grip. It was too late, as the keen edge was already badly dented and turned over, as a result of being used as a miniature crowbar. Looking at my other chisels I saw that they also been damaged in the same manner.

Wullie saw that I was simmering with rage, but because he was much bigger and heavier than me he just laughed in my face. I took the butchered chisels over to the bench-mounted grindstone and oilstones. It took much careful work to restore all three chisels to the keen sharpness required to be of any use. Having been brought up in an environment where telling tales was greatly discouraged, I said nothing to the instructor, which turned out to be a serious error. Returning to the bench, I placed the chisels as far from Wullie's thieving hands as possible. Carrying on with my trawler superstructure, with Wullie being constantly disruptive, proved to be very difficult.

Wullie continued to taunt me. He kept reaching over to touch my chisels, withdrawing his hand quickly when I noticed him doing it out of the corner of my eye. I spun round to face him. "Stoap yer stupit noansense, ya fuckin' bampot, or ah'll loass mah temper wi' ye awthegither, then ye'll be sorry," I hissed at him to prevent being overheard by the instructor. "Aye, you an' who else is gonnae dae anythin' tae me, ye stupit wee cunt," he said.

He blatantly reached out a hand again towards my newly sharpened chisels. Without thinking I lashed out, forgetting that I was holding the narrow chisel with the blade downwards, striking down on his creeping hand. The chisel went straight through the back of his outstretched hand as if it wasn't there, pinning it solidly to the wooden bench top.

My face turned as white as Wullie's, as he looked down at his hand which was now enthusiastically spurting blood. He started screaming like a banshee. The instructor raced over, followed by the rest of the class. "Whit happened here?" he asked, trying not to panic. One of two men who were working at the adjoining bench spoke up. "That rotten bastart has been tormenting the life oot o' wee Allan ever since he goat here, we wur jist aboot tae gie him a good kick up the arse, an' a good skelpin' roon' the ear when Allan here loast his temper, an' gave him whit he was askin' for," one of them said. The instructor nervously wiggled the chisel free from the bench, and then out of Wullie's hand. Wrapping the punctured hand in a tea towel, he led the loudly wailing white-faced Wullie out of the door. "Whit should ah dae noo?" I asked the man who had stuck up for me. "Get aff yer mark son, an' run hame, oot o' the wey, ye'll likely hear fae the polis, but Alec here an' me wull stick up fur ye, so dinnae worry too much aboot that nasty wee shite, he hid it comin' tae him."

Taking this advice literally, I ran home. "You're hame early, whit happened tae get ye oot o' the widworkin' class afore chuckin' oot time?" asked Mammy. "Ah hope this disnae mean that mah furniture order'll be cancelled." I was still trembling and lost for words. "Ah goat intae a wee bit o' a fight Mammy, wi' a right heidcase that jist started the night," I replied. "How did that happen? Ah thoat that ye would be as safe as hooses at the widwork class", said Mammy. "Ah stabbed him through the haun' by mistake wi' wan o' mah widworkin' chisels, but it wisnae mah fault Mammy, honest it wisnae", I stammered.

Mammy stood thunderstruck, her face turning pale, as she said "Ye must be jokin', ye must think that ah'm daft tae believe that ye widnae ever stab anybody, it's no' in yer nature." "Ah know, but he wis tormentin' the life oot o' me an' ah jist meant tae gie him a right good bang on the knuckles wi' the haundle, but Ah was haudin' the chisel the ither wey roon'. The shairp end went straight through his haun afore ah could stoap it."

Mammy put on her coat and told Bobby that we were going round to the school to find out what was going on, and to look after the younger ones until we got back. We went straight to the classroom. There was no sign of Wullie, and the blood had been mopped up. Two hulking policemen were taking statements from the instructor and pupils. I wanted to run for it but Mammy held me tightly by the arm.

"Ah think ye'll be wantin' tae talk tae mah boy, if whit he telt me wis true," said Mammy to one of the constables. "Right ye are Missus McLachlan, we've goat his name and address written doon, but we've talked to everybody here already, an' it's fairly clear that your wee boy was severely provoked by this Wullie Magee. We'll take doon his side o' the story anyway, an' then you can take him hame. You can bring him roon tae Lawmoor Street efter school the morrow, but don't worry too much, that Wullie Magee is a real bad yin, an' we know him only too well." The police seemed to be treating the whole thing quite casually, but I was so relieved I felt like singing out loud. Mammy looked the same.

When we got home Daddy was there and asked what all the fuss was about. Between Mammy and me he heard the whole story, without saying a word. "Ah well," he said when we had finished explaining, "Ah wid likely have done the same in your place, only a damn sight quicker. Get intae yer bed wi' nae supper, tae make ye think a wee bit aboot whit happened the night." After school the next day Mammy took me to the police station to find out what was to happen to me. A grim looking sergeant led us into a small room and closed the door. Sitting down at the table he spent a long time reading through the reports and statements, making an occasional note in the margins.

Finishing at last, he looked at me in the eye for some time before speaking. "Right son, ye've done somethin bad that ye shouldnae have done, an' its nae laughin' maitter. Ah've read through a' the statements, an' it looks like this Wullie Magee boy caused a' the bother right enough, but that disnae mean that ye can jist go aroon' jabbin' shairp chisels intae other folks' haunds. Ah can tell you that Wullie Magee was only at the night school last night because his probation officer, who must be the usual bliddy eedjit bampot, had him enrolled tae learn somethin' useful, an' tae keep him aff the streets, an' oot o' aw the trouble that he always gets intae."

"Despite a' that Ah have tae dae mah joab, an'gie ye some sort o' punishment, so that ye don't think that ye're gettin' aff scoat free", he muttered whilst he pondered. "Ah hear that ye really enjoy the widwork classes, so if ye're no' allowed tae go back, that'll be punishment enough." He was exactly right, and I was devastated. I so much wanted to finish off my trawler.

Walking back home, Mammy was thrilled that the police had been so understanding and had let me off with only a severe warning and expulsion from the night classes. I was not so sure, as I would have preferred sweeping the police station floor for a month, or something similar. The only consolation was that I had acquired some woodworking experience and now knew how to handle and look after tools properly.

Chapter 17

During the war, we awoke on Christmas mornings early in a frenzy of excitement, eager to open the few brown paper parcels that Santa Claus had laid on top of our blankets. To find a simple cheap colouring-in book, some wax crayons, or a small second-hand toy motor car which had seen better days, and been passed on by one of our aunties, was more than enough to keep us happy. It was the best that my mother could do. Additionally, instead of just plain porridge and rolls for breakfast, we had two fried potato scones and two slices of black pudding each. Eggs, fruit, chocolate, and many other goodies were only available on the black market, at prices well beyond our reach. We had never seen any of these things except in films.

Scotland at that time didn't observe Christmas as a public holiday, so apart from children's excitement it was another workday like any other. The New Year was the real celebration looked forward to by everyone. New Year's Day was the only proper official public holiday in the Scottish calendar, as far as I can remember. Every year, about two or three weeks before the New Year, more usually referred to as Hogmanay, or Ne'erday, it was customary, at least within our extended family, to strip the existing wallpaper from the walls, and with new wallpaper and/or paint, completely redecorate the house before New Year's Eve.

Luckily for us my lovely Aunties, particularly Jean, Annie, and Bella, were skilled in redecorating houses with minimal spending on materials. During the course of the year, as they went about their daily business, they always watched out for any bargains in wallpaper and paint. These were purchased and stored under someone's bed until needed. The modest costs were met cooperatively, as enough material was purchased to decorate the house of everyone in the material pool.

When the time came to prepare for redecoration, we all joined in with great excitement. Wielding wet rags, we stood on kitchen chairs, and soaked a section of wallpaper at a time. As it visibly swelled we attacked it with any suitable tool or just our fingernails, peeling it off in great swathes, and carrying great armfuls down to the midden, as it piled up on the floor. Once the paper was removed it was startling to see the vast difference in appearance between the paper that had been exposed to our indoor environment and the places which had been hidden behind an occasional overlap.

Our house wasn't very large, so the wallpaper removal didn't take any more than a day. Came the big day when Auntie Jean and Auntie Bella arrived, complete with rolls of wallpaper under their arms and a large can of distemper gripped in a spare hand. Auntie Annie was working two jobs as usual, so nobody expected her to do decorating as well. I liked listening as Jean and Bella prepared everything, all the time using technical terms that I had never heard before. The first task was to whitewash the ceilings, so the kitchen table and floors were covered in newspapers.

Standing on the kitchen table, and using a proper whitewash brush, Jean didn't take long to do the kitchen ceiling. The contrast between the new whitewash, and that of a year earlier, was a revelation, as the year-old surface now looked dull grey in comparison. It was decided to do the kitchen completely first as the table would have to be dismantled to get it through the lobby and into the bedroom. After finishing the ceiling, the top section of the walls was given two coats of pastel yellow distemper.

Now came the difficult part. Bella had been trimming the protective selvedge from the wallpaper, which was a critical and painstaking job. Next came the part that we children liked best, making the paste by adding flour gradually to a basin of water, stirring all the time, until the mixture was the consistency of thin porridge. Jean and Bella worked as a team, hanging the wallpaper. Mammy laid the next drop upside down on the table ready for pasting, which I did with gusto. At the same time, we three kids were dipping our fingers into the basin and licking off the paste. We thought that it tasted just fine, until Auntie Jean threatened to kick our arses for slowing things down and making a mess of our clothes.

It took about two days to have the house looking tip top. I was very impressed with my Aunties' skills and sheer competence. Their houses were next, so we trooped along with Mammy, as she acted as decorator's labourer, and helped in stripping paper and carrying the rubbish down to the midden.

Another task undertaken just before Hogmanay was the making of a very large suet pudding known locally as a dumpling. Mammy had been buying the necessary ingredients for some weeks, in order that we weren't caught out at the last moment.

During the mixing of the ingredients, which included currants and raisins, we were banished from the house, as the temptation to scoff handfuls of everything was just too much for us to resist. When mixing was finished, some silver sixpenny pieces were added. The dumpling was then rolled around the floured table until it assumed the size and shape of a soccer ball.

This was then placed inside a freshly laundered pillowslip tied tightly above the raw dumpling. Cooking was accomplished by suspending the pillowslip in the copper boiler in the washhouse from a broomstick handle spanning the boiler. This took most of the day, whilst we fed firewood into the grate underneath, as if our lives depended on melting the whole thing down for scrap.

By the time Hogmanay arrived our excitement was at fever pitch. Christmas had nothing on this. We were allowed to stay up until after midnight to see the New Year in. The table was covered by a brand-new dazzling white tablecloth. As far as we were concerned, the very best goodies known to man were laid out, with the large aromatic dumpling as the centrepiece. Bottles of 'ginger' (all soft drinks of whatever flavour or manufacture were generically referred to as 'ginger' in Glasgow) were laid out in rows, together with a large bottle of ginger wine.

Until Daddy was demobbed from the army no alcoholic beverages were bought. Apart from Auntie Jean, all my mother's sisters were implacably opposed to strong drink. Mammy herself didn't drink but wasn't quite as fanatical as the others about opposing it. Whisky then was strictly rationed, with people queuing up for hours on Friday nights outside each 'off licence' store to collect their gill of spirit, which they would decant at home into a larger bottle to save for the Hogmanay night celebrations.

At around ten pm visitors, mainly relatives, would begin to arrive. This was the signal for us to hoe into the goodies, taking no prisoners. With a bottle of ginger each, clamped in a death grip in our left hands to swig from periodically, and with our right-hand conveying goodies to our mouths like a demented soldier repeatedly saluting, it was easily the best night of the year. While we rapidly transformed the plates of food into plates of crumbs, we were mindful that we had to leave room for at least one or two large slices of dumpling when this was cut. "Wull you weans mind leavin' somethin' fur everybody else," Mammy would call out every few minutes. We would stolidly ignore her, as we wouldn't get a chance like this for another twelve long months.

When the minute hand of the clock neared midnight, our large 'Echo' push-button cabinet wireless would be tuned into the local radio station, in order to hear the commentary and midnight bells in George Square, where large numbers of mostly drunk people had already congregated. By the time that the bells started chiming, over half of those present could easily have been certified as being clinically blind. They swayed dangerously, holding on to each other to prevent themselves falling over.

Safely at home, everybody in the house cheered as the bells chimed midnight, singing 'A guid New Year tae wan an' aw", and all the following verses. Now was the time to take lumps of coal from the lobby bunker to hold as we knocked on neighbours' doors and went 'firstfooting'. We were invariably greeted with great enthusiasm and given a small glass of non-alchoholic ginger or elderberry wine. After visiting the neighbours, and them visiting us, we were given our long-awaited slice of dumpling, and packed off to bed in the adjoining room, leaving the grown-ups to carry on celebrating.

Hogmanay was the only time during the year that I left the table without feeling that I could eat another two or three meals immediately. The dumpling would be last us for some weeks, and when it got stale the slices were deep fried before serving.

You may think that our family lived on the brink from payday to payday. We did, but many families were much worse off than we were. Some kids didn't attend school, as they literally had no clothes to wear. Attempts by the parish authorities to clothe them, admittedly in the easily identifiable rough brown tweed jackets, grey shirts, brown jerseys and socks, finished off by solid hobnailed boots to be worn by both sexes, were frequently thwarted. Their drunkard fathers, and sometime mothers, would often pawn even these rough clothing items in order to buy alcohol.

One of my best friends at primary school was Jimmy Meachan, who lived in Thistle Street. In contrast to most of us he was invariably well turned out, wearing smart tweed jackets, well pressed shorts, smart shirt and tie, and highly polished shoes. His brother, about four years older, was also always dressed immaculately. My mother was always impressed by Jimmy's turn-out. "How is it that Jimmy kin play wae aw youse at school and then go hame jist as smairt as when he left, withoot gettin' a' covered in glaur an' clabber like you dae?" she would ask as I dumped my schoolbag on top of the coal bunker. The answer to that riddle eluded me also. "Ah dinnae know how he dis it Mammy, maybe his claes are jist like the wans that Superman an' Captain Marvel wear, fur they fly aboot the hale world, crashin' straight through mountains and skyscrapers, withoot gettin' their claes torn or even a wee bit durty.".

It wasn't the local practice for kids to be allowed to enter other people's houses. We might knock on the door to talk or to collect our playmates, but we always waited outside on the landing. One day Jimmy and I were going to the Palace picture hall together, and Mammy had ensured that I was well turned out, as Jimmy undoubtably would be.

I walked to his close in Thistle Street and knocked on the Meachans' first floor door. The door was opened by a woman dressed in a wraparound apron; her hair hidden under a turban. I assumed that this was Jimmy's mother, as I had never seen her before. She looked older than I would have expected, with a sallow olive skin, and dark circles under her eyes. "Is Jimmy ready tae go oot?" I asked. "Ye're a wee bit early, so he's no quite ready, son. Ye might as well as well come in an' wait fur him," she said.

I stepped inside hesitantly. Jimmy was busily polishing his shoes as if his life depended on the result. "Ah'll no' be long, Allan," he said. As I waited I couldn't help but look around the room. It was about the same size as our kitchen, with the bed recess curtains fully drawn, but there the similarity ended. The centre piece of the room was a peculiar sort of armchair. The seat and wooden armrests were normal, but the covering and upholstery of the outer chair wings and chairback had been removed, and the cavities created now contained rows of narrow shelves on which were located tins of boot polish, brushes, and all sorts of small paraphernalia, which would normally be stored within a kitchen cupboard. I could see no other furniture apart from a small table situated against the wall underneath a windowsill and four dilapidated kitchen chairs. On the table, about half a dozen small size jam jars were sitting upside down. "Wid ye like a wee cup o' tea while Jimmy finishes getting himself ready?" asked Mrs Meachen. Anxious to be polite, I said "aye please". She removed an ancient, enamelled tin teapot from the small sink side counter and picked up one of the jam jars, (jeelyjaurs), and sitting this the right way up, put a large spoon into the jar before pouring tea into it. Adding milk and sugar, she handed me the jar. "It might be a wee bit hoat yet, so leave the spoon in tae it's cauld enough tae drink withoot burnin' yer mooth," she counselled.

I had vaguely heard of families who were too poor to afford crockery, but the Meachans would have been the last family to be included in this category, if I had been asked to guess one. She then poured tea into another two jam jars, after putting in spoons, for herself and Jimmy. Neither showed the least hint of embarrassment, so I concluded that they thought that drinking tea out of used jam jars was perfectly normal. When the tea had been drunk, Jimmy and I set off. Looking at Jimmy's immaculate appearance in the street, anyone seeing him could be excused for assuming that he was a junior member of a well-to-do family.

After the pictures Jimmy and I split up at the end of Caledonia Road to make our separate ways home. Mammy was in the almost daily habit of using Jimmy's appearance and polite behaviour as an example, as she railed at me for kicking the toes out of my shoes or boots and getting filthy playing football and other street games. I couldn't wait to get home to tell her about the spartan appearance of the Meachans' house and the apparent absence of furniture or crockery. "Ah'm telling ye Mammy, we hid tae drink oor tea oot o' jeelyjaurs," I said in exasperation, as she refused to believe me. "An' they've only goat an auld chair wi' the back an' sides full o' wee shelves, fur keepin' a' the things thit ye keep in the kitchen press."

Mammy paused, as the description of the weird chair was too outlandish, even for someone of my fertile imagination to have thought up. "My God! She must spend everythin' oan her weans' backs, nae wonder that her boys are always dressed tae the nines. Ah wid raither spend oor money oan things tae eat an' drink, an real cups, saucers an' plates tae put oan mah table, than oan fancy claes that ye only grow oot o' afore ye get yer money's worth," said Mammy. This put an absolute and final damper on her daily comparisons between me and Jimmy Meachan. She never mentioned his name again in that context.

Chapter 18

My pals and I grew older, but most definitely not wiser. We roamed far wider than our immediate home territory. One place that we found that we could venture to, to explore and play in the non-asphalted or unconcreted outdoors, and without encountering the snarling wrath of park attendants, was a large expanse of swamp, bog, burns and scrub known as Mall's Myre, wasn't too far from the famous Hampden Park football stadium. It took about half an hour to get to the fringe of this sodden miniature wilderness by tramcar or about an hour on foot. In many ways this was a potentially dangerous place to be, but once we were there we were free to do almost anything that we wanted to without check, including being maimed, drowned, poisoned, or incinerated.

On arrival at the Myre the first place to head for was the imposing slag heap, which was constantly growing in area as the slag trains arrived to dump their half egg shaped loads, twenty-four hours a day. As the dumping face became overcrowded the top was bulldozed, and the complete rail line moved closer to the freshly created escarpment edge. This allowed the 'half egg' shaped slag wagons to tip their molten contents over the edge for a few months. When the tipping face became too crowded, the bulldozing and line repositioning was repeated. It was some time before I realized that the slag train came directly from the furnaces of Dixon's Blazes, at all times running on land owned by the ironworks.

Our lengthy journey from home, which directly abutted the ironworks, to the "Mallsy", as we called it, created an impression of great separation in terms of distance. We had no idea that the activities of the ironworks were spread over such a vast area of land.

As the slag train chugged along the top edge of the ever-expanding slagpile, my friends and I gathered about fifty yards away, directly under the anticipated dumping spot. The tank locomotive pushed the heavy slagwagons along the rails and stopped, with the thick black smoke which had been issuing from its chimney changing to a light grey. Two men descended from the engine footplate and walked along the track to the first wagon. Rearranging the heavy chains looping around a large projecting lug on the near side of the wagon they prepared the vessel for dumping. The heavy cast-iron container, shaped like a monstrous egg cup without a base, was decoupled from the others, and the handbrake locked on.

As the locomotive reversed, the chain tightened, pulling down on the lug, tipping the container through ninety degrees, and releasing its load of slag to tumble down the steep slope. This procedure was repeated until all the vessels were empty. Afterwards the locomotive and empty vessels chugged back to the furnaces for the vessels to be refilled. Depending on the amount of time that the slag had been sitting in the vessel, the dumped slag would behave in one of three different ways.

If fresh, the slag would pour out of the vessel just like white-hot molten lava and run splashing down the face to the bottom. If it was not so fresh, it would exit the vessel like half of a gigantic egg, to burst open as it smashed its way down the face, releasing the molten contents in a thick spray from the solidified outer shell. If the slag had compacted after having been waiting around for some considerable time before dumping, the solid lump of slag would bounce down the face without bursting, leaving the half egg shaped lump intact and able to roll past the bottom of the face, forcing us to scatter out of the way as it bounced erratically towards us.

The men carrying out the dumping never seemed to pay any attention to the crowd of kids standing at the bottom. We would edge as closely to the freshly dumped slag as the radiating heat permitted. To us this was exciting stuff, and well worth the trip. Having collected a large pile of tree branches in readiness, these were now thrown on top of the new slag, where they instantly exploded into flame, to be reduced to fine ash in a matter of minutes. Edging ever closer to the new slag until forced to stop by smoking boots or shoes and overheating feet, we continued to muck around with the hot slag, until we got bored and wandered off to the nearest area of swamp or pond.

One thing can always be guaranteed when a group of small boys plays in or near water. Sooner or later, everybody will be totally or partially soaked to the skin. During the war, anti-aircraft batteries had been located on Mall's Myre, being sited on raised clay mounds which dotted the swamps and connected by raised causeways. The causeways had been removed on cessation of hostilities, leaving the barbed wire enclosed overgrown mounds as islands.

As you might expect, these islands made ideal pretend forts, for us to defend and invade, by splitting up into two groups. Wooden swords and bamboo bows and arrows, supplemented by piles of small pieces of slag for throwing at the enemy position, constituted our armouries. We took turns at attacking or defending. The elected chief of each band tossed a penny to decide who would attack or defend first. The winner invariably chose to defend. The attacking band was forced to ford the intervening swamp from their fort, whilst the defenders' rained arrows and stones down on them. The footing between the islands was totally unpredictable. The attackers carried homemade wooden shields of all shapes and sizes, to protect themselves against the hail of stones and blunt arrows let loose by the defenders.

By the time the attackers reached the fort, most if not all were soaking wet from head to toe, as they stumbled over underwater tangles, falling into areas of deeper water on the way across. Now they had to climb up the steep sides and negotiate a way through the tangles of rusty barbed wire surrounding the defenders. Thoroughly soaked, shivering, and frequently bleeding from various injuries inflicted by stones or arrows, the attackers seldom made it to the top, where the defenders in warm dry clothes were eagerly waiting to engage them in hand-to-hand combat.

Rather than face further injuries, it was almost mandatory for the chief of the attackers to call out to his men at this point, to retreat from this one-sided battle to their own island. As they headed back, another hail of stones followed them. Walking backwards through the swamp, in order to protect themselves with their shields, they fell over into the murky water even more frequently than before. Reaching their own island, they rested for a while before calling out to the other side to commence attacking.

Now everything happened in reverse, with a similar result, leading to everyone eventually heading home sopping wet, shivering, and looking like they had just been hauled through a muddy swamp backwards, which was in fact exactly what had happened. We discarded our hurriedly made weapons, except for the bows and arrows, and made for home.

Returning home by tram from the nearby terminus was always problematic, as invariably the conductress, or clippie in the vernacular, would swiftly spread her arms wide and block our way on to the platform. "Holy Jesus Gallopin' Christ!!! Whit big pile o' soakin' wet rotten shite hiv you weans been rolling in? Ye're no' gettin' oan mah caur in that state. If Ah was stupit enough tae let youse oan the caur an' everybody in it wid hivtae be inoculated against ten thousan' diseases," she would howl, with her nose firmly clamped between her fingers. Her piercing voice probably reached as far as the English border and beyond. "Ah widnae like tae be any o' youse, when ye chap oan yer mammie's door tae be let in. She'll nae doot tell ye tae go straight doon tae the side o' the midden, an' wait fur the middenmen tae take ye away during the night, alang wi' the rest o' the rubbish."

The passengers waiting to board the tramcar hung back, waiting for our departure before venturing anywhere near the tramcar. As we shivered in our saturated clothing and footwear we had to decide on one of two choices. We could run all the long way home shivering and wet or walk all the long way home shivering and wet. I always chose to run, as did the majority. The minority walked, getting colder and more miserable by the minute. Running at least kept us warmer, if not totally comfortable. As I ran the soles of my saturated cheap shoes began to separate from the uppers, making a shloop slap shloop noise at every step.

The moment of truth arrived when I got home and knocked at the door. The clippie was dead right, Mammy would go berserk when she saw the state that I was in. She opened the door, and shrieked "In the name o' the wee man, did ye dive heid furst intae Jenny's Burn, an' swim aboot in it a' day?" Jenny's Burn was a massively polluted stream which fed into the River Clyde near Richmond Park. It looked and smelt dreadful, with the water, if you could call it that, resembling thick dark green porridge, interlaced with large everlasting bubbles. It was rumoured that rats, cats and small dogs could walk safely across the surface without sinking, but their paws dissolved within half an hour, leaving them hobbling around on the stumps. The peculiar acrid smell, if one was brave or silly enough to approach closer than fifty feet, was so bad that it took the breath away. We knew that nothing in the whole world could possibly be as polluted as Jenny's Burn.

We now had a standoff, with Mammy keeping the door on the chain as we conversed. She went away briefly, returning with the ubiquitous galvanized bathtub, saying "If Ah open the door jist a wee bit tae let the bath through, ye kin jist take aff a' yer claes an' put them intae it. Then ye kin leave it ootside an' run inside an' get yersel' straight intae the sink this minute." I undressed in a flash, in case anybody came up the stairs, dashed to the sink, and climbed in shivering violently.

Mammy filled a pot from the freezing cold running tap, and tipped the water over my head, as she muttered grimly, "Ah dinnae know whit we're goin' tae dae wi' you, ye cannae be trusted tae go oot an' play withoot ye comin' hame covered in clabber an' god knows whit else, where the hell hiv ye been playin' a' day?" "We aw went tae Mall's Myre tae watch the train tippin' the rid hoat slag, an' then played auld fashioned sodgers, wi' widden swords, shields, an' bo' n'arras," I replied. "Ye didnae get intae that bliddy disgustin' state jist playin' wi' thae things, waur did ye get so wet an' durty?" she retorted angrily.

"Everybody fell intae the swamp while we were attackin' the ither side's fort, ye cannae help it 'cos ye hiv tae cross a loat o'durty watter tae get there," I replied, truthfully but lamely. Mammy had never been to the large area of swampland and was never likely to.

There was no way out. I shivered increasingly, as Mammy scrubbed me from head to toe with red carbolic soap, rinsing me at intervals with potfuls of freezing water. At last, she pronounced me fit to rejoin the human race. I leapt out of the sink, grabbed the waiting dry towel and stood as close to the fireplace as my behind could stand, scrubbing away as vigorously as I could, my teeth chattering.

As I dried myself by the fireplace, Mammy brought the bathtub inside. She dumped the whole shebang into the sink and proceeded to rinse the stinking mess under the tap at full bore. Our normal water pressure was so high that you risked losing a finger or two, if a hand was placed under the tap when it was turned on to maximum flow. She rummaged around to find my shoes. Picking these up, she exploded in another bout of fury. The cheap soles looked like rapidly delaminating cardboard, peeling away from the shoes as we watched. "That's the last o' thae shoes, unless ye want tae wear them tae school as spats, wi yer bare feet stickin' oot below them. How dae ye think that Ah'm gonnae get new wans fur ye tae wear tae school? Ah hivnae any spare money tae buy any, unless ye don't mind everybody in the hoose starvin' tae yer Daddy gets his next week's pey."

As always Auntie Annie came to the rescue, when Mammy told her what had happened. She rummaged around her cupboards until she found a hardly worn pair of shiny shoes that my older cousin Bobby had grown out of. They were about two sizes too big for me, which was instantly fixed by ramming pieces of crumpled newspaper into the toe space. "Ye should try tae keep away fae watter, an' think aboot a' the trouble ye cause yer poor mammy, by ruinin' yer shoes an' claes a' the time," said Auntie Annie.

I sheepishly hung my head and resolved to do much better in future. I kept to my promise for a few weeks, but eventually succumbed to the call of the wild one warm Saturday morning, when the rest of our gang were setting out for Mall's Myre. They were jeering at me for being a mammy's boy. So I tagged on behind, unable to resist temptation as usual. This time I removed my shoes and socks as soon as we arrived at the swamps. I tied the laces together and hung them round my neck, keeping to relatively shallow water no deeper than my knees.

This time my shoes kept dry for most of the day, until I eventually tripped over an underwater obstacle and fell face first into water so deep that I was totally submerged. Wetting my new shoes was bad enough but losing them as I thrashed around underwater was a major calamity. Spluttering to the surface I realized that my shoes had gone.

Once I reached dry ground, or more correctly, less boggy ground I started to think about what I was going to tell my long-suffering mother. I set out for home, saturated and with bare feet, and thinking hard. For Glasgow it was a very hot day. By the time that I tiptoed all the way home, avoiding walking directly on the tender soles of my feet, my clothes were relatively dry, if a little smelly.

I knew for sure that Daddy would flay my backside unmercifully with his heavy army webbing belt with brass buckles, if he or Mammy found out that I had lost my shoes in Mall's Myre. Taking the easy way out, I told my furious mother that I had removed my shoes and socks at the side of the concrete paddling pool in Richmond Park, to paddle around, and returned to find that someone had stolen them and run away. Thankfully, this story was believable, as theft was rife locally. I received nothing more than a relatively mild skelping from Daddy using his bare hand. From then on I was careful not to walk in the swamps at all when playing at Mall's Myre.

Chapter 19

From a very early age, there were two things that I most wanted. The first was a proper leather football (a 'blether'). The other was a proper aquarium.

On the morning of my ninth birthday, my father pulled a brand-new three-quarter size bicycle from under the kitchen recess bed where it had been hidden. It was still wrapped in protective corrugated brown cardboard. "It's an Elswick, the very best bike that ye kin buy, nae doot aboot that," he said proudly as he removed the wrapping. "Whit dae ye think aboot tha' fur a birthday present?" he said to me, positively glowing with pride.

I had never had a birthday present before and was not expecting one. I couldn't even ride a bicycle, and I knew nobody that had one as sophisticated as this. I could just imagine the reception that I would receive, trying to learn to ride such a posh bike in the street, while everybody jeered. The nastier individuals would no doubt jealously thrust a stick through the spokes of the front wheel, when I was wobbling around, and badly damage both the bike and me. There would be no escaping these vicious bastards, the curse of the slums.

I had no concept of hurting Daddy's feelings, as I had never really seen him exhibiting any, apart from him telling jokes or demonstrating his undoubted prowess in confounding us by solving mathematical puzzles with ease. We knew that he used some sort of trickery but could never figure out how he did it. "Ah dinnae want a bike, Ah wid rather hiv a blether or an aquarium," I replied. There was no doubt that he had spent a relatively large sum on the bike and was taken aback by my response.

For once he looked stunned and disappointed. "It's nae use buying ye a blether, fur it wid only get stolen by bigger boys the furst time that ye took oot it tae play wi'," he said with conviction. I should have agreed with him, as he was right, but I was in too contrary a mood at the time to do so. "Well, how aboot an aquarium?" I asked boorishly. "An aquarium wullnae get ye oot o' the hoose an' take ye away fae these durty streets, an' get ye oot intae the fresh air o' the country," he grunted with a grim face.

"Ah cannae even go a bike, an' ah don't know how tae get tae the country by maself," I countered. "Ah'll show ye how to go yer bike, ye'll soon learn how tae dae it. If ye don't want tae learn in the street, ah'll take ye tae the Queens Park fitba' pitches, so ye wull hiv plenty o' room tae fa' aff wi' naebody tae see ye," my father replied.

An Elswick bicycle was top of the range, and Father had spent seven pounds to buy it, even though he had bought it from a fellow bus conductor who always had something to sell. This man must have spent every waking hour when he was not working running behind lorries, which invariably had goods precariously balanced on the open tailgate which fell off when the driver accelerated. Performing his civic duty by keeping the road clear, he took home for safekeeping whatever had fallen off the back of the lorry. When an hour or so had passed without the goods being claimed by the owner, he exercised his illegal right to sell them to defray the considerable out of pocket expenses incurred during collection and storage.

I continued to act like a fully paid-up spoilt brat when it came to learning how to ride the new bike. Every time that my father tried to take me to Queens Park, I made myself scarce, or claimed to be suffering from a migraine headache, which I was known to be prone to. This wasn't necessarily a lie, as I genuinely suffered from these at all too frequent intervals.

Inevitably, my father grabbed me one summer afternoon, as he held the bike in his other hand. He marched me all the way to the Queens Park recreational grounds. Patiently he demonstrated how easy it was to ride a bike. Determined to be as difficult as possible, I repeatedly fell off, as soon as he let go of the saddle which he had been steadying me with.

The surface of the football pitches consisted of coarse cinders, the size and texture of pieces of volcanic scoria, obviously designed to encourage and train players to stay on their feet at all times. Falling over meant that any skin, knees or elbows contacting the ground were instantly shredded, leaving a myriad of puncture holes which precious blood could spurt freely from. The cinder surface efficiently served another purpose, as it was capable of absorbing gallons of escaped blood, without showing any visible signs of the spillage.

Falling on the face was to be avoided at all costs. If this inadvertently happened, it was certain that even your own mother would fail to recognise you when you arrived on her doorstep. Additionally, the terrible pain caused by injuries to the face was dreadful, with the shredded wound retaining numerous minute razor-sharp particles of grit deeply embedded in the flesh.

The grand finale of learning to ride the bike occurred when my father realised that I only fell off when I knew that he had let go of the saddle. Despite my determined arseholeosity, I was learning to ride whether I liked it or not. We had finally completed four or five circles around the outside perimeter of the pitches, without me falling off, when my father cried in exultation, "Ye've been riding the bike a' this time by yersel' while Ah wisnae even haudin' oan tae the saddle." Hearing this I immediately fell off, adding to my numerous wounds.

For my father this was the last straw. He was totally silent and grim as he pushed the now not so pristine bike home as I painfully walked beside him, nursing the injuries received from falls from the bike. Only when we reached home and were sitting at supper around the table did he break his silence, saying to my mother, "That's the last straw fur me Jessie, Ah'm gonnae sell that bloody bike, fur the determined wee bugger disnae deserve it. Ah know a guy at the garage who wants wan like that fur his boy. At least it might be appreciated." I pretended that I didn't care what he did with the bike, but deep down I was really ashamed of how I had acted towards my father. I just had no idea how to admit this openly.

Just some months after the bike had been sold off a derelict shop in Camden Street was taken over by an enterprising young man. He hired out old decrepit bikes of all types and sizes at thruppence an hour, at the same time being kept busy fixing the elderly rattlers as they were often returned with various faults. Riding these often brakeless machines around the block became so popular that every kid that I knew was doing it, teaching themselves to ride a bike in next to no time.

Cycling had now become the latest neighbourhood craze. I was keen to join in but knew that asking for thruppence from my parents to hire a rubbishy old bike would be seriously suicidal. I had to be content with begging for a brief ride from someone else who had hired a bike. Of course, I found that I could ride a bike with no problem. Within a few months the majority of my playmates were riding around proudly on bicycles of their own, even if they were mostly second hand. I was left right out of things now, as everybody rode off to one of the many parks which were within easy riding range.

In sheer desperation I summoned up sufficient courage to broach the subject with my father. Trying to pick a suitable moment I sidled up to him as he was sitting by the fire after supper, reading the evening paper and smoking his Capstan cigarette. "Daddy, ah know that Ah didnae want a bike when naebody else in the street hid wan, noo everybody except me has goat wan. Ah don't want a new wan, any auld bike wull dae me," I said in voice hardly louder than a whisper. He sat still, giving no sign that he had heard me.

Encouraged by the fact that he hadn't jumped to his feet and skelped me hard on the nearest ear, I stupidly started to repeat my request. Before I got more than the first word out, he slowly lowered his newspaper until I could see his rapidly reddening face and bulging eyes. I now knew that I had been extremely unwise, to the point of lunacy, in broaching the sore subject of bicycles.

He jumped to his feet, shouting at the top of his voice. "Ah'll gie ye bike!!! Ye cantankerous wee bastart, ah'll gie ye bike!!!! If ah live tae ah'm a hundert years auld, an' won the treble chance oan the fitba' pools every second week durin' that time, ah widnae gie ye as much as a frozen green snotter tae buy a bike." Needing no further warning that my father was seriously considering the most painful method of killing me, I wheeled around and sprinted towards the door, wrenching it open in desperation, and jumped straight down to the next landing without touching a step.

I repeated the downhill long jump from the landing to the close and ran away down the street without breaking my stride. I knew that I would cop a severe hiding when I eventually returned home. In this I was not wrong. but despite this major setback within weeks, I was the owner of a passable bike, which I built from various old parts. The majority of the parts were obtained from climbing over the high brick wall of the scrap metal merchant at the Govanhill end of the Gushet.

The loaded freight wagons ready for dispatch to the steelworks proved to be an excellent source of all necessary parts, except for tyres and inner tubes. The tyres I got second hand from the man who ran the hire bike shop, in return for helping him to repair his old bikes. The inner tubes I had to buy from a cycle shop in Rutherglen Road, with money loaned by my mother as an advance on months of pocket money. Now that I had a reasonably reliable cobbled together bike I was able to join my pals as we explored places wide afar.

Chapter 20

Just before my father left his bus conductor's job, he and his regular driver arranged to take all members of their respective families on a Saturday trip "Doon the Watter" to Rothesay. Rothesay is the principal holiday resort town of the Cowal peninsula, and was most easily reached, by those without cars (99.9% of the population at that time), by the numerous paddle steamers operating from the Broomielaw wharf in central Glasgow, serving many towns on the Clyde coast. The pride of the fleet was the Queen Mary, which I and many others initially confused with the large ocean passenger liner of the same name.

As soon as we were told about the planned trip, I found it hard to think of anything else. Getting books from the public library about the Clyde holiday resorts, particularly Rothesay, and the majestic passenger liner Queen Mary, I read them from cover to cover, and then all over again. By the time that only a few days had to pass before we embarked, all of us were keyed up to fever pitch. The weather was reasonably warm and dry during the school week. On the Friday night, we helped my mother to get some things together for the trip. Getting to sleep was difficult due to supressed excitement.

At the crack of dawn, we were up and dressed. Disappointingly, we found that it was now raining steadily outside, with heavy greasy dark clouds lowering just above the rooftops. We were so used to lousy miserable weather, frequently much worse than this steady drizzle, that we were determined to enjoy the trip regardless. Mother and father were still fast asleep in the kitchen recess bed. I shook my father's shoulder. "Time tae get up Daddy, so we kin a' get tae the Broomielaw in plenty of time, so we don't miss the Queen Mary," I said excitedly. He opened his eyes and looked at the rain dribbling down the outside of the kitchen window with a definite lack of enthusiasm.

"It's nae good goin' oan a boat tae Rothesay in this wet weather, it'll be a waste o' good money. Ah arranged wi' Tam that if it turned oot tae be rainin' we widnae even go tae the Broomielaw, "he said, then continued, "Besides, Ah cannae even mind when Ah last had a whole Setterday aff work, Ah wid faur rather spend the day tucked up cosy in mah bed, readin' a good book." I was stunned, stunned, stunned, stunned, stunnedy stunned, as I howled in disbelief, "But Daddy, we don't care whit the weather is like, we jist want tae go tae Rothesay oan the Queen Mary. The rain wullnae matter a bit, it's a luxury liner with everythin' that ye kin think o', so we kin stay inside oot o' the weather an' no' get wet at a'. You kin play billiards an' drink pints at the baur, while we kin play in a' the special places that they hiv oan the ship tae entertain weans," I said hopefully, quoting from my library book about the Queen Mary. "Mammy kin even watch pictures in wan o' the onboard cinemas, Ah've seen pictures o' everythin' in the book that ah goat fae the library."

"Don't be a daft wee bampot, there's nae such things anywhere oan a Clyde paddle steamer, there's hardly enough room fur the passengers, never mind billiard tables, baurs, an' cinemas. Ah think that somebody has been pullin' yer leg, ye must be safter than ah thought ye wur, tae think that ye were sailin' oan the real big Queen Mary. Besides, it wid never fit intae the Clyde at the Broomielaw onywey," scoffed my father, continuing to laugh his head off at the very thought of travelling to Rothesay and back on a transatlantic liner.

He continued to laugh hysterically, as we weans tried to drown him out with our howls of disappointment. "Allan, the weans are that disappointed that they are a' in tears, dae ye no' think that we could go anyway, there'll be next tae nae passengers oan a day like this anyway. We'll be bound tae get plenty o' room inside, an' oot o' the rain an' weather", said my mother. "There'll no' be many passengers because maist folk are sensible enough tae stey at hame in bliddy weather like this," he responded, then burst out laughing hysterically again. No doubt he was thinking of me expecting that we would be travelling down the Clyde to Rothesay and back, on cheap day excursion return tickets, on the famous ocean-going Queen Mary.

Despite our tears and entreaties, he refused to budge from his cosy bed. We had to make do instead with the Cinerama Saturday Morning Cinema Club. I sat through the programme, without taking a word in, in my abject misery. Some weeks later my father arranged for us to go for a day trip to Rothesay by paddle steamer, but not on the Queen Mary, as he found a much cheaper day return excursion fare offered by another company. He had to work so we set off with Mammy in charge.

My mother wasn't too confident about being in sole charge of all the family, particularly as she had never been on a boat before.

Father arranged for Granny McLachlan to accompany us, in order to help mother cope with any problem which might occur. On the day we were out of bed and fully dressed ready to go at 7am. Mother spent some time making a large pile of jam sandwiches, sufficient to keep us fed until we got home.

Everything, including spare clothing and swimming costumes, was packed into three message bags to be carried by Mother, Bobby and myself. On our best behaviour we boarded a tramcar to the nearest stop to the Broomielaw, walking the rest of the way. At the dockside, a medium sized paddle steamer was berthed, decorated with a flock of screeching seagulls perched on every available surface. It was some time before Granny turned up to join us on the wharf. We trooped up the gangplank, overwhelmed by the sheer excitement of it all. We rushed to claim a seat on a slatted bench nearest to the bow. Mother called to us to sit beside her and Granny in the deck saloon. Pretending not to hear her we stayed where we were, anxious to get the most out of the voyage.

It wasn't raining for a change, but it was cloudy with a keen biting wind. The bad conditions were greatly magnified when the boat got under way, complete with the flock of noisy seagulls, screeching, wheeling, and swooping around the stern. We extracted our coats from a message bag and put them on back to front, helping each other to do up the buttons. This offered more protection from the wind, leaving no gaps for it to penetrate. All the way down the Clyde we hung over the bow railings, oblivious to the choppy swell that made the bow rise up and plunge down, at the same time rolling from side to side.

Mother and Granny sat inside the saloon looking white faced and grim, staring down at the deck, too scared even to look at the view, as the boat bucked, wallowed and heaved its way down the rapidly widening waters of the Firth of Clyde. We looked down at the bow wave, and the clear water being churned to a froth by the large paddlewheels resulting in a broad white wake stretching behind us -- I felt so exhilarated and imagined that we were sailing off to exotic foreign places.

All too soon for me the boat docked at Rothesay, with a lot of shouting between ship and shore, and noisy thrashing of the side mounted paddlewheels. We peeled off our back to front coats and stuffed them back into the bags, and we rushed to the saloon to collect Mother and Granny. Despite the fact that the boat was now safely tied up to the quayside, they were both still sitting bolt upright and pale faced, clutching at the arms of their seats with white knuckles.

"Come on youse two! We want to get aff an' dae things oan the beach, an' in the watter," I called, desperate to make the most of our limited hours on shore. Joining the others on the quay, we waited as Mother and Granny slowly released their cramped fingers and tottered shakily down the swaying gangplank to join us. "Ah wish that Ah was as good as youse lot at runnin' a' aboot the boat, as if it was jist anither street. Ah kin still feel ma stomach goin' up an' doon an' roon an' roon. Ah hope tae God that there's nae big waves oan the wey hame," said my mother. Granny nodded in agreement.

"Ah'm sorry Jessie, but Ah' hiv tae find a toilet right away fur Ah'm fair burstin' tae go," wheezed Granny, and hurriedly shuffled off down the nearest street. Rapidly recovering, mother gave us terse instructions, "Ah dinnae want anybody gettin' soakin' wet or drooned, so dinnae stray fae mah sight while we're here an' supposed to be enjoyin' oorsels. Ah'm trustin' ye Allan, tae make sure that naebody does anythin' that might be dangerous. Ah dinnae want tae be goin' hame wi' hoaspital cases or deid bodies, Ah'll have tae wait here untae yer Granny gets back fae the toilet, an' then ah'll hiv tae go masel' fur ah'm fair burstin' tae go."

Paying heed to my mother's warning, I led my brothers and sister down to a shingle beach at the end of the stone quay, within easy sight of mother as she hopped rapidly from foot to foot, waiting for Granny to show up. I ran back to her side, saying "Mammy, away ye go tae the toilet, ah kin watch the rest o' weans fae here nae bother at a'.".

In desperation she nodded her agreement, and sprinted off down the street, looking for a public toilet. Having been successful in avoiding an embarrassing accident, she returned within ten minutes looking much more relaxed and cheerful. Of Granny, there was not a sign. We waited for another half hour, but without success. It was clear that my mother was rapidly getting up a fair head of steam.

"Ah'll bet ye that the auld besom is sittin' doon in some bliddy pub wi' a gless o' whisky in her haund She was supposed tae come alang tae help me wi' youse weans," she muttered in disgust. "How we're gonnae find her ah don't know, ah'm no' goin' in tae every bliddy pub in Rothesay tae look fur her. Ah widnae cheapen masel' doin' that, fur a' the tea in China."

In exasperation, she followed me down to the narrow strip of shingle where the other kids were happily playing and sat down on a towel. After throwing large pebbles into the water until I got bored, I suggested to mother that it would be a good idea to dish out the jam sandwiches which she had packed for our lunch. She agreed, but she was obviously very worried about the whereabouts of our errant Granny, despite her anger.

With Mother's permission, Bobby and I went back to the quay to see if anything of interest was there. Finding a large steel grille set into the wooden deck, we lay down on our stomachs and peered down into the crystal-clear water. Excitingly, what we saw was wall to wall fish, swooshing about underneath us in large shoals. These were much bigger than any fish that we had seen before, changing direction by 180 degrees in the blink of an eye. "Mammy, Mammy," we shouted as we ran back to the others, "Ye should see the millions o' big fish that ur swimmin' aboot under the jetty. Kin we hiv some money tae buy a fishin' line?" "Sorry boys, ah've goat nae spare money, 'cos we might need a' the money ah've goat in mah purse fur an emergency, ye never can tell whit might happen afore we get hame," she said ruefully.

Dejectedly, we walked back to the grille, and lay down to watch the magical display of dexterity being displayed by the shoals. The fish swooshed backwards and forwards underwater too fast for our eyes to follow. We stood up and saw that some anglers were fishing off the outer edge of the quay. Very interested in what they were trying to catch, we sidled up close enough to feel that we were part of this whole marvellous environment. I looked down into the crystal depths, but I couldn't see any fish, apart from a few tiddlers hovering close to the piles.

"Hey mister, there's millions o' big fish, scooshin' aboot right under that big iron grille at the back o' the deck," I blurted out to the nearest angler. "Is that right, son?" asked the man. He reeled in his line, laid his rod down, and followed us over to the grille. He kneeled down and stared into the depths. "Dae ye know son, you're dead right', he said, getting to his feet and going back to get all of his tackle together. We spent the rest of the time watching him reel in fish after fish until his ex-army pack was full, bulging with large glistening herrings.

"Dae ye want some herrins tae take back tae yer Mammy fur yer supper boys?" he said as he packed up his tackle and bits and pieces. "Aye mister we wid, we've never had fresh herrins straight oot o' the watter before," I answered eagerly. He took four herrings from his catch, wrapped them up in a sheet of newspaper, and passed them over. Bobby and I ran back to mother and the others.

"Jist look at whit we've goat, Mammy," I said breathlessly, unwrapping the newspaper parcel to reveal our nice shining herrings. "Whit ur ye gonnae dae wi' these fish?" she asked to my surprise. "Eat them of course Mammy, we kin hiv them fur oor supper when we get hame", I replied, "whit else wid we dae wi' herrins?" "Ah widnae allow youse to eat herrins that didnae come fae a proper fish shoap, God only knows where they've been afore the man caught them." We protested in vain, but she was adamant in her refusal to let us take them home. She snatched the parcel from me and walked over to the nearest rubbish bin and chucked it in.

Realising that our normally even-tempered mother was upset and edgy because Granny hadn't reappeared, I didn't protest about the dumped herrings. There was only an hour left before the steamer would sail back to Glasgow. "Kin youse two go and see if ye kin find yer Grannie afore Ah go aff mah heid wi' worry aboot her?" she asked in a strained voice. We had no idea where to start looking and didn't have the faintest clue about the street layout of Rothesay. We hadn't even been off the quay so far, but set off at a run anyway, worried about getting left behind as none of us had any means of telling the time, apart from the town hall clock.

Walking up and down the immediate locality, with no sighting of Granny, we gave up and ran back towards the waterfront. As we passed the pub closest to the Quay, we were relieved to see Granny staggering out on to the pavement. "Where hiv ye been a' day Granny? Mammy has been worried oot o' her wits fur hours, an we were jist runnin' back tae her when we saw ye comin' oot o' that pub." Granny swayed dangerously, as she tried to put an index finger to her lips but missed by miles each time. Uncrossing her bleary looking eyes, she mumbled in what she thought was a conspiratorial whisper, "Ah've been loast a' day in this toon, tryin' tae get back tae yer Mammy, an' youse, Ah cannae tell ye hoo many miles ah must hae walked an' still steyed loast".

We took an elbow each to support and steer her as she swayed and staggered in turn. As we slowly made our way back to Mammy, she muttered, "Don't let oan tae yer Mammy that ye saw me comin' oot o' a pub, fur she'll jump tae the wrang conclusion that ah've had a wee drink." A teetotal blind man a block away would have known for certain that she was highly intoxicated, as the fumes from her breath would have knocked him silly. When mother saw our wavering trio slowly approaching, she came running to meet us. All other passengers were already safely aboard the boat.

As she approached, she caught the strong whiff of whisky fumes which Granny was inflicting on the general population at large. She screwed up her face as we met. "We'll hiv tae get a move on, or we'll miss the bliddy boat efter hingin' aboot a' day waitin' fur ye, ye drunken auld bugger," she hissed in anger. "Ah suppose that youse found her as she fell oot o' a pub door?" Being stone deaf when it suited her, Granny carried on ignoring my mother's out of character caustic comments. "Ye'll never guess hoo much trouble ah hid, Jessie. Ah've been oot o' mah heid a' day tryin' tae get back tae ye. Ah thought that ah wid be deid o' thirst afore ah found yese," she said. "There's nae chance o' you dyin' o' thirst Kate, ye wid drink every bliddy distillery in Scoatland dry afore that happened, ye lyin' auld bugger ye," Mother yelled into her better ear. Granny staggered forward up the gangplank to where the deckhands were waiting impatiently to cast off.

"Come on missus fur Christ sake, ye kin walk faster than that, ye're haudin' us up somethin' terrible," yelled one of the more impatient deckhands, "we've a' goat families waitin' at hame fur us back in Glesca, an' we'll never get there the night wi' you haudin' up proceedins." As Granny swayed past him her breath stopped him dead in mid-tirade. We helped Granny to the nearest bench seat, swinging her round until her behind was in close proximity to the seat. She gratefully slumped on to it and was fast asleep before we let go of her, wheezing and snuffling to herself.

"Whit the hell are we gonnae dae wi' her when we get tae the Broomielaw, she's faur too heavy tae cairry, we'll hiv tae ask wan o' the crew tae help us get her off the boat," Mother moaned in anticipated embarrassment. The sail home was even rougher than the trip down to Rothesay. Bobby and I had to sit each side of Granny, holding her by the arms to prevent her falling off the bench. Mother sat on an adjacent bench, no doubt wishing that she was safely home. As it happened we needn't have worried. When I shook Granny awake after the boat docked at the Broomielaw, she rose from her seat, and trotted off down the gang plank as if she had just spent all day in church singing hymns.

Poor mother was in much worse condition, with her face pale white and looking ill. She had been sitting rigidly all the way, willing herself not to succumb to the vomit which kept rising up in her throat. When we reached solid ground she instantly threw up, to her great mortification. She staggered to the ladies' toilet, and rinsed her mouth out and washed her face before reappearing, looking considerably better, with some colour in her cheeks. "If ye don't mind Jessie, ah'll walk through tae Argyle Street," said Granny, "an' get a number 9 Auchenshoogle caur hame, afore they stoap runnin' fur the night. Ah'll jist say cheerio the noo an' thanks fur the day oot doon the watter. Ah really enjoyed the sail an' the company."

Mother was struck dumb, no doubt stuck for a suitably caustic reply. We walked along the riverbank to Crown Street, where we climbed into a tramcar and were home in next to no time. Father let us in the door, seeming very pleased to see everybody home safely. "Tell me a' aboot the boat trip an' Rothesay, ye a' look as if ye're ready fur bed." Mother sat with her face between her hands, in total silence, as we all spoke at the same time babbling on about our day on the water. "An' Daddy, a man gied us four big herrins tae take hame fur oor supper that we saw him catchin', it wis great." I had to yell to be heard above the babble. Father pricked up his ears at the mention of free food.

"Where ur they then?" he asked. "Mammy threw them a' intae a rubbish bin," I responded without thinking. Father looked at mother in disbelief. "Tell me that ye're pullin' mah leg son, ye widnae throw away good freshly caught herrins, wid ye Jessie hen?" Mother hesitated for some time before answering. "Ah widnae allow ye tae eat fish that was caught by a man oan a pier, ye never know whit they hiv been eatin' afore gettin' caught."

Father threw up his hands in horror. "Who gives a monkey's fuck whit they've been eatin'! It's no' as if they pick their grub oot o' a bliddy menu fur fish, afore they get wired intae anythin' that they kin swally. Besides, ye gut them afore ye pit them intae the fryin' pan." This put the tin hat on the whole trip. It was days before he forgot about the freshly fried herrings that he so nearly got for his supper. Mother was tempted to berate him over Granny's performance in Rothesay, but she was too good natured to hold any sort of grudge for any length of time. It would keep for another day, to be brought up if necessary.

Chapter 21

My father was fond of animals, and so it wasn't surprising that he was gradually worn down by my almost constant moaning about not having a pup to play with.. Several times I got him as far as the pet shops at the Saltmarket, where we looked at everything for sale, especially the baskets full of pups frolicking with their siblings. I could see that he was sorely tempted, but we were both aware that my mother was dead set against having a puppy in the confines of our cramped home.

Uncle Shug arrived one night, to take my father for a quick pint. Mother bridled at this, telling both of them in no uncertain terms, "it'll have to be jist wan pint. Ah don't want tae hiv ye rollin' hame at chuckin' oot time laughing at anything at a' that catches yer fancy, an' keepin' the weans fae sleepin' wi yer noise." A couple of hours passed before Father returned home, looking sheepishly at Mother, obviously seeking forgiveness for his transgression.

"Don't think for a minute that Ah'm gonnae sit here darnin' everybody's holey soacks, while ye go gallivantin' aboot wi' yer bampot pals. Whit bliddy pub did ye go tae, the wan oan the

Greenock pier?" she asked in a sarcastic tone. "Jesus Christ Jessie, it's no' very oaften that ah go oot at a', it's only nine o' cloak at night fur Goad's sake," he replied. Mother looked at him more closely, for he was clearly hiding something inside his jacket. "Whit hiv ye goat in yer jaicket, don't kid me that your wallet has grown wee legs, and is trying tae escape afore ye spend any mair o' oor money."

Father reached inside his jacket, and brought out a tiny cream coloured pup, which he held out for everybody to see. He had bought it from some man in the pub. I was ecstatic. "Kin ah haud it Daddy? Ah jist want tae haud it fur a wee minute, a'll no' hurt it, honestly ah widnae," I whined. Mother chipped in before anybody else got a chance." "An' who the bliddy hell is gonnae watch it, feed it, clear up its mess, an' take it fur walks roon the streets? Youse are at work or at school fur maist o' the day. Ah dinnae want any mair things tae drive me daft a' day, ah've already goat too many things tae worry aboot, withoot any mair."

Poor mother was right, of course, but lost the battle after the pup was passed eagerly from hand to hand, with everybody going ga-ga over the tiny bundle. Bowing to the inevitable, she warned us about the consequences if we didn't honour our promises about taking turns in looking after the little pup. Finding a name for the tiny bundle was easy, with everybody except Mother agreeing on Sandy. That night Sandy slept in our bed. At last, we had a pup.

For the first few weeks everyone fought over who was next to look after Sandy. As time passed with Sandy now growing quickly, the novelty wore off, leaving only me still interested in looking after him. As Mother had clearly predicted, she was the only person at home all day, apart from little Grace, and was saddled with the chores associated with a growing dog whether she liked it or not.

At that time many people living in tenement buildings owned dogs. The problems associated with the dogs defecating or urinating were easily solved by the owners, but at the expense of everyone else. As the dog owners went off to work, school or shopping, the dog was simply biffed outside to look after itself. This was the status quo and had been as far back as anyone cared to remember. The public was so conditioned to seeing dog shit everywhere, particularly on footpaths, that it was never seen as a problem, unless stepped on personally.

My mother had grown up with this attitude. When Sandy was half grown, she decided that he could be left outside in the street, for at least a few hours each day. I wasn't even aware of her intention, as I still regarded him as far too young to cope with being alone on the streets. Many of the roaming dogs were aggressive in nature and wouldn't hesitate to attack any other dog to trespass on their marked-out territory. A dogfight to the death in these circumstances was not unknown.

I was very proud to have a dog and took him out on his lead after school for a good runaround with my pals, as we did whatever was flavour of the month. As a result, Sandy was well known and practically part of our gang. It was summertime and I was in the habit of playing football in the school playground after school with my classmates, before they dispersed homewards.

I was doing this this one afternoon when a boy who lived across the street from us ran into the playground through the open school gates, yelling at the top of his voice, "Hey AAAAllan, AAAAllan ye better come quick, yer wee dug Sandy has been tramped oan by a big Clydesdale hoarse, an' he's a' burst wide open." I followed hard on his heels as he ran back to where Sandy was lying outstretched in a gutter. The team of Clydesdales were still waiting patiently for the driver of the loaded lorry of Barrs Iron Bru and other Barrs soft drinks to emerge from the shop to which he was delivering.

I ducked under the belly of the Clydesdale that had inadvertently stood on Sandy and crouched over him. He had lost a lot of blood, which was now coursing down the gutter. Still crouching, I wriggled both hands under him, and lifted him clear, taking great care to avoid the clattering hooves of the Clydesdale, which was getting fairly skittish with me under his belly. I was blinded by tears as I wriggled backwards to get clear. Holding Sandy, who was whimpering in agony, closely to my chest, I hurried home as fast as I could, calling out to my mother to open the door to save time.

Luckily my father was at home, having taken a break between split shifts. I laid Sandy on the table as gently as I could manage. He was still bleeding copiously from his various wounds, particularly from his ruptured stomach. To give full credit to my father, he didn't waste any precious time asking questions, but gently wrapped Sandy in the nearest towel, and took off out the door saying that he was taking him to the vet's rooms in Crown Street. I was still too upset to speak. Looking at myself in the wardrobe mirror, I saw that I was saturated with blood from my chin to my shoes.

The sticky feeling and warmth of the blood was rapidly making me feel sick. Without saying a word my Mother held a large bowl underneath my chin just in time, as I retched and vomited until I had nothing else to bring up. After some minutes passed she helped me to get out of my red sodden clothes. My shoes were full of blood also. She undressed me and wrapped me in a bath towel, as she washed my discarded clothes to get rid of the blood before it congealed completely.

I was still too upset to speak. By the time that she had rinsed my clothes, put them through the sink mounted wringer, and hung them on the pulley to dry overnight, she had boiled two kettles of water to give me a warm bath in the tub. After drying myself, I sat at the table which a short time before had been wetly stained with Sandy's blood. "How did Sandy get oot Mammy?" I asked. "Ye widnae believe it Allan but this efternin was the first time that Ah let him go oot by himsel', ah thought that he wid be awright fur an 'oor or two, an' get himself some exercise, fur it's no' right tae keep a wee dug cooped up inside a hoose a' day," Mother sniffled through her sodden hankie.

"Dae ye think that the vet wull be able tae sort him aw right," I asked her. She hesitated before answering me. "If ah wis you ah widnae get mah hopes up too high son, yer Daddy wull dae his best ah'm sure, but Sandy wis hurt real bad fur a poor wee dug, so we'll jist hivtae wait an' see whit happens." It was some hours before Daddy got back from the vets. My heart soared when I saw that he was carrying Sandy in his arms, but so nearly hidden beneath many layers of bandages. Only Sandy's head was showing, and with both back legs in plaster he looked like a small mummy.

He was weakly whimpering as Daddy gently laid him down in front of the fire to keep warm. "How are we gonnae feed him an how is he gonnae go tae the toilet?" I asked. "That's somethin' that we'll hiv tae figure oot as we go alang, we must jist try tae dae oor best fur him, an' you'll hiv tae dae the maist o' the work yersel'. Ah'll hiv tae get back tae work noo as I'm runnin' too close fur comfort," he replied. I sat with Sandy until long past my normal bedtime, trying to get him to drink some milk from an eye dropper. It just trickled back out of his mouth, to my sorrow. I didn't know what to do to alleviate his obvious suffering, as he lay perfectly still, weakly whining.

In the morning, before I went to school I tried again to feed him, but with no success. My mother promised to do her best during the day to get him to accept some milk. When I rushed home after school, he was worse rather than better, whining and yelping weakly. For three days he hung in there, but I could sense that his condition was worsening. Father was still on the same split shift, so was at home when I ran in from school. "Ah'm sorry son but ah'm gonnae take him roon' tae the vet an' hiv him put tae sleep so he disnae suffer any mair, it's no' fair puttin' a poor wee dug through agony like this," he said, obviously distraught.

As he picked up Sandy from the fireside, the pup yelped in pain. I volunteered to go with my father to the vets. Deep down I was glad that Sandy was shortly to be put out of his suffering. At the vets we handed Sandy over to a female assistant, who assured us that we were doing the right thing and advised us that we shouldn't wait around. Father paid the bill, and we walked home in total silence. At home he said nothing as he gave my mother a gentle kiss, which was so out of character that I knew he was very sad. Dogs played no further part in our family life, until many years later when Laddie the clever collie became my father's beloved companion.

Chapter 22

Working as a bus conductor, my father didn't get to spend time with us, or our mother for that matter, due to the split shift system which resulted in early starts and late nights, with little or no paid overtime. His basic wage was two pounds ten shillings only. When possible he supplemented his income by using the long breaks spent in the Larkfield Garage canteen to gamble on his prowess at billiards and card playing. As he couldn't afford to lose any money, he had to be good enough to win more times than not, and he was good.

This ability turned out to be a double-edged sword. Most of his workmates soon worked out that he was too good for them and refused to play him for money. This meant that he was always on the lookout for people in the canteen whom he didn't know, to invite to play a game of cards, or billiards, or snooker, or anything at all, where he could introduce playing for money, after playing a few games for fun, losing every time, but not by too much.

The money that he made in this way, he shared out generously between mother and ourselves, not so much in cash but in small, unexpected treats. One of his workmates was a driver named Johnny

Blackwood. Johnny was one of those characters who were always ahead of the game of life. One day, over a pint in a pub in Govanhill, Daddy asked Johnny how he always had enough money to buy a few drinks in the pub whenever he wanted.

Johnny was only too pleased to tell him of some of the things that he did on the side to provide himself with extra spending money. One was bribing the clerk who was responsible for the ever-changing rosters, to put him on rosters that paid the best for the least effort and avoided the onerous split shifts whenever possible. He had to ensure that he was free at least one night per week, on Wednesdays, if not more. He revealed to father that he was a sergeant in the Territorial Army unit right next door to the bus depot, a Medical Corps unit, and had to attend at least one parade a week to qualify for his weekly bounty payment of twenty-five shillings.

Although father had vowed after being demobbed that he would rather do time in Barlinnie prison than put on another army uniform, the thought of being given twenty-five shillings for one night a week playacting in a drill hall had a strong appeal. He knew that he couldn't bribe the roster clerk, as he'd had many run-ins with the man over rostering practices which had seemed manifestly unfair to him. The last time that this had happened the clerk slammed his office door and locked it as my father pounded and kicked the door.

The clerk hadn't reported the incident to the depot manager, as father had expected him to do. He now knew why, and that he had been dead right about the rotten dirty bastard and the unfair rostering. Now he regretted that he hadn't persisted in kicking the door in at the time and giving the clerk a good hiding. Johnny Blackwood offered to recruit father to the Territorials, telling him that as an experienced non-commissioned officer in wartime he would automatically qualify for the rank of sergeant. Additionally, Johnny would receive a hefty bonus payment for recruiting a new sergeant.

Very tempted by the whole idea, father didn't take long to make his mind up. Less than two weeks later he announced to our surprise, including mother's, that he had found himself a new job and that he would be starting it the following Monday. His new job was working in the central kitchens of the school meals programme, located at Polmadie (pronounced poh-mah dee). His wage wouldn't be much more than he got as a bus conductor, but it was an eight to five thirty job, only five days a week, which was a real doddle compared to before.

Having got the hurdle of seven days a week shiftwork out of the way he immediately enlisted in the Territorials with the rank of sergeant, just as Johnny Blackwood had promised. As this was a Medical Corps unit, he had to undertake some basic training and studies in order to be functional as a senior NCO. He found the training enjoyable, as it exercised the mental ability which had lain dormant for the larger part of his life. The fact that he was paid extra for doing the medical training and work was an unexpected bonus.

The unit commanding officer was Captain Skelly, a competent and quietly spoken officer who was excellent at gaining the trust and affection of all members of his part-time unit. As he was the only officer, with his immediate lower ranks consisting of one warrant officer and four sergeants, the officer's and sergeant's messes were combined. Although my father had served in the regular Army for about ten years in all, he had never before had the opportunity to have a meaningful or friendly discussion with an officer, particularly a Commanding Officer. He genuinely admired Captain Skelly, despite the fact that every time Daddy mentioned his name we all fell about laughing and giggling. In broad Scots, the word 'skelly' is applied to anyone with a pronounced squint.

Since leaving his job with Corporation Transport, working in the school meals kitchen complex, and joining the Territorials, father was essentially a changed man, less likely to dish out severe beltings at the drop of a hat.

He spent more time reading library books and taking me to the Calder Street swimming baths. He had taught me to swim as soon as he was demobilised, but I had been going with friends for years to either Calder Street or the Gorbals Baths. The latter was a lot nearer but was much gloomier and old fashioned. The Gorbals pools were segregated, the main pool being reserved for males, and a smaller pool set aside for females. The pools also had a "Steamie" attached on the other side of the boiler room. Above the main swimming pool was a mezzanine floor where a large number of booths containing heavy duty baths were located. A long queue normally wound around this level, patiently waiting for a sixpenny bath in clean piping hot water; the bathers were expected to add cold water as desired.

We were used to the system which was employed by all Municipal swimming pools to regulate the entrance and exit of customers, and thought it to be perfectly normal, although it might sound weird to anyone living in more enlightened times. By official opening time a sizeable queue would have already formed outside the pool entrance door. Filing past the box office and handing over our fourpences, we ran like hell to claim a changing box, undressed, and put on our woollen swimming trunks, which were all identical except for the colour, most frequently crimson, with a white cotton belt buckled at the front.

Throwing open the door, we raced to be first to hurl ourselves into the pool. Having slowly graduated from the shallow end to the deep end, we were now competing to be the first of our gang to dive from the high diving platform which dominated the deep end. This platform, for some strange reason which I was never able to discover, was known as the "Diving Dale". Sturdy flights of non-slip stairs led to the top from each side, with a handrail on one side only, leaving each step available to be dived or jumped from without impediment. This sensible arrangement allowed potential divers to gain confidence as they slowly progressed to diving off the actual dale.

Once thirty minutes had passed the chief pool attendant blew his piercing whistle and called out "clear the pool" over and over until the last swimmer got out of the water. This took a little time, as the more obstinate swimmers tried to stay in as long as possible. The pool attendants would get highly annoyed, as there were always stragglers at the end of each half hour session. Using a very long pole with a fine net on the end, designed to scoop up the various rafts of detritus floating on the pool surface after every session, the chief attendant skilfully reached out and banged each one repeatedly on the head with the metal base of the net, until they climbed out. When even this treatment failed to flush the more stubborn from the pool, the attendants then walked up and down the rows of cubicles.

Upon finding an unoccupied cubicle containing somebody's clothing and footwear, they assumed that these belonged to one of those still in the pool. Nonchalantly, the attendant would call out to the likely owners "Dae these claes an' shoes belang tae you?" If the answer was in the affirmative, as it usually was, the attendant would call out "catch the buggers then" as he threw the bundle of clothing into the pool, well out of arm range of the culprit, to float or sink, depending on the specific gravity of the article. This was repeated until every booth was cleared. Those who hurriedly climbed out of the pool before their clothes were dumped were just as unlucky, as they watched their clothes being fired into the centre of the pool regardless.

By this time the rest of the swimmers had vacated the booths, and the next session of swimmers were swarming in to claim them. The troublemakers climbing out of the pool with their sodden bundles of clothing were grabbed by the attendants and propelled through the exit at high speed, to be deposited into the street dressed only in their trunks, shivering in the subtropical warmth (not!) of a typical Glasgow morning as they clutched their sodden bundles of clothing to their chests. It was rough justice, but it worked, and it prevented anarchy reigning at the end of each half-hour session.

Parents at that time were much more realistic in terms of the disciplining of their offspring by others in the community when they transgressed. I never heard of a complaint being lodged against a pool attendant, or anyone else for that matter. It was much more likely that the father would administer an additional thrashing upon hearing about any incident where their kids had received a belt round the ear, or had their arses soundly kicked by someone other than themselves.

When I got the strap at school for anything, which happened frequently, I was very careful to pull down the cuffs of my jersey to hide the prominent weals on my palms and, even more importantly, wrists. If I carelessly exposed them in sight of my father he would invariably give me a hiding for just getting the strap. "A'll jist gie ye somethin' else tae go whi' that strappin', so ye'll be better behaved at school the next time," he would say as he put me over his knee and started to tan my behind with his bare hand. This was his lightest form of punishment. The next step up was to get the same treatment, but on the bare bottom. The most painful was being thrashed with his trusty old army webbing belt on the bare bottom. Stupidly I would grit my teeth, determined not to cry. This only prolonged the beating, as he never stopped until I could hold my tears back no more.

My father had only worked in the school meals kitchen in Polmadie for a month or so, before being noticed by the lady nutritionist in charge of the operation. She was very impressed by his native ability and rapid innovation skills. He had quickly mastered the overall process of beginning with raw foodstuffs each day and delivering tubs and trays of excellently prepared and nutritious meals to a wide network of schools throughout Glasgow by 11am. He made many suggestions as to how the system could be improved. I can't remember if he was the only male employee, apart from the delivery van drivers, but I have the distinct feeling that he was. Once he felt that he was firmly established, he sat down at home for two or three nights with a heavy-duty cotton sheet, cutting and sewing. When he finished, he proudly displayed his handywork by putting it on. It was a sleeveless waistcoat of generous proportions.

"Ah don't know whit it's meant tae be but it's faur tae slack oan ye, ye'll have tae pit oan aboot five stane afore it fits ye," remarked my mother, laughing out loud as he rotated, showing off his creation for us all to admire. "Youse wullnae be laughin' when ye see whit I'm gonnae use it fur, ye'll be laughin' oan the ither side o' yir faces, so yese wull," he responded huffily. The next evening, he came through the door beaming, and looking a little bit like the Michelin man. Removing his outer jacket, he unbuttoned his oversized waistcoat, and held each side wide open, revealing that the inside had rows of roomy pockets. These now contained jam-jars with screw-on lids.

Behaving like Dante the famous magician, he withdrew one jar at a time, and flourished it for all to see. Each jar contained (separately) stew, mince, soup, rice, custard, stewed apples, and various other goodies which were hard to get even if you could afford them. My mother's face turned pale as she said, "Ye cannae bring stolen things intae this hoose, it's no' right, an ah wullnae staun fur it. Ye kin jist throw that waistcoat intae the fire this minute. Ah wullnae speak tae ye if ye don't." "But Jessie, a' this stuff was goin' tae the piggery anywey. It's jist a tiny wee bit o' the stuff that comes back fae the dinner halls tae Polmadie, efter everybody has been fed," my father explained.

We kids were far more interested in getting high quality food for supper than any moral considerations. "If it's only gaun tae the piggery, then it might be awright ah suppose. It'll help oot a loat in stretchin' oot mah hoosekeepin' money between peydays, ah'm hivin' a helluva joab tryin' tae make ends meet," mother replied. Father was much more of a cook than mother, and enjoyed cooking just as much as mother detested it. Within a short time, we were all sitting down to a veritable feast, compared to our normal fare. There was no further discussion on the subject, with father continuing to bring home a varied selection of leftovers each night, which only required reheating to be ready for the table.

One evening my father came home after his weekly Territorials session with his face positively beaming. "Guess whit, Jessie?" he asked mother. "The caretaker o' the drill hall has chucked it in, it was jist gettin' too much fur him. We wur jist talkin' in the mess aboot gettin' somebody else, when ah heard how much he wis gettin' peyed. Two pound ten a week! Kin ye believe that!" "So, whit's that tae dae wi' us?" asked mother. "It's goat everythin' tae dae wi' us Jessie, it wid be a great help tae hiv that comin' in oan toap o' mah wages," father replied. "How would ye manage tae cope wi' a' that work, it's a big place tae look efter, an' keep spick an' span a' the time?" asked mother grimly.

"Ah could manage it if you an' the boys mucked in tae help me aboot three nights a week, that's a' it would take Jessie.". Mother was loathe to contradict him in front of us, but she was getting worked up. "Ah'm sorry Allan, but Ah dinnae want tae put a dampener oan yer best intentions. There's nae wey that we could cope wi' that, ye cannae expect young boys tae work tae late at night three or four nights a week, as well as daein their school hamework, an' ah don't see masel daein the same, an' runnin' a hameful o' weans at the same time, ah'm tired oot as it is," she said with a note of finality.

Father sat down in his fireside chair and lit up a Capstan, obviously surprised by mother's rejection of his great idea, saying nothing for some minutes. Staring into the fire, he smoked his cigarette down to his fingers in silence, flicking the cigarette end into the flames. "Ah'm sorry hen, but ah've already said that ah would take the joab, an' ah've signed aw the papers already, so that we cuid start right away. Ah didnae think that ye'd mind, an' would be gled o' the extra money comin' every week," he said. "Ah'm no' goin back oan mah word efter signing everythin', ah'll jist hiv tae manage somehow." "If ye're that determined ah suppose that we'll jist hiv tae gie it a go, an' see how it works oot," said mother.

The next night we all trooped up to the drill hall, where we played about amongst the vehicles while father, with mother in tow, drew up a schedule of tasks and times. Despite everything, helped by mother and (reluctantly) us, my father's job as caretaker carried on for some years. Most allocated jobs I didn't mind doing. The only exception was sitting in front of a small mountain of discarded grey-green denim overalls. Before they could be sent off to the laundry, small metal split rings had to be removed from the rear of the numerous metal buttons on each overall, the rings and buttons being chucked into two separate buckets. This was a soul-destroying and long slow job and caused painful fingernails. When we had finished the task and had loaded the overalls into substantial laundry bags for collection, we were rewarded by having to refit the buttons and rings on to each of the overalls from the sacks of freshly laundered ones which were waiting for us.

After a while I did everything possible to avoid this job of the overall buttons after school, even if it meant hiding until I was sure that father had given up and had set out without me. My usual hiding place was on the far side of our wash house galvanized roof. One summer afternoon I had gone into my usual hiding spot and was sure that he had gone. Just to be on the safe side I decided to jump down into a back court in Crown Street, instead of ours. I jumped off the high wall onto a straggly crop of grass, landing on my hands and toes to take the shock. As I landed, my left hand hurt terribly. Lifting the palm first I was shocked to see that the thick bottom of a large green beer bottle was stuck firmly to the palm, and that I was bleeding profusely. Turning my hand over I nearly passed out in horror. Sharp triangular spikes of glass had penetrated my hand and were sticking prominently out of the back.

With the base of the beer bottle still firmly impaled in my palm I rushed home, hoping that mother had not gone to the drill hall with father. Pounding on the door I was relieved when she opened the door. "Your daddy wull gie ye a right hid...." She trailed off suddenly, as she noticed the blood freely dripping from my hand onto the lobby floor. I silently held up my left hand to where she could see it better. I might as well have held up the Devil himself. Staggering backwards, she instantly turned pure white, turned away from me and held on to the top of the coal bunker for support. Rapidly pulling herself together as good mothers do, she took hold of my wounded hand with violently shaking fingers.

She turned my hand over and when she saw the long razor-sharp shards of green glass protruding from the back, she nearly passed out cold. Recovering, she grabbed a tea towel from the sideboard, and wrapped it loosely round my hand. Without pausing to grab a coat or anything she banged on the Leydens' door. "Could ye jist watch the weans, while ah run tae the doactor's? Wae Allan, he's goat the bottom o' a big beer boattle right through his haund." As Mrs Leyden nodded her assent, we hurried along Crown Street to the nearby doctors' surgery. Mother spoke up as the doctors' nurse glanced up from the paperwork on her desk. "Kin ye have a look at this one's haund right away please, ah'm frightened tae touch it in case ah make it worse."

The nurse nodded, and I put my still bleeding hand on her desk. Unwrapping the bloody tea towel she held my wrist and looked at both sides of my hand. Still holding my wrist, and ignoring the waiting patients, she tapped on the doctor's door, and led me straight through. "Doctor, this wee boy has made a right mess o' his hand, can ye sort him right away?" The doctor looked at me. "What have you done to try and kill yourself this time?" He asked. I couldn't think of any reply, as I was apprehensive of what might be necessary to remove the glass. The nurse held my forearm firmly, as the doctor rattled around in his tool drawer, probably to find a small crowbar or something to lever the bottle base from my palm. I gritted my teeth and looked up at the ceiling, rather than watch.

The doctor found what he no doubt thought was an appropriate instrument, and said in a reassuring voice, "This is going to hurt a bit as I remove the glass from your hand, but it won't take long, son." He wasn't wrong, as I gritted my teeth and screwed my eyes tightly shut to prevent tears starting. When I heard the glass clunk as he dropped it into a nearby bin, I knew that the worst was over, or so I hoped. I waited until the nurse prepared an antiseptic solution in an enamel bowl large enough to immerse my hand in. She swabbed away at the penetration wounds, until both she and the doctor were satisfied. My hand was now throbbing with pain. "You've been a good soldier, son, so just keep it up while I stitch up the holes, and then you can relax," said the doctor.

The stitching took some time, and then the nurse did a great job of bandaging my hand and fitted a neck sling for support. The nurse took me through to the waiting room to be reunited with mother, and I could see the look of relief on her face. The nurse attended to the necessary paperwork. "Right Mrs McLachlan, just make sure that he keeps the wounds clean and dry. He can go tae school, but he must stey away from any rough play, an' bring him back in in aboot a week's time tae get the stitches oot.". We set out for home. "Noo ye hearad whit the nurse telt ye, ah want ye tae promise me that ye'll dae that, wi' nane o' your usual stupit nonsense." said mother. I wasn't in a position to argue.

Once home we thanked Mrs Leyden for stepping in and helping. My mother had promised father that she would join him at the drill hall, with all of us, as soon as I got home. Hours late, we hurried up Cathcart Road. He wasn't impressed when he saw me with my arm in a sling. "Whit's next? Wan o' these days ye'll come hame wi' yer heid in a sling, an' we'll hiv tae hing ye up oan a hook tae sleep," he said, as he tried to think of a job that I could do with one hand. He led me into the stores, and pointed at a large open packing case, saying "This joab should be right up your alley, ye kin unpack a' these bandages, an' put them oan thae shelves in order, fae the wee'ist tae the biggest." It was very late when we started out for home at the end of the day, but every job had been completed.

During the following week I tried hard to keep the bandages and sling clean, but by the time mother took me to have the stitches out, they looked as if I had got them second hand from a coalman. Kindly, the nurse removed the bandages before taking me into the doctor's room. He looked closely at both sides of my hand. The contrast between my grubby fingers and the rest of my hand was startling. I looked away as he busied himself picking the stitches out. "Try to keep a clean glove on your hand for the next two weeks, to stop dirt from causing any infection," he said. This I did but suffered stupid taunting from my classmates who called out "Run fur yer lives, here comes The Clutching Hand (the subject of a popular 'chapter' series) at every opportunity. My hand healed just fine, but the scars took years to fade away.

Chapter 23

Whenever we could we attended football matches on Saturday afternoons. At that time Hampden Park held the world record for the largest number of spectators at a match. I seem to remember that this was in the region of 140,000. Apart from the relatively small grandstand there was no seating, with spectators standing on the terraces. Tubular metal barriers were interspersed along the terraces to prevent fans being crushed. The strange thing about Hampden Park was that the huge stadium was the 'home' ground of Queens Park Rangers, then a Third Division team composed entirely of unpaid amateurs. My brother Bobby was a dedicated Third Lanark fan. His particular hero was 'Wee Jocky Henderson', an anomaly amongst goalkeepers, being only five feet tall. Despite this he had the spring of a jumping jack and was known and admired for his spectacular saves. 'Thirds" home ground was Cathkin Park, at Cathcart, not very far as the crow flies from Hampden Park. We could join in the surging columns of fans walking up both sides of Crown Street, and walk to either of these two venues, depending on which match appealed. Riding on public transport was not an option, as all buses and tramcars were packed solid, with the overflow grimly hanging on to each other and the vertical platform poles, with the clippies struggling to get close enough to boot them off. "Come Oan, Get Aff," the well-known war cry of the clippies, could be heard frequently above the hubbub of the thousands of simultaneous conversations of the army of fans on foot.

The other main football teams and grounds in Glasgow at that time were 'Celtic', based at Celtic Park in Parkhead, 'Rangers' based at Ibrox Park in Ibrox, 'Clyde', based at Shawfield Park in Shawfield, and 'Partick Thistle' based at Partick. I was not a devoted fan of any particular team, but enjoyed going to any match I fancied on the day. Despite my lack of allegiance to a particular team I had favourite players, such as Geordie Young of Rangers and captain of Scotland, Wullie Miller the Celtic goalkeeper, Neil Mochan, and Bobby Evans, also of Celtic.

Each stadium had separate gates for schoolchildren to get in at half price. As far as we were concerned any kid using these gates was either rich or seriously mentally disabled. With a hessian sack rolled up tightly under an arm, we walked straight up to the head of any of the long queues leading to a turnstile. Mounted policemen, riding very large and impressive horses, kept the surging crowds under firm control by using their horses to barge against any unruly elements, driving them backwards, and freely using their very long batons to crack any intransigents on the head and shoulders before they got out of hand. At the turnstile we tapped the next-in-line man on an arm. Without a word being exchanged, he would lift us by the armpits ('oxters' in the vernacular) and leaning over the turnstile would deposit us on the other side. It was universally accepted that any child able to be lifted over the turnstile got into the match free.

Once safely inside the ground, we found each other and then squirmed our way down through the rows of tightly packed terraces, until we arrived at the chest-high wall separating the spectators from the pitch. Waiting patiently until play was underway we climbed over the wall and dropped down on to the gravel track encircling the pitch. We now had a better view of the game and players than even those sitting in expensive seats in the grandstand. A number of policemen on foot walked slowly round the track, facing the crowd, being on the alert for any disturbances.

When one of the constables approached us to tell us to get back over the wall pronto, it was easy to explain to him that we only climbed over to escape being crushed on the other side. He would look at the crowd now tightly packed against the other side of the wall, and reluctantly nod his agreement. This ploy never failed to work, so that we could enjoy the best view of the match without it costing us a penny, along with the row of paraplegics and cripples who were allowed to drive their invalid cars right on to the track. Our behaviour was unfailingly impeccable, as we were far too accessible to the policemen, but we had no need to do anything which might have attracted their attention as we were in the box seats.

When the match was over, we scrambled back over the wall, and unrolled our hessian sacks. As the fans slowly cleared the terraces, literally thousands of large beer bottles, known as 'screwtaps', were left behind in their wake. We climbed back up the terraces, picking up bottles and putting these in our sacks, and it didn't take long to accumulate as many as we could carry on the long walk home. Once again we couldn't use public transport, as the clippies refused to let us on with our heavy sacks of bottles. "Youse lot kin get tae buggery aff mah bliddy caur this minute, it' no' a smelly brewery lorry ye know, it's fur decent folk, no' a bliddy bunch o' scavengers," they would shout in a shrill voice that would have toppled the walls of Jericho if their tramcar had been on the Israel route.

Our backs felt like they would never straighten again by the time we reached home. In theory, each bottle was worth tuppence as a return, but there was a major catch as I have mentioned earlier. The pub where the bottles had been originally purchased from, had stamped its name on the label. Only the correct pub would refund the tuppence. Some of the bottles bore the stamp of some faraway pub and were just tipped into the midden. The rest we swapped between ourselves, about six of us, to make the job of travelling around a large number of pubs to get refunds a bit easier than it might have been otherwise. We could only collect bottles from Hampden and Cathkin Parks, as they were within walking distance, and even then it nearly killed us walking home. If we went to Ibrox, Parkhead, or Shawfield, we had to use the tramcars or buses to get there. Partick Thistle we never watched.

Now that our family was a little more financially secure, father made a list of all daily tasks to be carried out. This was tacked up on the kitchen wall, with the price to be paid for each alongside the task as an increment to our sixpence pocket money. Alex, Bobby and I were delighted. Now we would be paid for doing jobs that we had previously done anyway. We all slept in the same bed. When I awakened first thing in the morning I was keen to get washed and dressed and go to the dairy for the milk and rolls as I had been doing for years. I would now get a credit of tuppence for this. I was still rubbing the sleep from my eyes, when I heard our door banging shut. Wandering into the kitchen I looked around. Mother was still asleep, but father had gone off to work.

The message bag was missing from where mother kept it handy. Not only was it missing but so was Bobby. Alex was still sound asleep even although his eyes were disconcertingly wide open. Sleeping like that was quite normal for him. We were used to it but it could give other people a bit of a fright. As I was washing my hands and face in the sink, I heard Bobby knocking on the door in family code. I opened the door to let him in. "Whit ur you daein gettin' the rolls an' mulk? That's mah joab, Ah 've been gettin' them fur years," I said in an angry tone. "It disnae maitter who gets them noo, it jist depends on who's ready furst," he replied. "How the hell did ye get washed and dressed withoot wakin' me up?" I asked. "Ah went tae bed wi' mah shoes socks an' claes oan, that's how," he replied defiantly.

Bobby could smell money from miles away and made every penny a prisoner. Despite trying, neither Alex nor I could make any headway in the jobs for money stakes, as Bobby would somehow get there first. I tried the time-honoured method of giving him a good thumping, but the lure of cash was stronger than his fear of me and it made no difference.

The family had grown too large for mother to cope with the laundry by using the wash house on one morning a week. For some time, she had been also going to a bagwash shop which was located quite a long way away down Crown Street, between Ballater Street and thc Saltmarket. Twice a week, on Tuesdays and Thursdays, I had to load the dirty washing into a very substantial white kitbag, pull the drawstring tight, load it over my shoulder and trudge to the bagwash shop. The bag was heavy enough, but at the shop the dry unwashed clothing was exchanged for the previous load, now soaking wet; this was much heavier. By the time I made it home my shoulders and back were cramped and aching, and my clothes were wet through where they'd been in close contact with the kitbag. Because of the heavy weight involved, this was at least one job that Bobby couldn't do. I earned sixpence for each return trip.

Now that I was ten years old and had more money to spend, I was allowed to go to the pictures, but only to cinemas which my parents approved. There were about four cinemas in Govanhill, and one in Shawlands, which were deemed to be acceptable. I can't remember all their names except for the Calder and the Embassy. These ran two movies at a time, with patrons entering at any time and leaving as the film reached the same scene as when they had entered.

Between the two cinemas we could always rely on seeing our favourite actors. These were mainly comedians or cowboys. Some of their names were ingested, well chewed, and regurgitated with the typical Glaswegian mispronunciation. For example, we would chatter on about seeing "Baw Dabbit and Lucas Teller" (Bud Abbott and Lou Costello) and "Jee Notry" (Gene Autry). Favourite comedians were The Three Stooges, Charlie Chaplin, Buster Keaton, The Keystone Cops, The Marx Brothers, Laurel and Hardy, The Bowery Boys, and some more that I can't remember. Cowboys were Roy Rogers, with on screen wife Dale and his horse Trigger, Gene Autry, Hopalong Cassidy, Tom Mix, Tex Ritter, and The Lone Ranger with his trusty Indian sidekick Tonto. More serious contenders were John Wayne, Audie Murphy, James Stewart, Henry Fonda, Victor Maclaglen, Alan Ladd, and a raft of sidekicks like Andy Clyde who appeared in just about every one of their films, usually driving the chuckwagon.

Tarzan was another favourite, played by the musclebound former Olympic gold medal swimmer Johnny Weissmuller. After some years playing Tarzan, he became too corpulent to carry on with the role, wearing only a tastefully tailored leather loin cloth. With little delay he returned to the silver screen as Jungle Jim, who did everything that Tarzan did, except that he was dressed immaculately in a loose-fitting safari suit at all times. He must have missed the now unemployed Jane very much. I certainly would have.

The series of musical swimaganzas starring the beautiful and highly athletic Esther Williams, who had been a champion swimmer in her own right before being 'discovered' by Hollywood, featured marvellous aquatic sets, complete with hundreds of synchronized swimmers. I sat through every one of her films two or three times, only going home about 8pm to avoid a repeat of the Crownie episode.

War films were also a favourite. The American ones were full of action, and the heroes were the same bunch of guys from the more epic Westerns, with John Wayne and co wearing US Marine helmets, sometimes embellished with the odd bullet hole, and permanently sweat-saturated fatigues, rather than white Stetsons and dust encrusted cowboy outfits.

The British ones were entirely different, with a small number of prominent actors, such as John Mills, Richard Attenborough, Jack Hawkins, Alec Guinness, Trevor Howard and David Niven taking most of the leading parts. The supporting cast were always the same bunch of actors and actresses, remixed and repackaged from film to film. If it wasn't for the amount of live action wartime footage procured from the vaults of the War Department, covering all three services, these films would have been dead boring and less than half an hour in duration.

The Elstree studios' battle scenes featuring shoddily constructed cardboard model warships, supposedly battling through heavy seas whilst being bombed, shelled, or torpedoed, were usually so cheaply and poorly shot that they were embarrassing to watch. Even we children could see that the footage depicting an embattled convoy braving the U Boat wolf packs prowling the northern approaches of the Atlantic was filmed using a large tin tray containing no more than six inches of tap water. I suppose that we should have been thankful that the studio hands making the waves with soup spoons or wooden school rulers were kept out of shot, at least in the edited footage.

The British film industry continued to churn out comedies with poor scripts and silly plots. Norman Wisdom, Benny Hill, and others 'starred' in utterly forgettable black and white productions. The 'Carry On' films, with the ongoing cast of Sid James, Kenneth Williams, Bernard Bresslaw, Hattie Jaques, and Barbara Windsor, aided and abetted by a semi-permanent collection of odd looking and untalented over actors, were only funny the first time around.

Chapter 24

When I was young, although I had no cognisance at the time, no attention whatsoever appeared to be paid to environmental issues. Pollution was rife across the board, notably in connection with waterways quality, and with the smoke and soot particle emissions from the hundreds of tall factory chimneys which dotted the cityscape, belching columns of thick black smoke every day of the year. The smoke must have contained just about every type of potentially dangerous chemical, known or unknown. This smoke had, over a period of years, coated the surfaces of all buildings black. This had been going on for so long that no one still living had seen the stone and brickwork before it had become blackened. The only spots that revealed the underlying surface and colour of the stonework, were where the corrosive action of the chemical-laden soot had attacked the stonework, causing the eroded blackened surface to spall off. The outer texture of the exposed surface was invariably soft and crumbling.

A large number of older factories which were still operational had been deliberately sited on the banks of, or in some cases were straddling, waterways, in order that free cooling or process water was readily available. After being utilised for production purposes, this often highly contaminated effluent was simply discharged into the nearest waterway, mostly without any attempt to undertake even primary treatment. Secondary or tertiary treatment was not even an issue to be discussed. Eventually all of these waterways, open or piped underground, emptied into the Clyde. The once pristine river, which had been famous for its salmon runs, was by the mid-1940s so polluted that it ran turgid, discoloured, and stinking of God knows what, to discharge into the Firth of Clyde, and eventually into the Atlantic.

From time to time someone fell, was pushed, or jumped into the Clyde from one or other of the various bridges, or from the steep banks. The Parsonage family, by means of some sort of tradition, had cornered the market on dragging the murky depths to recover the corpses of these poor unfortunates. When I lived in the Gorbals, Ben Parsonage was the man who invariably carried out this task. The jungle telegraph was very efficient. In no time at all, after he started to row his boat backwards and forwards across the river, usually between the last upstream traffic bridge and the large weir between Glasgow Green and Adelphi Street on the southern bank, large crowds jostled to get the best view of proceedings.

One day my younger brother Bobby and I were watching Ben doing his stuff, in the hope of seeing him actually retrieving a corpse. We coped with the boredom by feeding the large squalls of seagulls which were wheeling and screeching around. Competition was tough; only those gulls which were really on the ball were able to snatch the piece of bread in mid-air, before it had gone a yard. Our grisly hope of seeing Ben snagging the corpse with the grappling irons was rewarded late in the afternoon, as it was getting dark. We were too far away to see any detail as the body was hauled over the stern, but we could now boast of seeing a dead body. We knew that the body would be taken straight to the mortuary, which was located near the riverbank, close to the Saltmarket.

We had to walk past this large sombre red brick building on our way home. As we reached it we decided to risk clambering up one of the iron grilles which protected each tall window, so we could see in. The bottom two thirds of each window were painted white on the inside, so we had to climb up to the upper part of the window which was clear glass. The windows were plenty wide enough to allow us to climb up side by side. As we reached the top and readied ourselves to look into the inside of the mortuary, a big ghostly white face appeared on the other side of the window and let out a loud moan. In shock we fell from our perches and crashed to the ground. Despite the distance of our fall and the pain we suffered as a result we were up and away in a flash, running the rest of the way home without talking or stopping for breath.

Once home we immediately felt the pain caused by our sudden and unexpected collision of our feet and ankles with the pavement outside the mortuary. Despite the pain we couldn't wait to tell mother about our scary experience. "Mammy, ye'll never guess whit we've jist seen doon at the Clyde. That man wae the big rowin' boat caught a deid boady wi' his chains an' hooks. Oan the wey hame we climbed up the ootside o' a windae at the mortuary, tae see if we could see whit wis inside. We saw a great big white ghost oan the ither side o' the windae, honest we did, it wis a real ghost Mammy. It wis pure white an' made a horrible noise. We fell aff the windy an' ran a' the wey hame."

Mammy looked at us for a while before replying. "That serves yese bliddy right, fur climbin' up windaes when ye shouldnae be. Ye're lucky thit the ghost didnae grab the baith o' yese an' sook a' the blood oot o' yese, tae ye looked jist like him. Then ye wid huv been a' dressed up in white sheets, an' been made tae spend the rest o' yer lives waitin' fur somebody as stupit as youse two tae climb up the mortuary windaes an' frighten the shite oot o' thim." After our well-deserved fright at the mortuary, we always walked on the other side of the road when walking towards Glasgow Cross.

Street games were played all year round, but far more intensively during summer evenings when our apology for a sun didn't properly set until ten pm or even later. Our sense of the changing seasons was governed more by the length of day rather than by temperature, as summer weather could be consistently grim with plenty of cold wet miserable days.

One activity that we engaged in from time to time during summer was unusual in that we provided a public service to the community in doing so. Starting early in the morning, boys scoured the neighbourhood, collecting all the paper and cardboard that they could lay hands on. Another couple of boys climbed on to the roof of one of the abandoned wash houses in the back courts. The windows and door of the derelict wash houses were already solidly boarded up, in order to keep kids out. The iron railings which had originally separated each back court had long since been prised loose, to be used as crowbars, spears, or poles to prod the lumps of wood that we sailed as battleships in the filthy puddles which were a semi-permanent feature of the back courts; the poles saved us from having to wade in amongst the turds when a piece of wood became becalmed in the middle.

While one group was gathering paper etc, another was collecting lengths of rope: usually some poor housewife's clothesline. The rope was cut into pieces about a yard and a half long. When we guessed that we had sufficient pieces, the next job was to patrol through the streets and back courts, collecting about twenty of the local dogs which were allowed by their owners to roam free during the day. Each was secured by a length of rope, and led to the back court which contained our wash house of choice. During the time spent collecting dogs, the others on the wash house roof were stuffing paper and cardboard down the chimney. Another group had been collecting as many stones, slates, and pieces of brick as possible, and piling them up about twenty feet from the wash house. The boys on the roof continued to ram the paper down the chimney, using a broomstick handle to help out if the chimney became blocked. It took some time and effort, but eventually all the paper had been stuffed inside.

Now came the fun part, as a final bundle of paper was set alight and rammed down the chimney. Most of the dogs had been corralled into this activity before, and now strained on their rope leads barking and yelping in excitement. As the boys holding the ropes had about four or five in each hand, it was a job and a half restraining the dogs. We waited impatiently for the fire to take hold inside. Smoke was belching from the chimney for some time before it started to seep thickly from under the door and around the windows. Every boy and dog were tensed up and waiting for the next part.

As if under the strict control of a general, a solid phalanx of rats, amazingly like a living brown carpet, rushed out from under the door. The yelping dogs were let loose to pounce on the frantic rats like a pack of bloodthirsty wolves. We let loose with our piled-up missiles as fast as we could pick them up and throw them, trying to hit the rats and miss the dogs, not always successfully. Noisy bedlam ruled for about five minutes, the boys making just as much noise as the dogs, with housewives leaning out of their windows shrieking and squealing at the sight of so many rats at one time but joining in vicariously in the slaughter.

As suddenly as the horde of rats emerged, the scrabbling survivors disappeared into middens and under the doors of the adjacent derelict wash houses. The back court was now littered with the corpses of hundreds of rats. Our 'rent a dog' pack was still charging around in frenzied circles tossing dead rats into the air, trying to find a live one to scrunch between their slavering jaws. One of the more prominent spectators, Mrs McCafferty, leaned a bit farther out of her kitchen window and called down to us in a voice that would have frightened all the rats to death, and deprived us of our version of 'blood sports', if she had called out earlier.

"Hey, youse boys doon therr, ye've done a bliddy good joab wae a' thae rats, but ye better dae as good a joab clearin' up a' thae deid yins, or ah'll get the polis tae yese. Ah know a' yer mammies as well, sae ye better get stuck in fast. If ah wis youse, ah'd be gettin' coal shovels fae hame, tae save pickin' up the buggers wi' mah bare haunds." This was advice that had to be taken seriously. Mrs McCafferty was a woman well known for her willingness and ability to thump anyone of either sex, if she thought that they had it coming to them.

We scattered off home to borrow coal shovels. As the blaze inside the wash house petered out, the thick grey smoke was replaced by a thin streak of white emerging from the chimney. We returned from our homes bearing every variety of fireside and coal bunker shovels known to man, and shovelled up the dead rats as quickly as we could, having to contest each dead rat with the marauding dogs which were still eagerly nosing around for any live rats to kill. The more rats that we dumped into the nearest midden, the more the dogs contested the remainder. A couple of boys had to stand guard at the midden wielding their coal shovels to bash the heads of dogs trying to grab a corpse from the accumulating pile. It was some time before we were able to retrieve every corpse, untie the ropes of the dogs which were still hoping for more rats to appear, and then give them a good kick up the arse to speed them on their way home. We were now exhausted; our adrenalin rush having receded. Despite the amount of work and trauma involved in our slum version of fox hunting, we would do this all over again in a few weeks' time, choosing a different derelict wash house as the battlefield.

I was very lucky in having in having older cousins, ranging from teenagers to adults. Two of them in particular, Nancy and Grace Patterson, were just fantastic in giving Bobby, Alex and me lots of their spare time and treats that my parents could never have afforded. On the occasion of the annual Glasgow Fair, which was held in July, the huge grassy expanse of Glasgow Green, located on the northern bank of the Clyde, became almost invisible under large numbers of canvas marquees and the 'Big Top' of the circus. The whole shooting box and dice was known universally as 'The Shows'.

Under the protection of the marquees, the individual rides and many other means of parting eager children and their parents from their savings were located. Everything that spun around or moved up and down was driven by an individual steam engine. The engines also ran electric generators to provide power for the multitude of coloured light bulbs that festooned the rides and marquees. From the time I was old enough to ride on the younger child-oriented rides of buses, cars and aeroplanes, one or both of these cousins would take me for an evening of wonder and euphoria. The sound of the classic fairground music emanating from the individual steam-driven organs of each ride, clamouring to be heard above the general background hubbub of scores of differing tunes, was excruciatingly exciting for me, and is still deeply imprinted in my mind.

As soon as Bobby and Alex were each considered old enough they were included in these wonderful outings. My cousins' close friend, Margaret Ballagh, also came along most of the time. We knew Margaret already, as she worked in the fishmongers shop just around the corner from Kidston Street, in Caledonia Road. Filleting and handling fish amid crushed ice all day, in a climate which could well have made the ice superfluous for most of the year, was hard on the fish girls' hands, leaving them raw and swollen from day to day. Despite her sore hands, and the thick glasses that she habitually wore to correct very poor sight, Margaret was the most good-natured and kind person that I had ever met. As an interruption to the story being told, I would like to digress a little, and write a few heartfelt words about our own Saint Margaret.

Whenever my parents were too strapped for cash to buy food for our supper, I would be sent round to the fishmongers with sixpence to buy 'fish for the cat', despite the fact that we didn't have a cat at the time. I tried to ensure that I would be served by Margaret, even if meant that I had to act like a half-witted idiot in the queue, letting others be served first. When I asked her for 'sixpence worth of fish for the cat', she would poke around in the steel bin where all the scraps and bones were thrown into during filleting and roll up a large amount of them in white wrapping paper.

When the parcel was unwrapped at home, there, hiding miraculously under the filleting scraps, would be at least four lovely fresh and gleaming herrings. I don't know if my father ever thanked Margaret personally, but my mother certainly did, from the bottom of her heart. The fish scraps themselves were never wasted, as they were all we got if Margaret wasn't at the counter. Father would boil the scraps until the flesh came away from the bones. Carefully straining the water away, he removed every trace of fishbones. The remaining flesh was then simmered slowly in milk, seasoned with plenty of pepper, salt, and a little vinegar, and served up as a nourishing fish stew.

Now back into the story proper. We were thrilled just to be at the Shows, even if we never got a ride. There was so much to see and listen to as the stall barkers competed in loud penetrating voices to round up as many passersby as possible, to spend their money on tossing rings or throwing darts etc. Our cousins would make sure that we got rides on just about everything that was safe, and a few that weren't. They started off by giving each of us a large handful of copper pennies that loaded down our pockets, in order that we felt independent to a degree. The coins weighed so much that our short trousers would have been around our ankles if it wasn't for our industrial-strength braces buttoned very securely to our trouser tops.

The highlight came after we had exhausted our trove of pennies. Armed with large dollops of candy floss on sticks, we were guided to the queue waiting to enter the 'Big Top' of the circus. The clowns entertaining the waiting crowds performed acts which we could see close up. Despite being so close to the clowns I was still at a loss in working out how they did their tricks. Sitting down in the front row of seats, we were enthralled by each act, even if we were frightened stiff by the risks taken by the aerial gymnasts and the trapeze acts. Our eyes were screwed tightly closed for much of the time in case someone crashed to the ground. The hilarious acts of the clowns, and performing poodles, had us laughing so much the tears were running down our cheeks.

Everything would be going just fine until the large cage was erected for the lion taming act. Remembering my last encounter with the roar of an unseen lion which frightened me out of my wits, I was determined to redeem myself and brave it out. Before the lions appeared I closed my eyes tightly shut and jammed my index fingers into my ears, my body rigid. Until I was convinced that the lion tamer had packed his cage and gone, I resisted the temptation to have a quick peek. I unscrewed my eyes and fingers only when I could feel everybody screeching as the clowns came on again.

For weeks after one of the Shows we drove our mother bananas by swinging on a rope tied to a large hook above our bed and trying to do somersaults off the top of our wardrobe onto the bed. Before we could perfect these moves, the top of the wardrobe was badly split, and the recess bed crashed to the floor as the springs gave way and its long-suffering legs collapsed. The mattress cover had long before been ripped in many places by being used as a surrogate battleground, ocean, prairie, and desert. My father was just as unimpressed as usual, and thrashed my behind despite my yelled explanation that we were only training ourselves to be circus performers.

In December each year, the large Kelvin Hall complex was taken over by another circus and sideshows. These were more modern than the ones at Glasgow Green and were plugged into the mains electricity. Without the puffing steam engines and chorus of wailing organs, the special atmosphere of the 'Shows', could not be recreated.

Nevertheless, Kelvin Hall was an exciting venue, and we eagerly looked forward to this for many weeks beforehand.

Now that I was nine years old, my father presumed that I was perfectly able to do most things, particularly babysitting the younger children. This premature introduction into a whole range of what nowadays would be regarded as adult responsibilities changed my daily life significantly, but that is another story!

Printed in Great Britain
by Amazon

49135103R00169